Elements
of
Musical
Understanding

Elements
of
Musical
Understanding

ALLEN WINOLD

School of Music, Indiana University, Bloomington

PRENTICE-HALL, INC.,
Englewood Cliffs, New Jersey

Elements of Musical Understanding
ALLEN WINOLD

Current printing (last digit):
10 9 8 7 6 5 4 3 2 1

Library of Congress Catalog Card Number: 66-14356
Printed in the United States of America. C-26812

Photograph on the title page by Marc Bomse.

PRENTICE-HALL INTERNATIONAL, INC., London
PRENTICE-HALL OF AUSTRALIA, PTY. LTD., Sydney
PRENTICE-HALL OF CANADA, LTD., Toronto
PRENTICE-HALL OF INDIA (PRIVATE) LTD., New Delhi
PRENTICE-HALL OF JAPAN, INC., Tokyo

Preface

This book presents a general introduction to the elements of music theory and to the periods of music literature. Although it is designed primarily for college courses such as Music Appreciation, Introduction to Music, or Fundamentals of Music, it can also profitably serve the individual reader.

The basic approach of the book is through active musical experience. The student is encouraged to develop an understanding of the language and literature of music through analysis, composition, performance, and listening. Explanations of notation, terminology, and concepts and descriptions of styles, composers, and individual works are concisely written to allow maximum opportunity for the student to work directly with actual musical materials.

The organization is intended to be flexible enough to meet the individual needs of teachers and students. The introduction provides a general discussion of the nature and meaning of music and information on the physical and psychological characteristics of sound. Each chapter in Part I introduces one of the basic elements of music and traces its usage through the periods of music literature. The chapters in Part II are devoted to a concentrated study of each of these periods. If a unified chronological approach is preferred, this may be achieved by beginning with Chapter 6 and continuing to the end of the book, referring back to material in the first five chapters as needed.

I wish to express my gratitude to the following who have contributed so much to the writing of this book: to my teachers, faculty colleagues, and Dean Wilfred C. Bain of Indiana University School of Music whose wisdom and inspiration have shaped much of the content; to my students whose enthusiasm and patience have tested and refined much of the material presented here; to my wife, Helga, my children, Claire, Erika, and Bettina and to my parents, whose devotion and love have encouraged and sustained me in the writing of this book.

Special thanks are also due to Patricia Gardner and Mary Cooper of the Indiana University School of Music staff for their invaluable assistance in the initial preparation of the copy and to Mrs. Raeia Maes and the College Book Editorial-Production Department of Prentice-Hall for advice and encouragement far beyond the formal requirements of editorial supervision.

The photographs on pages ii-iii, 20, 48, 88, 114, and 166 are of the Queens College Orchestral Society of Queens College of The City University of New York. Dr. Boris Schwarz, Professor of Music at Queens College, is the conductor.

ALLEN WINOLD

Contents

Introduction   2

*Physical and Psychological Characteristics of Sound.   The
Elements of Music Theory.   Musical Style and the Periods of
Music Literature.   The Use of the Exercises.*

PART **|**

*The
Elements
of
Music
Theory*

1

The Temporal Element   14

*Beat.   Meter.   Tempo.   Rhythmic Notation.   Time
Signatures.   Rhythmic Patterns.   Rhythmic Characteristics.
The Temporal Element in Music Literature.   Temporal Element
Summary.   Exercises.*

2

The Tonal Element   40

*Tone.   Pitch Designation.   Pitch Notation.   Melodic Intervals.
Scales.   Key Signatures.   Scale Properties.   Tonal Characteristics.
The Tonal Element in Music Literature.   Tonal Element Summary.
Exercises.*

x

3

The Timbre-Dynamic Element   80

Dynamics.   Articulation.   Character.   Instruments. The Orchestral Score.   Voices.   Vocal Ensembles.   The Timbre-Dynamic Element in Music Literature.   Timbre-Dynamic Element Summary.   Exercises.

4

The Textural Element   110

Harmonic Intervals.   Chords.   Harmonization.   Homophonic Texture.   Polyphonic Texture.   The Textural Element in Music Literature.   Textural Element Summary.   Exercises.

5

The Formal Element   158

Musical Units.   Repetition, Contrast, and Variation.   Theme and Transition.   The Analysis of Music.   Specific Forms of Music.   Types of Music.   Formal Element Summary.   Exercises.

PART II
The Periods of Music Literature

6

The Pre-Baroque Period   180

The Formal Element in the Pre-Baroque Period.   Sacred Vocal Forms.   Secular Vocal Forms.   Instrumental Forms. Representative Composers of the Pre-Baroque Period.

7

The Baroque Period   196

*The Formal Element in the Baroque Period.   Single-Movement
Vocal Forms.   Multi-Movement Vocal Forms.   Single-Movement
Instrumental Forms.   Multi-Movement Instrumental Forms.
Representative Composers of the Baroque Period.*

8

The Classical Period   224

*The Formal Element in the Classical Period.   Single-Movement
Instrumental Forms.   Multi-Movement Instrumental Forms.
Single-Movement Vocal Forms.   Multi-Movement Vocal Forms.
The Marriage of Figaro, Act One.   Representative Composers
of the Classical Period.*

9

The Romantic Period   276

*The Formal Element in the Romantic Period.   Single-Movement
Instrumental Forms.   Multi-Movement Instrumental Forms.
Single-Movement Vocal Forms.   Multi-Movement Vocal Forms.
Representative Composers of the Romantic Period.*

10

The Contemporary Period   340

*Schools of Contemporary Music.   The Formal Element in the
Contemporary Period.   Forms of the Contemporary Period.
Representative Composers.*

Index   384

Elements
of
Musical
Understanding

Introduction

T here is a story told of a man in a small isolated village in central Europe who loved to play on his cello, which had just one string. It was his custom to put his finger on one note in the middle of the instrument and play this note for hours at a time. His wife listened patiently to his playing for years until one day when she had to journey for the first time to a large, nearby city. She came back in great excitement to tell her husband that she had seen other cellists there, playing on instruments with four strings, moving their fingers up and down to various notes all over the instrument. Her husband, quite unimpressed, continued to play his one note. Finally he looked up and said, "Wife, they are looking for the right place. I have found it."

Although few people have such a limited outlook, many people are unaware of the incredible richness and variety of music. The literature of music extends from primitive pagan war chants to sophisticated symphonic tone poems, from simple folk songs to complex string quartets, from euphonious Renaissance choral works to cacophonous modern electronic compositions.

It is difficult to find a satisfactory definition of music that will include all its various aspects. Some early definitions are extremely limited. The tenth-century theorist, Odo of Cluny, defines music as "the science of singing truly and the easy road to perfection in singing." Later definitions are often so broad and vague as to be almost meaningless. The nineteenth-century poet and musician, E.T.A. Hoffmann, defines music as "the mysterious language of a distant spirit world whose wondrous accents echo within us and awaken us to a loftier, more intensive life." Another nineteenth-century writer, Eduard Hanslick, produces a somewhat more cogent definition of music in his famous phrase, "Music is form moving in sound." George Bernard Shaw, in his play, *Man and Superman,* calls music "the brandy of the damned," which is hardly a definition but is no less helpful than some other attempts at defining music.

We seek a definition that is general enough to cover all the facets of music and yet specific enough to give us a concrete conception of its nature and purpose. To meet these criteria, the following is proposed:

Music is an art, a craft, and a science involving the conscious organization of sound and silence in the framework of time for the purpose of effecting communication between men.

We might say that such a definition is so general and inclusive that it could be applied to many things which are not usually regarded as music. Ordinary conversation, for example, might seem to be included in this definition of music. Is it music? Probably it is not; however, if we add instrumental accompaniment to it and emphasize the natural melodic rise and fall of the voice and the inherent rhythmic characteristics of the words, as operatic composers have done in *recitative,* then we would clearly recognize the result as music. Is the sound of a fog horn on the river at night

3

to be called music? Probably it is not; however, if we would record this sound, alter it electronically to produce various pitches and durations, and organize these as composers of the present-day electronic pieces have done, then we could legitimately label the product music. Are the notes a cat strikes accidentally as it walks across a piano keyboard to be termed music? Again, we would have to say they are probably not; but if we use these notes as the beginning of a fugue subject and build an extended composition on them as the Baroque composer, Domenico Scarlatti, is alleged to have done, then they would certainly become music.

Our definition of music emphasizes the relationship between music and other aural experiences. This kinship between natural and artistic experience is likely to be overlooked in music more than in any other art. In an art gallery we can relate pictures to other visual experiences we have had. In a theater we can relate the scenes of a play to incidents from our own lives. In a concert hall, however, we are often not able to relate the music coming from the stage to sounds we have heard in our daily lives; instead we are conscious of what might be called an "aesthetic distance" between ourselves and the music.

To overcome this feeling of aesthetic distance many writers describe music in similes and metaphors. Mozart's music is compared to a formal garden or a Raphael Madonna; Beethoven's music is likened to a storm or to a Michelangelo statue; Stravinsky's music is said to express the frantic pace of our modern mechanized civilization or to parallel the artistic work of Picasso.

Such colorful descriptions of music may at times be helpful in bridging aesthetic distance; more often they are obscure, inappropriate, or sometimes even nonsensical. Comparisons with other arts are especially problematic, not only because they may be inaccurate, but also because they may be based on material totally unfamiliar to the listener. Nor is it helpful to lay too much stress on the relationship between music and specific events in the life of the composer. (See Tchaikowsky's view on this, Chapter 9.)

A more recent and probably more fruitful approach to the understanding of music is based on psychological principles. Concepts from the *Gestalt* (German: pattern) school of psychology are applied to problems of musical form; aspects of Freudian psychology are applied to problems of musical meaning. The advantages of this psychological approach over the meta-phorical approach are that it deals directly with the music itself and it offers interesting hypotheses to account for the effect of music on the human organism. These hypotheses, however, are largely based on research in areas outside music, and their application to music has not yet been fully verified through controlled experimentation. Furthermore, some background in both music and psychology must first be achieved before this approach can be used effectively.

There is a third approach to bridging the aesthetic distance between listener and music, based neither on metaphorical description nor psychological explanation but rather on musical experience. The present text is based primarily on this experiential approach, although it does not completely neglect the possibilities afforded by the first two. The following chapters introduce the reader to a progressive series of musical experiences from the perception of a simple beat to the comprehension of a complex modern composition. These musical experiences include not only listening but also analysis, composition, and performance.

Rigid separation between composer, performer, and listener is a fairly recent and not necessarily salutary situation. The listener who comes to a performance with some personal experience in the creation or re-creation of music, no matter how rudimentary this may be, will inevitably be more actively and meaningfully involved with the music. For this reason the suggested exercises in the first five chapters should be carried out not only by classroom students but also by the individual reader, if full comprehension of the material is to be achieved. The student cannot expect to become a Van Cliburn or a Stravinsky through these exercises, but he can expect to appreciate more fully the accomplishments of the master performers and composers and to derive satisfaction from meeting the challenge which the exercises present. At the end of this chapter we shall consider how the exercises in this book may best be used; but first it will be helpful to gain a broad over-view of certain fundamental aspects of music, such as the physical and psychological characteristics of sound, the elements of music theory, and the periods of music literature.

Physical and Psychological Characteristics of Sound

The following simple experiments can be used to demonstrate some of the pertinent principles of acoustics, the science of sound. We shall use a string bass in these experiments, but if none is available a violin, guitar, or other string instrument can be used.

Pluck a string of the string bass and observe what happens. We *see* that the string has been set into vibration and continues to vibrate back and forth; we *hear* a sound. All sound involves *vibration* in a three-fold process: a *sound producing source,* such as a vibrating string; a *sound transmitting medium,* such as air; and a *sound receiving mechanism,* such as the human ear.

Pluck the bass string again and compare this sound to that produced by dropping some coins on a table. The sound of the bass string is produced by a regular and relatively simple vibratory motion and is called a *tone.* The sound of the coins is produced by an irregular and relatively complex vibratory motion and is called a *noise.*

Pluck the thinnest string on the string bass and then pluck the thickest string on the string bass. Notice that the thinnest string vibrates faster than the thickest string and that the sound of the thinnest string is higher than that of the thickest string. The speed of vibration—the number of back-and-forth cycles that the string makes in a given amount of time—is the physical characteristic of *frequency*; this produces the psychological characteristic of *pitch*. Frequency is measured in terms of cycles per second (cps). The faster the frequency is, the higher the pitch becomes. The higher string in the experiment has a frequency of 96 cps; the lower string has a frequency of 40 cps. The human ear can detect pitches ranging from approximately 20 cps to 20,000 cps.

Return to the lowest string and pluck it very lightly. Observe that the back and forth motion of the vibration is very narrow and that the sound is soft. Then pluck the string again very forcefully and observe that the vibration is wider and that the sound is louder. The width of the vibration is the physical characteristic of *amplitude*; this produces the psychological characteristic of *loudness*. The wider the amplitude is, the louder the sound becomes. Loudness may be measured in *phons*. More often, however, this aspect of sound is described in terms of the *decibel* (db), which is a measure of the physical energy or intensity of sound. Musical sounds range in intensity from approximately 25 db, the level of a single instrument played softly, to 100 db, the level of the full orchestra playing loudly.

Next, pluck the lowest string on the string bass and strike the same note, E_1 (see Chapter 2 for an explanation of pitch notation) on the piano. Notice that even though the pitch and loudness of these two sounds may be the same, they still sound differently. This difference is caused by the third physical characteristic, *overtone structure*. When we pluck the lowest string on the bass, the string is vibrating not only as a whole unit, it is also vibrating in halves, quarters, and other proportional units. The string vibrating as a whole produces the tone we hear most clearly, the *fundamental*. The smaller vibrations of the string produce what are known as *overtones*. Overtones are usually not heard as separate pitches; instead their number, position, and relative strength determine the third psychological characteristic of *tone quality* or *timbre*. Because of such factors as the difference in the construction of a piano and a string bass, the number, position, and relative strength of the overtones above a given tone on each instrument are different and therefore the timbre of the tone on each instrument is different.

Using the piano we can perform an interesting experiment to make these overtones more audible. First, we gently depress the keys for the tones b, e^1, g-sharp^1, and b^1 in such a manner that the tones do not sound but the dampers are released from the strings. Holding these keys down, we strike E_1 strongly and then release it. As we do this we hear the tones b, e^1, g-sharp^1, and b^1, produced by overtones and sympathetic vibration.

The fourth physical and psychological characteristic of sound is relatively easy to understand. The same term, *duration,* is applied to both the physical and psychological characteristic. The physical duration of a sound lasts from the onset of vibration to the cessation of vibration; the psychological duration lasts from the instant the sound is first perceived until the instant it is no longer heard. Duration can be measured in direct terms, such as seconds or milliseconds, or it can be measured in relative terms, such as describing one sound as half as long as another. The characteristic of duration is also applicable to the element of silence, which plays an important, though often overlooked, role in music.

We can summarize the characteristics of sound as follows:

Physical Characteristic	Psychological Characteristic	Relationship
frequency	pitch	the greater the frequency, the higher the pitch
amplitude	loudness	the wider the amplitude, the greater the loudness
overtone structure	timbre	timbre is determined by the number, position, and relative strength of overtones
duration	duration	the length of the time of vibration determines the length of the sound

For the sake of simplicity and clarity we have indicated only the most direct and obvious relationships between the physical and psychological characteristics of sound. These relationships are, however, more complicated than we could indicate in this necessarily brief and superficial discussion. The psychological characteristic of pitch, for example, is affected not only by frequency, but also, to a lesser degree, by the other physical characteristics of sound.

The Elements of Music Theory

We could describe all aural experiences, including music, in terms of physical or psychological characteristics; however, it is more helpful to discuss music in the specific terminology of music theory. In this text we have organized these theoretical terms into five basic elements: *temporal, tonal, timbre-dynamic, textural,* and *formal.*

These theoretical elements of music are related to the characteristics of sound. The *temporal* element, for example, is based on the physical or psychological characteristic of duration; it includes such factors as rhythm, tempo, and meter. The *tonal* element is based on the physical characteristic of frequency or the psychological characteristic of pitch; it includes such aspects as interval, scale, pitch motion, and tonality.

These two basic elements serve to define and delineate music in terms of what may be thought of as horizontal (temporal) and vertical (tonal) dimensions. Utilizing this conception we can represent a piece of music in a graph such as the one shown in Figure 1.

This graph actually represents the first line of a simple folk song "Frere Jacques." We shall use this tune throughout the text to illustrate various principles of music. It is particularly well suited for this purpose by virtue of its simple and recognizable construction.

Example 1 shows the same melody in modern musical notation. By comparing this to Figure 1 we can see the basic similarities between the two

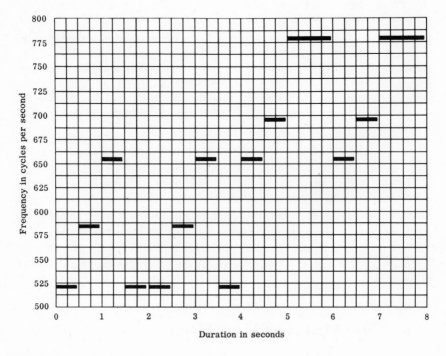

Fig. 1.

EXAMPLE 1.

representations. Musical notation is, in effect, a stylized symbolization of a graphic representation of music.

The two remaining physical and psychological characteristics of sound, amplitude (loudness) and overtone structure (timbre), may be grouped as a third element of music—the *timbre-dynamic* element. *Dynamic* terms or markings are used in music to indicate relative levels of loudness. Our discussion of the timbre-dynamic element will include consideration of such aspects as the tone quality of solo instruments and voices, instrumental and vocal ensembles, dynamics, and articulation. The timbre-dynamic element lends color and character to the basic dimensions of music provided by the temporal and tonal elements. "Frere Jacques," for example, could be performed by a flute or an oboe; it could be played loudly or softly; it could be articulated with smoothly connected tones or with heavily accented tones.

The textural element represents an expansion of the tonal element to include the relationship of simultaneously sounded sonorities; it embraces such theoretical considerations as harmonic intervals, chords, consonance and dissonance, types of polyphony, and types of homophony. The formal element constitutes a synthesis of the first four musical elements; it is concerned in general with relationships between structural units of a musical composition, especially considering such factors as the balance between unity and variety and the extension of musical material through repetition, variation, and contrast. The term *form* is also used in a specific sense to denote certain structural patterns in music such as binary form, sonata form, and others.

Although discussed separately in this book, these musical elements are generally heard in combination and interaction with one another. Melody, for example, results from the union of tonal and temporal elements. The textural element often serves to underline or delineate the temporal element. Any discussion of the formal element would involve some consideration of all other elements.

Musical Style and the Periods of Music Literature

Style in music involves a synthesis of the basic musical elements; a particular musical style may be defined in terms of its specific selection and combination of these elements. Musical style is not static; rather, it involves constant change in the usage and emphasis of the musical elements within certain limits. If these limits are consistently exceeded, a change in musical style occurs.

The study of these stylistic changes as shown in representative compositions, together with some consideration of the socio-cultural milieu in which they occur, constitutes the subject matter of music literature. Because of the dynamic nature of musical style, it is impossible to set precise chronological boundaries to the periods in which certain styles have prevailed. It is still possible, however, to organize music literature in terms of arbitrarily delineated chronological periods, recognizing that characteristic styles of one period generally extend to other periods. The following chronological division has been adopted for this book:

Period	*Approximate Beginning*	*Approximate Ending*
PRE-BAROQUE	—	1600 (beginning of Florentine opera)
Ancient (— -500)		
Medieval (500-1450)		
Renaissance (1450-1600)		
BAROQUE	1600	1750 (death of J. S. Bach)
Early Baroque (1600-1650)		
Middle Baroque (1650-1700)		
Late Baroque (1700-1750)		
CLASSICAL	1750	1827 (death of Beethoven)
Rococo (1725-1775)		
ROMANTIC	1815	1900
Early Romantic (1815-1850)		
Middle Romantic (1850-1890)		
Late Romantic (1890-1920)		
CONTEMPORARY	1900	—
Impressionism (1880-1920)		

Main periods are indicated with capital letters, sub-periods with small letters. Within each period and sub-period there are various national or stylistic schools. Individual composers, though they may be primarily identified with a particular period or school, generally reflect influences from other periods and schools, as well as their own individual traits.

The Use of the Exercises

The exercises in Part I are only suggestive of the types of musical activities that can profitably lead to a better understanding of music. For the amateur some of them may prove too difficult or time consuming. For the professional music student they would have to be supplemented with additional material. However, some exercises in each of the four categories should be done. The exercises in analysis are designed to test and strengthen the comprehension of the material covered in the chapter. The exercises in composition are of special importance, not only because they contribute to a better command of the material, but, more importantly, because they lead the student toward the development of his expressive possibilities. The exercises in performance must be adapted to the level of the student; they are intended to be challenging but not frustrating. The exercises in listening must also be varied according to the needs and interests of the student. It should be borne in mind that the exercises in stylistic identification will become progressively easier through the first five chapters. As each new element is added to the listening vocabulary, it facilitates the recognition of stylistic characteristics of the various periods of music literature.

No specific exercises are given in the last five chapters comprising Part II of this book. However, at least three types of activities are suggested in connection with these chapters. First, the musical examples discussed should be analyzed and listened to, not only from the point of view of formal organization but also according to the usage of the musical elements discussed in Part I. The themes should be sung or played, the instruments should be identified, and the texture should be analyzed, etc. It is especially helpful to have full scores for at least some of the works discussed, in addition to the musical examples and graphs given in this text. Second, it is valuable to compare works from various periods, to find the similarities and differences in musical style, for example, between Mozart's *Symphony No. 41 in C Major* (K. 551) and Bartók's *Concerto for Orchestra*. Finally, it is suggested that some historical or biographical study be done, supplemented by outside reading. The quotations given for several composers can also provide the basis for discussions of the meaning of music, the role of the musician in society, the creative process, and other subjects.

One word of caution, however, is in order at this point. The activities suggested above may lead to the conviction that music is an academic chore rather than an aesthetic experience. It is true that music can be performed, composed, or heard in a deliberate and objective manner, with intensive concentration on musical technique and historical perspective. However, these should not be ends in themselves, but only means to bring about what is essentially the basic purpose of all musical activity—communication. This communication may be in terms of a specific story which the composer is seeking to tell the listener through his music; it may be in terms of a general emotional experience that the composer seeks to re-create in the listener, or it may be in terms of a purely musical design which the composer wishes to share with the listener.

In music, as in any form of communication, some degree of technical understanding and experience is necessary if communication is to be effective. A reader of this text who has had training in English grammar, syntax, and vocabulary will undoubtedly receive more of the intended communication than one who has not had such training. This does not imply, however, that the trained reader always consciously analyzes parts of speech, sentence structure, punctuation, and orthography. He is aware of these factors and could, if necessary, identify them; in actual reading, however, he subordinates them to the over-all comprehension of the material. The untrained reader might be aware of the various shapes of the letters or even recognize a few words, but without some more specific understanding of the language he could not receive much communicative value from this book.

The analogy between reading a book and hearing a piece of music is by no means exact, but it is valid to a certain extent. Even on the purely emotional, non-intellectual level, the trained listener can expect to gain more from music than can the untrained listener. The trained listener may not always deliberately analyze music in terms of its theoretical elements, but he does hear them and he could, if desired, identify and describe them. In actual listening, however, he is mainly aware of what these elements contribute to the structure and meaning of the music. The inexperienced listener may not be able to verbalize nor even discern such details. He may have a superficial impression of the general sound and shape of the work, but he will miss the significant nuances of the music.

To test the validity of this relationship between knowledge and experience in music and understanding and enjoyment, the following experiment is suggested. Before beginning the study of the main parts of this look, listen to two unfamiliar musical compositions. Write a description and comparison of each work and indicate how meaningful and enjoyable each work is. After finishing the book, listen again to the same two works and write a new paper on them. Compare this to the paper written earlier to see if increased understanding and enjoyment are apparent.

PART I

The Elements of Music Theory

chapter 1

The Temporal Element

Music always exists in a "framework of time." The temporal element, therefore, may be regarded as a fundamental and universal element of music. It is also in many ways the most accessible and comprehensible of the musical elements. Many people claim they cannot "carry a tune" or tell a clarinet from a bassoon, but most people can at least feel the beat of a march or a waltz. Let us then begin our study of the temporal element with consideration of this idea of the beat.

Beat

The basic unit of the temporal element is the beat, a regularly recurring pulsation. In everyday life we find many examples of such regularly recurring pulsations from the tick of a watch to the beat of a heart. In music, beats may be organized by means of accents into groups (meter); their frequency or speed may be regulated (tempo); or they may provide a background against which other temporal units may be sounded (rhythm). In some music beats are enunciated; in other music beats are only implied; and in some music beats, in the sense of regularly recurring pulsations, may be obscured.

The opening of the minuet of Mozart's *Symphony No. 39 in E-flat Major* (K. 543) is an excellent example of enunciated beat. The woodwinds play a clear, regular beat pattern against the string melody. The second movement of the same symphony is a good example of implied beat. No instrument is sounding a regularly recurring pulsation or beat, but we can supply this ourselves as we listen to the flow of the music. For an example of obscured beat we could turn to a recitative passage, for example, the opening recitative in the last act of Mozart's opera, *The Marriage of Figaro,* in which it is difficult to find any clear beat.

We use the term beat to indicate duration as well as pulsation. A tone having a duration of "one beat" would sound from the beginning of one beat (in the sense of pulsation) until the instant preceding the following beat.

Meter

The organization of beats into groups of twos, threes, or larger units is termed meter. This organization is accomplished by placing on the first note of each group an accent or stress. Accents are usually achieved by sounding one note louder than the others (*dynamic* accent), but they may also be achieved by having one note higher than the others (*tonic* accent) or one note longer than others (*agogic* accent).

15

The most common metric groupings are those of two beats or *duple* meter and those of three beats or *triple* meter. While other groupings are possible and frequently employed in music, they are usually heard as combinations of these two basic meters. *Quadruple* meter, for example, is a four-beat grouping with a primary accent on the first beat, no accent on the second beat, a secondary accent on the third beat, and no accent on the fourth beat. In other words, quadruple meter is, in effect, a succession of two duple meter groupings. *Quintuple* meter can be regarded as a combination of duple and triple meter; larger groupings may be similarly analyzed.

These metric groupings of beats, with the first beat accented, are called *measures* and are marked off from one another with *bar lines*. The first beat of a measure is called the *downbeat* and the last beat of a measure is called the *upbeat*. These terms refer to the traditional patterns used in conducting music. In these patterns the first beat of a measure is indicated by a downward gesture and the last by an upward gesture. The conducting patterns for three meters are given in Fig. 1–1. In executing them it is helpful to snap the fingers at the end of each stroke to indicate the precise instant of the beat. Beats with primary accents are indicated > and should receive a more vigorous movement, beats with secondary accents are indicated — and should receive a slightly less vigorous movement, and beats with no accent are unmarked and should be executed with quieter movements.

The patterns given here are theoretical rather than artistic. A skilled conductor makes more supple, curving gestures and he places the last beat

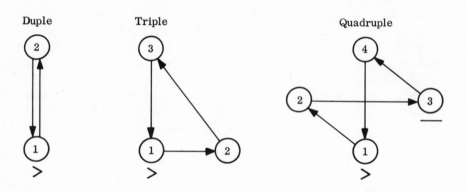

Duple   Triple   Quadruple

Fig. 1-1.

near the bottom of the pattern rather than at the top as we have indicated.

Using these conducting patterns it is possible to determine if a piece begins on the upbeat or downbeat and what basic metric grouping is being used. Listen first to a work, such as the third movement of Brahms' *Symphony No. 1 in C Minor,* which begins on the downbeat, and then to another, such as the main theme of the last movement of the same symphony, which begins on the upbeat, and accompany these with the proper conducting gestures. Notice that the upbeat has a feeling of tension somewhat like an inhalation of breath and that the downbeat has a sensation of release like an exhalation.

To determine aurally the metric grouping of a composition, first listen carefully for the beats and tap these. Then listen for accents and tap these loudly and note how often they come. If they come every other beat, the excerpt is in duple meter; if they come every third beat, the excerpt is in triple meter, etc. To confirm this, perform the appropriate conducting pattern while listening to the music and determine if it "fits"—that is, if the accents in the music coincide with the downbeats in the conducting pattern.

There is another aspect of meter in addition to the organization of beats into groups. We must also consider the manner in which the individual beat itself may be *divided*. If the beat is regularly divided into two equal parts, the meter is *simple;* if the beat is regularly divided into three equal parts, the meter is *compound*. A complete description of a meter would include a term denoting the regular division of the beat (i.e. simple or compound) and a term denoting the number of beats in each measure (i.e. duple, triple, quadruple, etc.). Simple triple meter, for example, would indicate that each beat is regularly divided into two equal parts and that there are three beats in each measure.

The terms simple and compound indicate the basic division of the beat. This does not imply that, in music written in these meters, every beat will be regularly divided. In a simple meter, for example, some beats may have two equal divisions, others may have one tone lasting one-half beat and two tones each lasting one-quarter beat, others may have tones lasting the full beat or longer. The basic effect, however, of a piece written in simple meter will be one of regular division of the beat into two equal parts. To determine whether a meter is simple or compound it is helpful to count aloud the patterns given in Figure 1–2 while listening to the music to find which pattern best fits the music.

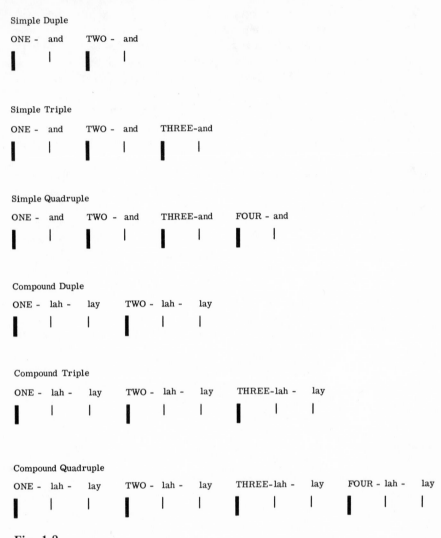

Fig. 1-2.

The following movements provide clear examples of various meters:

Simple Duple: Mozart, *Quartet in B-flat Major,* K. 458, last movement
Compound Duple: Mozart, *Quartet in B-flat Major,* K. 458, first movement
Simple Triple: Mozart, *Symphony No. 39 in E-flat Major,* K. 543, third movement
Compound Triple: Beethoven, *Quartet in F Major,* Op. 18, No. 1, second movement
Simple Quadruple: Brahms, *Symphony No. 1 in C Minor,* Op. 68, last movement, allegro section
Compound Quadruple: Bach, *French Suite No. 5 in G Major,* gigue

Tempo

The speed or frequency with which beats occur in music is referred to as tempo and can be indicated by verbal description or, more precisely, by metronome markings. The metronome marking indicates how many beats occur in one minute; for example, MM60 would indicate that 60 beats occur in one minute.[1] The following chart compares the English, Italian, German, and French tempo terms. Since most composers, regardless of national origin, use the Italian terms, these should be thoroughly learned. Tempo indications fall roughly into three main categories: slow tempos (fewer than sixty beats per minute), moderate tempos (sixty to eighty beats per minute), and fast tempos (more than eighty beats per minute). Composers and performers are by no means consistent in their interpretations of these tempo indications, especially since the terms often refer more to the character of the music rather than to the precise speed of the beat.

English	Italian	German	French
SLOW TEMPOS			
broad	*largo*	*breit*	*large*
slow	*lento*	*langsam*	*lent*
slow	*adagio* (literally, at ease)	*getragen*	*lent*
heavy	*grave*	*schwer*	*lourd*
MODERATE TEMPOS			
moderate	*andante* (literally, walking)	*gehend*	*allant*
	moderato	*mässig*	*moderé*
FAST TEMPOS			
fast	*allegro* (literally, cheerful)	*schnell*	*vite*
lively	*vivace*	*lebhaft*	*vif*
very fast	*presto*	*eilig*	*rapide*

Slight adaptations or modifications in these tempos can be indicated thus:

English	Italian	German	French
very	*molto*	*sehr*	*très*
somewhat	*poco* or *un poco*	*ein wenig* or *etwas*	*un peu*
more	*più*	*—er*	*plus*
even more	*—issimo*	*noch —er*	*encore plus*

[1] MM stands for Maelzel's metronome; it refers to the inventor of the instrument.

background for the temporal element in music. Against this, rhythmic patterns of various durations are sounded.

Let us tap a steady beat and sing the first two lines of "Frère Jacques." Notice that each syllable has a duration of one beat except for the word "vous," which lasts two beats. We could represent this as shown in Example 1–1.

EXAMPLE 1–1.

In actual musical notation, however, we use a set of symbols called *notes* to indicate the relative duration of tones. We use a parallel set of symbols called *rests* to indicate the relative durations of silences in music. Some of these basic symbols are given in Example 1–2.

EXAMPLE 1–2.

Whole Note	o	Whole Rest	▬
Half Note	𝅗𝅥	Half Rest	▬
Quarter Note	𝅘𝅥	Quarter Rest	𝄽
Eighth Note	𝅘𝅥𝅮	Eighth Rest	𝄾
Sixteenth Note	𝅘𝅥𝅯	Sixteenth Rest	𝄿
Thirty- second Note	𝅘𝅥𝅰	Thirty- second Rest	𝅀

In Example 1–2, each note or rest lasts exactly twice as long as the note or rest immediately below it. If we assume that the quarter note lasts one beat, then the half note would last two beats. We could then notate "Frère Jacques" as shown in Example 1–3.

EXAMPLE 1-3.

If we designate the sixteenth note as the beat note, then the notation would be as given in Example 1-4.

EXAMPLE 1-4.

Words: Frè - re Jac - ques Frè - re Jac - ques, Dor - mez vous?___ Dor - mez vous?___

Notation: ♪ ♪ ♪ ♪ ♪ ♪ ♪ ♪ ♪ ♪ ♪ ♪ ♪

Beats

Smaller note values, such as the 64th and the 128th notes, are written by adding additional flags to the note stem (Example 1-5).

EXAMPLE 1-5.

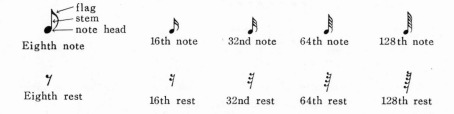

Groups of eighth notes or smaller values may be connected by straight lines called *beams*, which replace the flags and make the note groupings easier to read. Notes should always be beamed in such a manner as to make the main beat structures apparent (Example 1-6).

EXAMPLE 1-6.

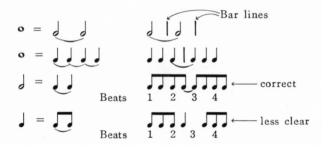

In instrumental music, beams should be used whenever possible. In vocal music, beams may only be used when several notes are sung on one syllable. If each note is sung on a separate syllable, flags must be used as shown in Example 1–4.

The symbol ⌢ called a *tie,* when placed over two notes of the same pitch, indicates that the two tones are to be sounded without any intervening pause or articulation. With this symbol it is possible to indicate relationships between various note values and also to unite two tones of the same pitch across bar lines or occasionally across beats, where its use makes the position of the beats clear.

EXAMPLE 1-7.

A dot (.) placed after a note indicates that one half the duration value of the note is to be added to the note. A second dot adds one half the duration value of the added note to the total duration.

EXAMPLE 1-8.

A *fermata* or hold (◠) placed over a note indicates that it is to be sustained longer than its normal duration.

Time Signatures

Theoretically any note may be designated as having a duration of one beat, but in actual practice the following note values are most frequently employed: ♩ , ♪ , ♩ , ♪ . The time signature at the beginning of a composition or section is a double number, which indicates in the lower figure the type of note which has a duration of one beat and in the upper figure the number of such beats in each measure. The time signature $\frac{2}{4}$ indicates that the quarter note (♩) has the value of one beat and that there are two quarter note beats in each measure.

Time signatures with 2, 3, or 4 as the upper number indicate *simple meters*. Time signatures with 6, 9, or 12 as the upper number indicate *compound meters*. In compound meters the bottom figure is generally not regarded as the beat note; instead the beat note is a note value three times as long. For example, $\frac{6}{8}$ indicates that there are six eighth notes in each measure; however, except for very slow tempos, the dotted quarter note (♩.), not the eighth note (♪) is regarded as the beat note, with two beats in each measure.

The following chart lists the most common time signatures:

	Duple			Triple			Quadruple		
SIMPLE	$\frac{2}{2}$	$\frac{2}{4}$	$\frac{2}{8}$	$\frac{3}{2}$	$\frac{3}{4}$	$\frac{3}{8}$	$\frac{4}{2}$	$\frac{4}{4}$	$\frac{4}{8}$
COMPOUND	$\frac{6}{4}$	$\frac{6}{8}$	$\frac{6}{16}$	$\frac{9}{4}$	$\frac{9}{8}$	$\frac{9}{16}$	$\frac{12}{4}$	$\frac{12}{8}$	$\frac{12}{16}$

The time signatures $\frac{4}{4}$ and $\frac{2}{2}$ are often represented by the symbols **C** and **¢** respectively.

Time signatures with 5, 7, and 11 as the upper figure indicate *complex* or *unusual* meters. The following are some of the possible complex time signatures: $\frac{5}{8}$ $\frac{5}{4}$ $\frac{5}{2}$ $\frac{7}{8}$ $\frac{7}{4}$ $\frac{11}{4}$ etc.

These meters are usually heard and performed as combinations of other meters. Quintuple meter, for example, can be regarded as a combination of duple and triple meter.

EXAMPLE 1–10.

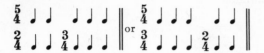

Time signatures or meters indicate nothing with regard to the speed of beats; this is established only through tempo terms or metronome markings.

Rhythmic Patterns

In any measure of music, it is possible to write a great number of rhythmic patterns using various note values, provided that the note values in each measure total the number of beats indicated in the given time signature. In performing and listening to rhythms, it is helpful to analyze the patterns in terms of beats, using ties to indicate the total value of notes lasting longer than one beat.

EXAMPLE 1–11.

In rhythmic patterns involving notes of shorter duration than the beat note, it is helpful to subdivide the beat so that the subdivisions are equal to the shortest note of the rhythmic pattern and then to indicate the value of the given notes with ties.

EXAMPLE 1–12.

Observe that the beams are used in such a manner that the division of the measure into beats is made clear.

Example 1–13 is a selection of some of the more common rhythmic patterns employed in music. Some of the patterns have names derived from their use in particular types of music or from their resemblance to poetic feet; others have no specific name and must be referred to by enumerating the note values used.

EXAMPLE 1–13.

NAME	SIMPLE METER	COMPOUND METER
Trochaic (long-short),also called "dotted rhythm" in simple meters)		
Iambic (short-long), also called "Scotch Snap" or "Hungarian rhythm" in simple meters		
Dactylic (long-short-short), also called "Siciliano rhythm" in compound meters)		
Anapestic (short-short-long)		
Spondaic (even long notes)		
Tribrachic (even short notes)		
(short - long - short)		

The term *triplets* is used when three notes are to be sounded in the time usually taken by two; the term *duplets* is used when two notes are to be sounded in the time usually taken by three. It is also possible to have other, more complex, irregular patterns of this nature, such as having five notes sounded in the time normally occupied by six. These are indicated in Example 1–14.

EXAMPLE 1–14.

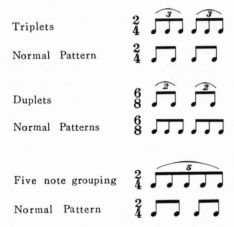

Triplets

Normal Pattern

Duplets

Normal Patterns

Five note grouping

Normal Pattern

Example 1–15 lists all the notes commonly used to express various beats or subdivided beats in simple and compound meters. Any beat value not listed in this table must be expressed by means of two or more notes tied together. For example, a note lasting $1^1/_3$ beats in $\frac{6}{8}$ meter must be expressed ♩. ♪, not ♩ , because the half note would not make the beat structure clear. Rests may be substituted for the equivalent notes, with the exception of a two-beat rest in any simple triple meter, which must be written as two one-beat rests ($\frac{3}{4}$ ♩ 𝄽 𝄽 not $\frac{3}{4}$ ♩ ▬). A rest on the *last* two three-part divisions of a beat in compound meter should be written as two rests ($\frac{6}{8}$ ♪𝄾𝄾♪𝄾𝄾 not $\frac{6}{8}$ ♪𝄽 ♪𝄽).

EXAMPLE 1–15.

Simple Meters			Beats $\frac{1}{8}$	$\frac{1}{4}$	$\frac{3}{8}$	$\frac{1}{2}$	$\frac{5}{8}$	$\frac{3}{4}$	$\frac{7}{8}$	1	$1\frac{1}{2}$	$1\frac{3}{4}$	2	3	$3\frac{1}{2}$	4
♪	=	Beat Note														
♩	=	Beat Note														
♩	=	Beat Note														
♩	=	Beat Note														

Compound Meters		Beats $\frac{1}{6}$	$\frac{1}{3}$	$\frac{1}{2}$	$\frac{2}{3}$	$\frac{5}{6}$	1	2	3	4
♪. =	Beat Note	♬	♪	♪.	♪	♪♬	♪.	♩.	♩. ♪.	♩.
♩. =	Beat Note	♬	♪	♪.	♩	♩♪	♩.	♩.	♩. ♩.	o·
♩. =	Beat Note	♪	♩	♩.	♩	♩♪	♩.	o·	o· ♩.	⋈·*

* ⋈ = Breve   ⋈· = Dotted Breve

Rhythmic Characteristics

The term *rhythm* (Greek: flow) is used not only in the sense of rhythmic patterns but also in the broader sense of "everything pertaining to the temporal quality (duration) of the musical sound."[2] In this latter sense, we can point to such rhythmic characteristics as the following:

Prominence. Rhythm in a musical composition can be prominent or subordinate depending upon whether it dominates other elements, such as timbre or texture. The rhythm of a dance movement like the *Gigue* from the *French Suite No. 5* by Bach is likely to be more prominent than that of a slow sacred choral composition, for example, Palestrina's *Missa Papae Marcellus.*

Complexity. A composition has a simple rhythm if the temporal factors, especially the rhythmic patterns, are regular and easily perceivable; it has complex rhythm if the temporal factors are complicated and more difficult to perceive. A folk song such as "Frère Jacques" is rhythmically simple; a modern composition such as Bartók's *Music for Strings, Percussion, and Celesta* is rhythmically complex.

Consistency. Consistent rhythm implies that the same or similar patterns, meters, and tempos are used throughout a composition; inconsistent rhythm implies considerable change and variety in these temporal factors. An example of consistent rhythmic usage is the slow movement of Beethoven's *Symphony No. 7 in A Major;* an example of inconsistent rhythm is Stravinsky's *Le Sacre du Printemps.*

Flexibility. Rhythm in music is termed rigid or strict when the onset of the notes of the rhythmic patterns coincides precisely with the beat or subdivided beat. When this is not the case, the rhythm is flexible or *rubato.* A waltz such as Strauss' *Blue Danube* is usually performed with more flexibility or *rubato* than the minuet of Haydn's *Symphony No. 104 in D Major.* We can test this by listening to recordings of the two works, conducting the triple meter pattern, and noting how the rhythms of the

---

2 Willi Apel, *The Harvard Dictionary of Music* (Cambridge, Mass.: Harvard University Press, 1950), p. 640.

waltz often come slightly before or after the beat. In contrast, the rhythms of the minuet occur precisely on the beat or on subdivisions of the beat.

   Syncopation.   Music is syncopated when the normal accents of the metric background are negated by the rhythmic patterns of the music; it is non-syncopated when the metric accents are confirmed. Syncopation may be achieved in a variety of ways. Example 1–16 is syncopated because it has some dynamic accents in normally unaccented portions of the measure.

EXAMPLE 1–16. Stravinsky, *Le Sacre du Printemps*, "Dance of the Adolescents. © 1921 by Edition Russe de Musique. Copyright assigned to Boosey & Hawkes, Inc. 1947. Reprinted by permission.

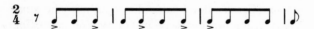

Syncopation is achieved in Example 1–17 by having agogic accents (longer notes) on the second beats of each measure, and by having rests on the first part of the downbeat in measures 2, 3, and 4.

EXAMPLE 1–17. Beethoven, *String Quartet in E Minor*, Op. 59, No. 2, third movement.

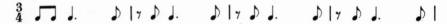

Example 1–18 illustrates another type of syncopation achieved by beginning notes on an unaccented beat and carrying their duration over a normally accented beat.

EXAMPLE 1–18. Schumann, *Symphony No. 3 in E-flat Major*, first movement.

Syncopation may also be achieved by beginning notes within one beat and carrying their duration over the following beat as shown in Example 1–19.

EXAMPLE 1–19. Brahms, *Symphony No. 2 in D Major*, second movement.

Syncopation and flexible rhythm, though sometimes similar in the final aural result, are not synonymous. Syncopation refers to aspects of the written music; flexible rhythm refers to aspects of performance practice. Other technical terms referring to the temporal element will be introduced in the historical section immediately following.

The Temporal Element in Music Literature

Pre-Baroque. It is difficult to discuss the temporal element in earlier music because of the ambiguities of notation and the lack of accurate information on performance practice. Musicologists are not agreed, for example, on the proper rhythmic interpretation of Gregorian chant. One likely theory holds that it should be sung with most of the notes of equal duration, and with no regular metric grouping. An example of Gregorian chant in the original *neumatic* notation and in conventional notation, according to this theory, is given in Examples 6–2 and 6–3.

The addition of other musical lines to the single line of Gregorian chant and the influence of the dance gradually brought about a greater use of metric music. In the Medieval period triple meter was held to be superior because of its reference to the Holy Trinity; it was called *perfect* because in its three beats it had a beginning, middle, and end. Gradually duple meter was accorded equal stature and, in the Renaissance period, was used frequently. In this period, metric accent was largely achieved through agogic and tonal accent, and the metric feeling was often deliberately obscured through the use of subtle syncopation and differing rhythms in the various voices. This is illustrated in the excerpt from Palestrina in Example 4–67. Originally this music was notated without bar lines.

Baroque. Instrumental music of this period is marked by a high degree of consistency in rhythmic usage. One meter (duple, triple, or quadruple in simple or compound form) is used throughout a movement. One rhythmic pattern may dominate a movement, especially in fast movements. Usually one tempo is to be maintained for each movement without change or *rubato,* but unfortunately this is not always observed in modern performances. Baroque dance forms may be characterized according to their temporal features as follows:

Dance	National Origin	Meter	Tempo	Rhythm
ALLEMANDE	German	quadruple	moderately slow	usually begins with up-beat, frequently uses dotted rhythms and short running figures

{ COURANTE OR	French	triple	moderate	often uses hemiola * at ends of phrases
CORRENTE	Italian	triple	fast	usually in steadily moving sixteenth notes
SARABANDE	Spanish	triple	slow	usually begins on downbeat, often has accent on second beat
GIGUE	English	compound duple	fast	often uses trochaic patterns

* Hemiola refers to the use of rhythmic patterns from compound duple meter in a work written in simple triple meter, or vice versa. This is usually indicated by note values rather than by a change of time signature. ($\frac{3}{2}$ ♩ ♩ ♩ |♩ ♩ |)

Much vocal music of the Baroque period shows the same consistency of meter, tempo, and rhythm. One exception to this general rule is the *recitative,* developed first in the operas, cantatas, and other vocal works of this period, and characterized by rhythmic inconsistency and rhythmic flexibility. In recitative, the rhythm of the music follows more or less closely the natural rhythmic inflection of the text, as can be seen in the recitative from Handel's *Messiah* in Example 7–1.

Classical. Composers of the Classical period achieved a balance in the temporal element between consistency and inconsistency, and between simplicity and complexity. Contrasting rhythmic patterns were used within a movement, and the strong rhythmic drive of a Baroque fast instrumental movement was replaced by a supple rhythmic flow, with occasional tempo changes. The meters of the Baroque period continued to be used.

The *minuet,* which actually originated in the Baroque period, became the standard third movement of the Classical symphony. Originally in moderate triple meter, its tempo was gradually increased until it was replaced by the faster *scherzo* (Italian: joke), especially in Beethoven's instrumental music. The *march,* which was also first heard in the Baroque period, appeared in the Classical period in at least three types—the slow funeral march, the moderate processional march, and the fast military march—all of which are in duple or quadruple meter.

Romantic. In contrast to the balance achieved by Classical composers in rhythmic characteristics, Romantic composers tended toward inconsistency, complexity, and flexibility. Changes of tempo and *rubato* became almost hallmarks of the style and the range of possible tempos increased. A greater variety of rhythmic patterns, more varied use of syncopation, triplets, and other irregular patterns, and rhythmic conflict between various parts add to the expressiveness and excitement of the music. Tentative experiments in the use of complex meters were made.

New stylized dance forms appearing in the music of the period include the following:

Dance	National Origin	Meter	Tempo	Rhythm
LANDLER	German	triple	moderate	heavy accent on the first beat
WALTZ	German	triple	in general fast, but some waltzes are moderate or slow	more flexible or "lilting" than the Ländler; often achieved by anticipating the second and third beats in the accompaniment
MAZURKA	Polish	triple	moderate	often accented on second or more usually the third beat
POLONAISE	Polish	triple	moderate	often uses this rhythmic pattern:

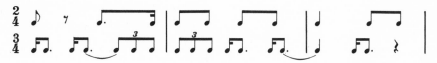

Dance	National Origin	Meter	Tempo	Rhythm
POLKA	Bohemian	duple	fast	often uses this pattern:
DUMKA	Bohemian	various	alternating slow and fast sections	

Contemporary.   Complexity, inconsistency, syncopation, and changes in tempo and meter are characteristics of the temporal element in most contemporary music. Contemporary composers have emphasized and expanded the possibilities of the temporal element, introducing such innovations as the following:

Polymeter. The *simultaneous* combination of two or more different meters (Example 1–20).

EXAMPLE 1–20.   Stravinsky, *Petrouchka*, first scene. © by Edition Russe de Musique. All rights assigned to Boosey & Hawkes Inc. Reprinted by permission.

Multimeter. Frequent changes of meter in *successive* measures (Example 1–21).

EXAMPLE 1–21. Stravinsky, *Le Sacre du Printemps,* "Sacrificial Dance." © 1921 by Edition Russe de Musique. Copyright assigned to Boosey & Hawkes Inc., 1947. Reprinted by permission.

Unusual meters. Metric groupings of 5, 7, or 11 beats, or more complicated metric indications such as in Example 1–22.

EXAMPLE 1–22. Bartók, *Mikrokosmos,* Vol. VI, "Dance No. 1 in Bulgarian Rhythm." © 1940 by Hawkes & Son (London) Ltd. Reprinted by permission of Boosey & Hawkes Inc.

Polyrhythm. The simultaneous usage of two or more strikingly different rhythmic patterns (Example 1–23).

EXAMPLE 1–23. Ives, *Three Places in New England,* "The Housatonic at Stockbridge." Used by permission of the copyright owner, Harmony Twitchell Ives, and Mercury Music Corporation.

Contemporary composers often write highly complex and irregular rhythms. An extreme example of this is the complicated rhythms used in some electronic music, which cannot be expressed in conventional notation, but must be indicated in precise mathematical measurements of duration as shown in Example 10–9.

Jazz has made unique contributions to the development of the temporal element of contemporary music, but this has come, to a great extent, from aspects of performance practice. Much of the distinctive character of jazz comes from an almost indescribable phenomenon known as "swing," which refers to a "loose" relationship between the strongly accented underlying pulse of the music and the characteristic rhythmic patterns played against it.[3]

The written aspects of the temporal element in jazz do not differ radically from other contemporary and earlier music. Despite differences between such jazz styles as *ragtime, blues, swing, bebop,* and *progressive,* most of this music can be described as being in duple or quadruple meter with frequent usage of characteristic accented syncopated rhythms. Although notated in simple meter, much jazz music has a feeling of compound meter in per-

formance. For example, the dotted figure ♩. ♪ is usually played thus ♩ ♪,

a practice that is also implied, interestingly enough, in certain Baroque compositions.

Among the characteristic musical styles and dances used in jazz and sometimes incorporated in other contemporary music are the following:

Type	*Meter*	*Tempo*	*Rhythm*
RAGTIME	duple	fast	often uses this characteristic pattern:

BLUES	duple	slow	often uses tango-like rhythms and syncopations
SWING	duple	fast	subtle *rubato* in solo instruments plus precision of attack in rhythm section
BEBOP	duple	various	more complex rhythms plus accentuation of second and fourth beats

Progressive jazz shows the influence of certain aspects of contemporary non-jazz music; some exponents play in complex, highly inconsistent and irregular rhythms, others play in a free, almost non-metric style.

In addition to these styles, which originated in the United States, other dance types originating in Latin America have been incorporated into jazz and other contemporary music. These include the *tango,* which is based on the earlier *habanera* and is in slow duple meter with syncopation, the *rhumba,* which is in fast duple meter with much syncopation and repetition,

---

[3] For a fuller discussion of swing and other aspects of jazz, see Jerry Coker, *Improvising Jazz* (Englewood Cliffs, N.J.: Prentice-Hall, Inc., 1964).

and the more recent *bossa nova* in which a highly syncopated melodic line is set against the following underlying rhythmic patterns:

Despite the importance of innovation in the temporal element of contemporary music, many contemporary composers display an eclectic approach and restrict themselves to previous rhythmic practices, relying on other elements to provide novelty in their music.

Temporal Element Summary

BEAT

enunciated, implied, obscured; downbeat beginning, upbeat beginning

ACCENT

dynamic, tonal, agogic

METER

regular division of the beat:
simple, compound
number of beats in the measure:
duple, triple, quadruple, quintuple, etc.
other:
non-metric, polymetric, multimetric
possible time signature ($\frac{2}{4}$, $\frac{6}{8}$ etc.)

TEMPO

basic tempo:
very slow, slow, moderate, fast, very fast
changes of tempo:
no change of tempo, some change of tempo, frequent change of tempo, possible tempo designations in Italian

RHYTHM

prominence:
very prominent, fairly prominent, subordinate
consistency:
highly consistent, fairly consistent, inconsistent
complexity:
simple, fairly complex, highly complex
flexibility:
rigid, fairly rigid, flexible
syncopation:
highly syncopated, moderately syncopated, non-syncopated
rhythmic patterns:
indicate with dots and dashes for short and long notes and with possible rhythmic notation

Exercises

Analysis

1. Indicate what equivalent notes could be used in place of the tied notes given in Example 1–24.

EXAMPLE 1–24.

a ♩♩ = 𝅗𝅥   f ♩♩♩♩ =

b ♩♪ = 𝅗𝅥.   g ♩♩♩ =

c ♪♪ =   h ♩♩♩♩♩♩ =

d 𝅗𝅥𝅗𝅥 =   i ♫ =

e ♪♪♪ =   j ♩♪♪ =

2. Indicate possible rhythmic notation for the patterns in Example 1–25.

EXAMPLE 1–25.

| 1 2 3 4 | = | $\begin{cases} \frac{4}{4} \\ \frac{4}{8} \\ \frac{4}{16} \end{cases}$ 𝅗𝅥 ♩♩ / ♩ ♫ / ♩ ♫ | 1 2 3 | = | $\begin{cases} \frac{3}{4} \\ \frac{3}{2} \\ \frac{3}{8} \end{cases}$ |

| 1 2 3 4 | = | $\begin{cases} \frac{4}{4} \\ \frac{4}{8} \\ \frac{4}{2} \end{cases}$ | 1 2 | = | $\begin{cases} \frac{6}{8} \\ \frac{6}{4} \\ \frac{6}{2} \end{cases}$ |

3. Refer to the music examples in Part II and to other music and find examples of the following: simple, compound, and complex meters; polymeter and multimeter; syncopation; triplets; inconsistent rhythms, etc.

Composition

1. Write examples (rhythm only, no pitches) according to the following specifications.

    a. downbeat beginning, simple triple meter ($\frac{3}{4}$ $\frac{3}{2}$ or $\frac{3}{8}$); andante tempo with no tempo changes; simple, consistent, non-syncopated rhythmic characteristics (8 measures).

    b. upbeat beginning, compound duple meter, allegro tempo with no tempo changes, fairly complex, inconsistent, moderately syncopated rhythmic characteristics (8 measures).

    c. 4 measures of polymeter, other temporal factors not specified.

    d. 7 measures of multimeter with frequent tempo change, other temporal factors not specified.

    e. free rhythmic composition, no temporal factors specified.

Performance

1. Practice conducting the various meters in various tempos.

2. Practice tapping and singing various rhythmic patterns given on page 27. Establish a meter and conduct it with the right hand, tap the beat or a subdivision of the beat with the left hand, and sing various rhythmic patterns. This may sound very complicated, but it can be done if kept simple and if the tempo is not too fast. For example:

EXAMPLE 1–26.

3. Disregarding other elements, perform just the temporal element of various musical examples from Part II.

4. Perform your original compositions.

Listening

1. Listen to the following examples and describe them according to the temporal element summary, *i.e.,* indicate if the beat is enunciated, implied, or obscured; if it begins on an upbeat or downbeat, etc. Refer to these sections for hints on listening:

  a. Palestrina, *Missa Papae Marcellus*
  b. Bach, *French Suite No. 5 in G Major*
  c. Beethoven, *Quartet in C Major,* Op. 59, No. 3
  d. Brahms, *Symphony No. 2 in D Major,* Op. 73 (Note changes in each section of the third movement.)
  e. Stravinsky, *L'Histoire du Soldat*

2. Using aspects of the temporal element as criteria, identify the stylistic characteristics of unfamiliar compositions and make an "informed guess," based on the characteristics discussed at the end of this chapter, as to the period in which the compositions were written. In the classroom situation, the teacher can select these compositions from those discussed in Part II of the text and from other music. The individual reader can approximate this situation by having another person play records for him, or by tuning in the middle of a good music program on radio and analyzing the work as it is played.

chapter **2**

The
Tonal
Element

For purposes of discussion we shall consider the tonal element by itself here, although in performance it is inseparable from aspects of the temporal element. The combination of the tonal and temporal elements is *melody.* The term melody is often erroneously used to indicate only the pitch aspect of music. In its most meaningful usage, however, a consideration of melody embraces both pitch and rhythm.

Although the study of the tonal element is more complex and challenging than that of the temporal, it is well within the grasp of the average student to develop the ability to perceive, appreciate, and perform its manifold aspects. Calvin Coolidge once claimed that he could only recognize two melodies—one of them was "The Star-Spangled Banner" and the other one was not. Most readers are already beyond that stage and can profit from a detailed study of this fascinating musical element.

Tone

The basic unit of the tonal element in music is the *tone,* a musical sound with a fixed pitch or regular rate of vibration. From the total spectrum of frequencies perceivable by the human ear (20 to 20,000 cycles per second), music employs only a selected number of pitches, which correspond approximately to the 88 tones of the piano. The term *note* is often used as a synonym for tone even though, in the strictest sense, note should refer only to the written symbol and tone to the heard pitch.

Pitch Designation

We can best understand the basic principles of pitch designation by referring to the piano keyboard which consists of 52 white keys and 36 black keys, with the black keys arranged in alternating groups of twos and threes. The lowest tone on the piano is to the extreme left when facing the keyboard; the tones rise in pitch from left to right. The white keys of the piano are designated by the first seven letters of the alphabet (A–G); the lowest white key on the standard piano keyboard is called A_2, the next white key to the right is called B_2, the next C_1, etc., as indicated in Example 2–1. As we proceed from left to right on the keyboard, the same seven letters are repeated several times for pitch designation. To distinguish between tones with the same letter designation, we add numerical sub- or superscripts and change from capital to small letters, changing to a new form always on a C.

EXAMPLE 2–1.

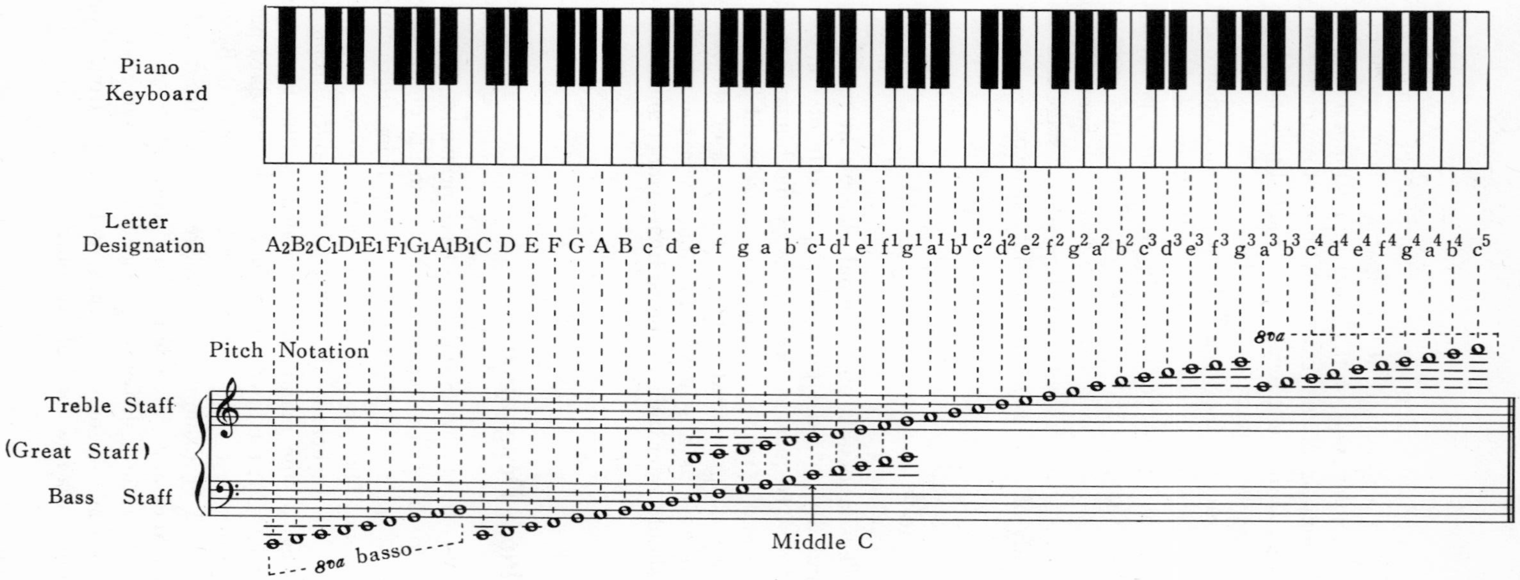
Piano Keyboard
Letter Designation
A2B2C1D1E1F1G1A1B1C D E F G A B c d e f g a b c1 d1 e1 f1 g1 a1 b1 c2 d2 e2 f2 g2 a2 b2 c3 d3 e3 f3 g3 a3 b3 c4 d4 e4 f4 g4 a4 b4 c5
Pitch Notation
Treble Staff
(Great Staff)
Bass Staff
8va
8va basso
Middle C

The arrangement of the black keys in groups of twos and threes facilitates the location of various tones. For example, all of the *C*s on the piano lie to the left of groups of two black keys. The location of the other white keys can readily be understood by studying Example 2–1.

The black keys are named according to their relationship to the white keys immediately above or below. This involves the use of the following special signs or *accidentals:* ♯ (sharp), indicating the raising of pitch, and ♭ (flat), indicating the lowering of pitch. The black key between *C* and *D* can be designated either as *C*♯ (C-sharp), indicating that it is above *C*; or it can be designated as *D*♭ (D-flat), indicating that it is below *D*. The other black keys may be similarly designated as can be seen by studying the keyboard and the bottom line in Example 2–2. There are no black keys between *E* and *F* or between *B* and *C*; therefore, *E*-sharp is the same as *F*, and similarly *F*-flat is the same as *E*, *B*-sharp is the same as *C*, *C*-flat is the same as *B*. Two tones having the same pitch but different letter designations (for example, *E*-sharp and *F*) are called *enharmonic* tones.[1]

Occasionally double sharps (✖) and double flats (♭♭) are used to indicate the double raising or double lowering of pitch. For example, *F* ✖ would be the same as *G, B* ♭♭ would be the same as *A,* etc. The relationship of these less commonly used accidentals to the piano keyboard can be seen by studying the top line of Example 2–2.

The natural sign (♮) indicates a return to the normal or "white-key" note.

---

[1] Enharmonic tones have the same pitch only when *equal temperament* is used; in other tuning systems, such as *just intonation,* there is a slight difference in pitch between the two tones. For fuller information, see the *Harvard Dictionary of Music* article on *temperament.*

EXAMPLE 2–2.

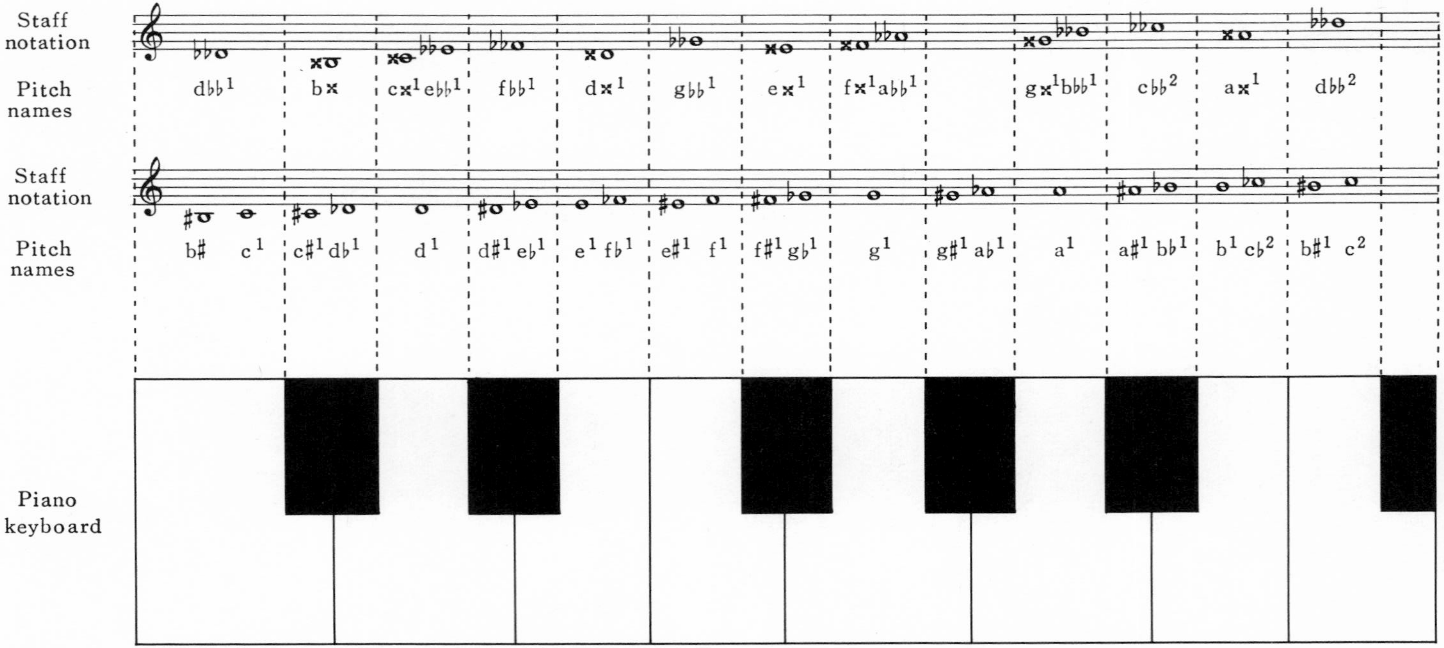
Staff notation
Pitch names
d♭♭1
b𝄪
c𝄪1 e♭♭1
f♭♭1
d𝄪1
g♭♭1
e𝄪1
f𝄪1 a♭♭1
g𝄪1 b♭♭1
c♭♭2
a𝄪1
d♭♭2
Staff notation
Pitch names
b♯ c1
c♯1 d♭1
d1
d♯1 e♭1
e1 f♭1
e♯1 f1
f♯1 g♭1
g1
g♯1 a♭1
a1
a♯1 b♭1
b1 c♭2
b♯1 c2
Piano keyboard

Pitch Notation

It would be possible to write music using only letter designations as described above. For example, "Frère Jacques" could be written as follows:

$$c^2 \quad d^2 \quad e^2 \quad c^2 \qquad c^2 \quad d^2 \quad e^2 \quad c^2$$

Frè - re Jac - ques, Frè - re Jac - ques, (etc.).

It is, however, more efficient to use a group of five parallel lines, called a *staff* and to indicate pitches by placing the head of the note symbols of rhythmic notation on the lines or spaces of the staff. A *clef sign* at the beginning of the staff indicates the location of one specific pitch; from this we can determine the location of other pitches, since adjacent lines and spaces on the staff correspond to adjacent letters in pitch designation. Music has a wide range of pitches so various clefs are needed to cover segments of this total range.

The earliest clef signs were actual letters; later these evolved into the present symbols as shown in Example 2–3. A staff is named according to the clef used; a staff with a treble clef is called a treble staff, one with a bass clef is called a bass staff, etc. The combination of the treble and bass staffs is called the great staff.

EXAMPLE 2–3.

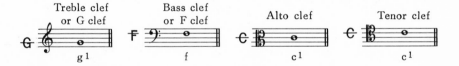

It would be possible to write music using only letter designations

Examples 2–1 and 2–2 illustrate the relation of pitch designation and the piano keyboard to pitch notation in the treble and bass staffs. For notes above or below the staff, short lines, called *ledger lines,* must be added. For notes requiring more than three or four ledger lines, it is customary to use the designations *8ve basso* and *8ve soprano* (or simply *8ve*) indicating that the actual note is eight notes (one *octave*) lower or higher than the written note. This is illustrated in Example 2–4.

EXAMPLE 2–4.

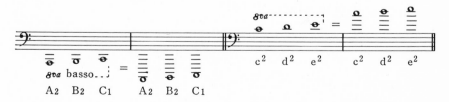

EXAMPLE 2-4. continued.

Sharps, flats, and naturals are indicated in pitch notation by placing the proper accidental sign immediately before the note-head. For notes below the middle line of the staff the stems should begin at the right side of the note-head and extend upward; above the middle line stems should begin at the left side of the note-head and extend downward; on the middle line itself stems may extend in either direction. Flags are always written on the right side of the note-stem. These principles are illustrated in Example 2-5.

EXAMPLE 2-5.

Before proceeding to the next section of this chapter, readers with little or no experience in pitch notation should study the preliminary exercises at the end of this chapter. A moderate degree of facility in reading the treble and bass clefs can easily be acquired in a short period of concentrated study. To attempt any further serious study of music without this ability would be like attempting to study Shakespeare without knowing how to read and write the English language.

Melodic Intervals

The musical distance between two successive pitches is called a *melodic interval*. The smallest interval used in Western music is the half step or minor second. Referring to Example 2-2, we see that half steps on the piano keyboard can be found between the white keys *B* and *C* and between *E* and *F*; in all other cases, they exist between a white key and an adjacent black key. Intervals larger than a half step can be named according to the number of half steps comprising the interval or according to the traditional theoretical terminology as given in the following list. The interval name consists of a *numerical* name (third, fifth, etc.) preceded by a *descriptive* name (major, perfect, etc.). Another system for determining intervals is given in the exercises at the end of this chapter.

Number of half steps from lower to higher tone	Interval name(s)	Example (from c)
0	prime, unison, (repeated tone)	c—c
1	augmented prime, (chromatic* half step)	c—c-sharp
1	minor second, (diatonic* half step)	c—d-flat
2	major second, (whole step)	c—d
3	augmented second	c—d-sharp
3	minor third	c—e-flat
4	major third	c—e
4	diminished fourth	c—f-flat
5	perfect fourth	c—f
6	augmented fourth	c—f-sharp
6	diminished fifth	c—g-flat
7	perfect fifth	c—g
8	augmented fifth	c—g-sharp
8	minor sixth	c—a-flat
9	major sixth	c—a
9	diminished seventh	c—b-double-flat
10	augmented sixth	c—a-sharp
10	minor seventh	c—b-flat
11	major seventh	c—b
11	diminished octave	c—c-flat^1
12	perfect octave	c—c^1
13	augmented octave	c—c-sharp^1
13	minor ninth	c—d-flat^1
14	major ninth	c—d^1

* A chromatic half step involves two tones with the *same* letter name but different accidentals. A diatonic half step involves two tones with *different* letter names.

Scales

A scale is a prescribed arrangement of successive pitches, usually running from the lowest pitch to the highest in ascending order (or vice-versa) like the steps of a ladder (Latin: *scala,* ladder). The most commonly used scale is the *major scale,* which can be written as in Example 2–6, using only natural notes.

EXAMPLE 2–6.

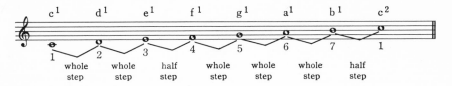

This scale contains seven different pitch names. The eighth tone has the same pitch name as the first and can be regarded as the end of one scale or the beginning of the next. It is important to know that there are whole steps or major seconds between all degrees of the scale except between the third and fourth degrees and between the seventh and upper first degrees. We can write major scales beginning on any note provided we maintain the proper intervals between adjacent notes, using accidentals when necessary. For example, to write a major scale beginning on D, we must use F-sharp and C-sharp to preserve the proper interval relationships.

EXAMPLE 2–7.

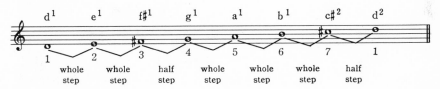

The next most commonly used scale is the *minor scale,* which can be found on the white keys of the piano between a[1] and a.[2] The scale in this form is called *pure* minor. Other forms of the minor scale involve various alterations of the sixth and seventh degrees of the scale as indicated in Example 2–8.

EXAMPLE 2–8.

Pure Minor (Natural Minor)

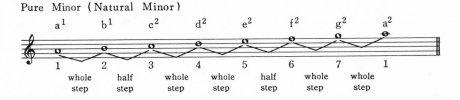

EXAMPLE 2–8. continued.

Harmonic Minor

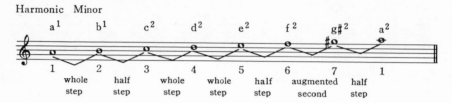

Melodic Minor (ascending)

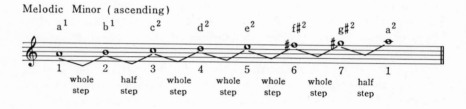

Melodic Minor (desending)

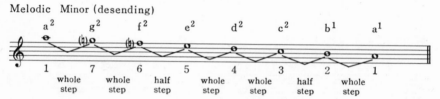

The major and minor scales are called *diatonic* (Greek: through the tones). If we alter tones of a diatonic scale by adding or changing accidentals, we produce what are called *chromatic* tones. The chromatic scale includes the seven tones of a diatonic major scale with five chromatic tones inserted between degrees 1 and 2, 2 and 3, 4 and 5, 5 and 6, and 6 and 7. We cannot insert chromatic tones between degrees 3 and 4 or between 7 and upper 1, because half steps already exist there; chromatic tones would merely introduce enharmonic duplications. It is customary to use sharps for ascending chromatic scales and flats for descending chromatic scales.

EXAMPLE 2–9.

Ascending chromatic scale

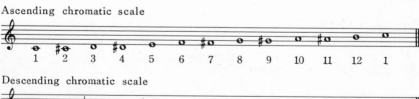

Descending chromatic scale

In addition to the major, minor, and chromatic scales, other scale forms may also be used. One of the earliest scale forms was the *pentatonic*. This scale of five tones is found in primitive and oriental music and also sometimes used, or at least implied, in popular songs.

EXAMPLE 2–10.

The *whole-tone scale,* as the name implies, consists exclusively of whole tones or major seconds.

EXAMPLE 2–11.

The predecessors of the modern major and minor scales were the *church modes*. The names of the various modes were taken from Greek tribes because when these scale forms were first formulated and discussed, it was thought that they were the same as scale forms used in ancient Greek music. Actually the Greek scale forms were considerably different. There is, however, no need for us to consider the Greek scale forms since we have virtually no extant music based upon them. The most commonly used church modes are shown in Example 2–12.

EXAMPLE 2–12.

Dorian

Phrygian

EXAMPLE 2–12. continued.

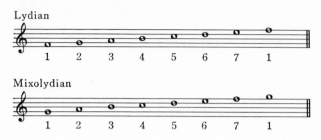

Key Signatures

    To save the labor involved in writing accidentals before each note in scales or compositions, it is possible to summarize all the appropriate accidentals at the beginning of each staff line. This collection of accidentals is called the *key signature*. Key signatures and a sample scale for all major and minor scales or keys are given in Example 2–13. The *relative* minor scale begins on the sixth degree of the major scale and uses the same key signature. The *parallel* minor scale begins on the same note as the major scale and uses the key signature of the major scale a minor third above. The key signatures for minor scales are valid only for the pure minor; extra accidentals must be added in the course of the scale or composition if the harmonic or melodic forms are to be used.

EXAMPLE 2–13.

D Major · B Minor · D Minor

A Major · F♯ Minor · A Minor

E Major · C♯ Minor · E Minor

B Major · G♯ Minor · B Minor

F♯ Major · D♯ Minor · F♯ Minor

G♭ Major · E♭ Minor · G♭ Minor = F♯ Minor

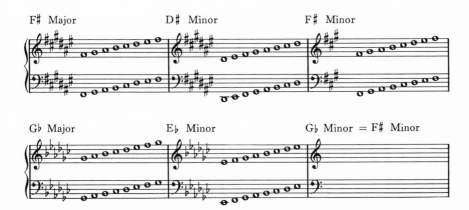

EXAMPLE 2–13. continued.

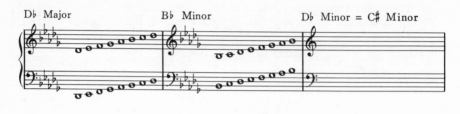

Db Major   Bb Minor   Db Minor = C# Minor

Ab Major   F Minor   Ab Minor

Eb Major   C Minor   Eb Minor

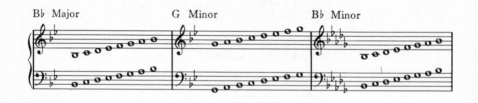

Bb Major   G Minor   Bb Minor

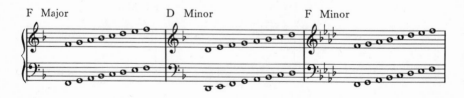

F Major   D Minor   F Minor

Accidentals in a key signature apply to all octaves of the particular note during the entire section of music or until a change of key signature. Additional accidentals, introduced during the course of the composition, apply only to the given octave of the particular note and only during the measure in which the accidental appears.

Scale Properties

In addition to the intervallic relationships between successive tones, the individual tones of a scale have commonly accepted designations and characteristics as indicated in the following listing:

Scale Degree	Name	Characteristics
first	tonic	often the beginning and ending tone of a composition, and usually the most frequently used tone in a composition; feeling of rest, stability, or "home base."
second	supertonic	active or unstable tone, generally leads to first or third degree.
third	mediant	rest tone, important in distinction between major and minor.
fourth	subdominant	active or unstable tone, usually leads to third degree.
fifth	dominant	rest tone, usually second most frequently used tone; often used for upbeats.
sixth	submediant	active tone, often leads to fifth degree.
seventh	leading tone	active tone, usually leads to first degree.

Tonal Characteristics

Tonality, key, mode. We have presented the concepts of single tone, melodic interval, and scale, and, in so doing, may have created the impression that music is made out of scales. Historically, however, this is false. Melodies were created before scales were formulated. Scales are only a theoretical summary of the tonal material available for a particular composition, or they can be thought of as a pedagogical abstraction. To understand this, let us examine the following melodic segment from the Lutheran chorale, "A Mighty Fortress Is Our God." If we arrange all the tones used in ascending order and indicate above each tone the number of beats it is used, we arrive at the following:

EXAMPLE 2-14. "A Mighty Fortress Is Our God."

We see that *D* is the first and last tone and the most frequently used tone of the composition, so that we can conclude that *D* is the tonic (see scale properties). A study of the scale above *D*, which we abstracted from the melody, shows that it has the interval structure proper to the diatonic major scale. We can say then that this piece is in the key of D major.

The example just analyzed is regular and relatively easy to analyze because the tonic appears as the first, last, and most frequently used tone, and the other tones used can be arranged conveniently in an ascending scale. The following examples are less obvious, but the basic principle remains the same: first seek the tonic, then arrange the other tones used above it in ascending order to determine the type of scale organization. Often tones beyond the eight tones of the one octave scale will be used; sometimes not all the tones of the scale will included. Occasionally, tones not normally in the scale are used. If these are not written too frequently, they do not disturb the basic key feeling. If these are used repeatedly (for example, if *F*-sharp is always used instead of *F*), it is possible that a key other than the one indicated in the key signature is being employed.

In Example 2–15, although D-flat is not the first tone of the piece, it is the last and most frequently used tone and should therefore be regarded as tonic. The melody extends beyond the eight tones of a one-octave major scale. The excerpt is in the key of D-flat major.

EXAMPLE 2–15. Dvořák, *Symphony No. 5 in E Minor*, second movement.

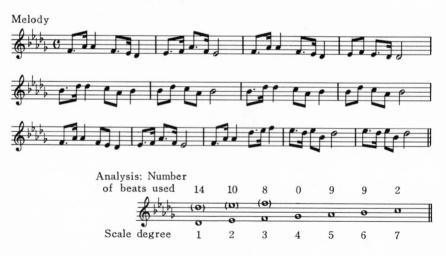

The next example is in the key of E minor. Only five tones of the scale are used, but the position of E as tonic is clearly established by its frequency and position as final note of the excerpt.

EXAMPLE 2–16. Dvořák, *Symphony No. 5 in E Minor,* third movement.

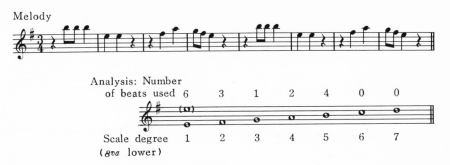

The following example is in the key of E-flat major. The use of one *B* natural does not destroy the basic key feeling of E-flat major.

EXAMPLE 2–17. Haydn, *Quartet in E-flat Major,* Op. 33, No. 2, first movement.

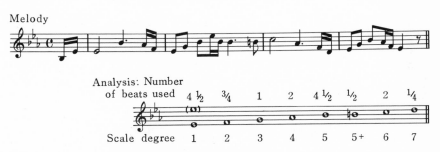

Example 2–18 has a key signature of E-flat major; however, the continuous use of *A* natural and the position of *B*-flat as first and last note indicate that the composition at this point is actually in the key of B-flat major.

EXAMPLE 2–18. Mozart, *Symphony No. 39 in E-flat Major,* first movement, (K. 543).

The term *key* refers to the particular tone used as tonic in a composition and to the intervallic ordering of the scale tones above this tonic. The term is limited to description of major and minor keys. The term *mode* applies specifically to the intervallic arrangement of scale tones above the tonic. It is used not only in major and minor but also for other forms such as the church modes. Indeed, the term *modal* implies that a piece is in one of the church modes.

Tonality is a broader term than either of these and refers to all the various possible relations between one central tone (the tonic) and the other tones used in a composition. The term *tonality* can be used as a synonym for key: we can say a composition is written in the key of G minor or in the tonality of G minor. It can also be used for complex, irregular tonal organizations. For example, the melody in Example 2–19 is not in any particular key, but it is possible to say the tonality is centered on E, with a secondary center or "dominant" on B-flat.

EXAMPLE 2-19.   Bartók, *Fifth String Quartet*, finale. © 1936 by Universal Editions ; renewed 1963. Copyright & renewal assigned to Boosey & Hawkes Inc. for the U.S.A. Reprinted by permission.

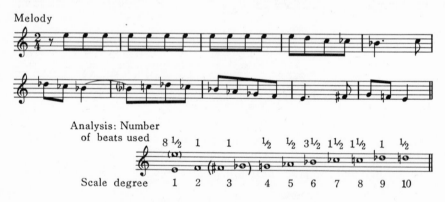

So far, we have been discussing tonal characteristics only in terms of written music. Of far more importance is the cultivation of the ability to distinguish tonal characteristics aurally, for music is, after all, an aural phenomenon. For maximum enjoyment, the listener needs to cultivate this ability to analyze aurally just as much as a spectator at a football game needs to cultivate an ability to recognize the various plays being used.

One basic distinction to be made in terms of tonality is that between major and minor. It is usually true that the major mode has a brighter, more cheerful, more positive character than the minor mode, but occasionally other musical elements, especially the temporal element, will tend to negate these characteristics. A more reliable method is to develop the ability to compare a particular composition to certain prototype compositions which have clear-cut major or minor characteristics. Particular attention should be paid to the third degree of the scale (mediant); if this is a whole step above the second, the composition is in major; if it is a half step above the second, the composition is in minor. The two melodies in Example 2–20 can be effectively used as prototypes.

EXAMPLE 2–20.

Sing, play, and listen to them several times until you have a feeling for their tonal organization, especially for the differences between the third scale degrees of each. Then play, sing, and listen to other melodies and compare them to the two prototype melodies. If they sound like the first, they are likely to be major; if they sound like the second, they are likely to be minor. It is not essential to learn to discriminate aurally between the various forms of minor since most compositions in minor modes use various forms in the course of the composition.

The ability to recognize the various church modes is more difficult to develop and of less importance for the listener. It offers, however, an interesting challenge for the serious student. One method, which is historically anachronistic but often effective, is to compare the church modes to the major and minor modes as follows:

Dorian sounds like pure minor with the sixth degree raised (Dorian Sixth).
Phrygian sounds like pure minor with the second degree lowered (Phrygian Second).
Lydian sounds like major with the fourth degree raised (Lydian Fourth).

Mixolydian sounds like major with the seventh degree lowered (Mixolydian
Seventh).

Another basic distinction to be made in terms of tonality is between
diatonic and chromatic writing. If a composition uses only the notes of a
major or minor scale, it is said to be diatonic. Such compositions will sound
stable, simple, and familiar (at least to a listener used to hearing popular
music, hymns, and folk songs).

EXAMPLE 2–21. Mozart, *Symphony No. 39 in E-flat Major*, third movement (K. 543).

If a composition is moderately chromatic, using only occasional altered
tones, it will sound less stable, simple and folk song-like, but will still sound
somewhat familiar.

EXAMPLE 2–22. Schumann, *Carnaval* (" Eusebius ").

If a composition uses extensive chromaticism, with a large proportion
of altered tones, it will sound unstable, complex, and totally different from
popular music, hymns, or folk songs.

EXAMPLE 2–23. Schoenberg, *String Quartet No. 3*, first movement. Reprinted by
permission of Gertrud Schoenberg.

We must not confuse the distinctions between sharps and flats, major
and minor, or diatonic and chromatic. Either sharps or flats can be used
in major or minor keys, in diatonic or chromatic writing.

    Change of tonality. Music does not always remain in the same tonality or key. The change from one tonality to another is called modulation. Some compositions have no modulation at all; that is, they remain in the same tonality throughout. Others have a moderate amount of modulation, changing tonalities occasionally in the course of the composition. Still others have extensive modulation with frequent change of tonalities.

Modulation may occur to *related* or *distant* tonalities. The simplest method of determining whether one tonality is related or distant from another is to refer to the diagram below. This so-called "circle of fifths" has the tonics of all major and minor keys arranged according to the interval of the perfect fifth. Adjacent keys are related; for example, the related keys of D Major would be G Major, A major, E Minor, B Minor, and F-sharp Minor. Other keys are more or less distant depending upon their separation in the circle from the original key. The one exception to this general rule is that parallel major and minor keys may be considered to be related even though they are not close together on the circle of fifths.

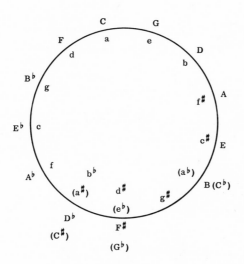

Pitch progression. The pitch motion of a melody may be described generally in terms of the type of intervals most frequently used.
Conjunct. progressing mostly by major and minor seconds:

EXAMPLE 2–24. Beethoven, *Symphony No. 9 in D Minor,* last movement.

Disjunct. progressing mostly by intervals larger than the major second:

EXAMPLE 2–25. Schoenberg, *Quartet No. 3*, first movement, second theme. Reprinted by permission of Gertrud Schoenberg.

Mixed. displaying a combination of conjunct and disjunct motion:

EXAMPLE 2–26. Beethoven *Quartet in F Major*, Op. 59, No. 1, first movement.

Pitch patterns. In a more specific sense, we can analyze a melody to determine if any particular pattern of interval relationships is prominent. The melody in Example 2–27, for example, is built mostly from the interval of a third.

EXAMPLE 2–27. Brahms, *Sonata in D Minor for Violin and Piano*, third movement.

The next melody has been given the nickname of *"Quinten"* ("Fifths") because it emphasizes the interval of a fifth.

EXAMPLE 2–28. Haydn, *Quartet in D Minor*, OP. 76, No. 2, first movement.

Pitch direction. The pitch motion of a melody may also be described in terms of its predominant direction.

Ascending. progressing basically from low to high:

EXAMPLE 2-29. Schumann, *Quintet in E-flat Major*, Op. 44 third movement.

Descending. progressing basically from high to low:

EXAMPLE 2-30. Schubert, *Symphony No. 8 in B Minor* (" Unfinished "), second movement.

Stationary. remaining basically on the same pitch level:

EXAMPLE 2-31. Bartók, *Fifth String Quartet*, first movement. ©1936 by Universal Editions; renewed 1963. Copyright & renewal assigned to Boosey & Hawkes, Inc. for the U.S.A. Reprinted by permission.

Mixed. displaying a balance between the three types of direction:

EXAMPLE 2-32. Mozart, *Symphony No. 39 in B-flat Major*, first movement (K. 543).

Pitch contour. The characteristic of pitch direction is useful in describing short segments of a melody. Since longer melodies almost always have a mixture of ascending, descending, and stationary direction, it is more helpful to describe them in terms of their over-all contour or shape. Every melody will have its own unique contour; it is possible, however, to organize these various contours into four general categories according to the location of the *climax* of the melody. The climax may be defined as the point of greatest tension in a melody; it usually occurs on the longest, loudest, and highest (occasionally lowest) tone.

Climax at beginning. The pitch direction of Example 2–33 is mixed; the general contour is that of a descent from the climax at the beginning.

EXAMPLE 2–33. Tschaikowsky, *Symphony No. 4 in F Minor,* fourth movement.

Climax in the middle. Many melodies have an arched contour with the climax in the middle. In Example 2–34 the climax is emphasized by repetition of the highest note.

EXAMPLE 2–34. Tschaikowsky, *Symphony No. 5 in E Minor,* fourth movement.

Climax at the end. Example 2–35 illustrates another common contour type. Here the melodic line makes two ascents, reaching the climax at the end of the second.

EXAMPLE 2–35. Tschaikowsky, *Concerto in D Major for Violin and Orchestra,* second movement.

Indefinite climax. Not all melodies have clearly recognizable climaxes as in the preceding examples. Sometimes, as in Example 2–36, no particular tone will stand out as a point of greatest tension.

EXAMPLE 2–36. Schubert, *Tod und das Mädchen* (*Death and the Maiden*), introduction.

Range.   The range of a melody may be defined as the distance between the lowest and highest tones and may be arbitrarily categorized as follows:

Narrow. having a range of a perfect fifth or less.

EXAMPLE 2–37. Beethoven, *Symphony No. 5 in C Minor*, Op. 67, first movement.

Average. having a range between a perfect fifth and a major or minor tenth.

EXAMPLE 2–38. Beethoven, *Symphony No. 5 in C Minor*, Op. 67, second movement.

Wide. having a range larger than a major tenth.

EXAMPLE 2-39.   Beethoven, *Symphony No. 5 in C Minor*, Op. 67, third movement.

Tessitura.   This term, which may be defined as that part of the range which is used most frequently, is commonly used to refer to specific instruments or voices. For example, if the range of the soprano voice is regarded as extending from c^1 to g^2, then high tessitura would be a concentration of pitches in the upper part of this range, (roughly from d^2 to g^2). We shall use the term in a somewhat broader sense to refer to that part of the *total* range of pitches (available for *all* instruments and voices), which is used most frequently. We shall categorize this aspect of the tonal element as follows:

EXAMPLE 2-40.

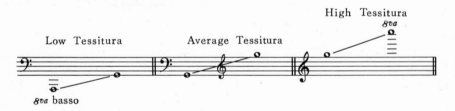

Examples 2–41 to 2–43 illustrate various types of tessitura.
Low tessitura:

EXAMPLE 2-41.   Mendelssohn, *Octet in E-flat Major*, Op. 20, last movement.

Average tessitura:

EXAMPLE 2–42. Mendelssohn, *Symphony No. 4 in A Major,* second movement.

High tessitura:

EXAMPLE 2–43. Mendelssohn, *Concerto in E Minor for Violin and Orchestra,* first movement.

It should be emphasized that the term *tessitura,* in both its specific and general connotations, refers not to the total range used, but to the part of the total range used most frequently in a melody.

Melodic ornamentation. Occasionally extra notes, called *ornaments,* are added to the main notes of a melody. These can be written out in music notation as shown in Example 2–44.

EXAMPLE 2–44. Wagner, *Tristan und Isolde,* " Liebestod " (Love-death).

They can be indicated by special signs such as the following:

EXAMPLE 2–45.

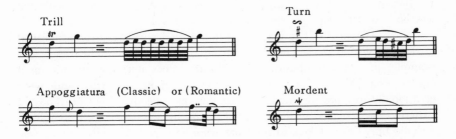

Ornaments may also be added freely by the performer in certain types of music. Some compositions have no melodic ornamentation; others have moderate or extensive ornamentation.

Prominence. The tonal element can be prominent or subordinate, depending upon whether or not it dominates other elements in a composition. The tonal element is more prominent in the slow movement of Beethoven's *Quartet in E-flat Major,* Op. 74 than it is in the *Scherzo* of the same quartet, where the temporal element dominates.

The Tonal Element in Music Literature

Our recognition of style characteristics of the various periods of music literature is greatly enhanced when we add aspects of the tonal element to those of the temporal element discussed in Chapter 1.

Pre-Baroque. The vocal nature of most pre-Baroque music conditions the characteristics of the tonal element so that the music generally has narrow range, average tessitura, and conjunct motion. The tonal organization is basically that of the church modes; however, this is sometimes altered by the use of chromatic notes (*musica ficta*) supplied by the composer, editor, or performer. Many pre-Baroque works remain in one tonality throughout; others have occasional modulations to closely related tonalities.

Baroque. Beginning in the Baroque period, the major and minor modes gradually replaced the church modes and moderate modulation to related keys replaced the practice of remaining in one tonality. Chromaticism was not extensively used but was sometimes employed to meet certain dramatic or emotional considerations of a text. The development of instrumental music in this period influenced the tonal characteristics of both instrumental and vocal music. Range and tessitura were somewhat extended, and disjunct motion was used more frequently than in the previous period. Melodic patterns were often repeated throughout a composition, and some scholars have pointed to the affective or emotional connotations implied in certain characteristic melodic patterns of the Baroque period, especially in the music of J. S. Bach. Ornamentation was both written and improvised fairly extensively.

Classical. The major and minor modes were clearly established in the Classical period. The moderate amount of chromaticism used (for example, in many compositions by Mozart) does not obscure this tonal organization. Modulation became somewhat more frequent and went occasionally to more distant keys. The Baroque melody, based on repeated patterns, was replaced in the Classical period by a broader "folk song-like" melodic line. Often Classical melodies were based on chordal outlines (see Chapter 4). One significant contribution of this period was the development of the "singing allegro," a sustained lyric line in a fast tempo. Especially in certain instrumental compositions, the range was extended and higher and lower tessituras became more common. Melodies were somewhat less ornamented than in the Baroque period.

Romantic. Although use of diatonic major and minor modes continued, chromaticism was more extensively employed than in earlier periods. In the works of the late Romantic composers in particular, extensive use of chromaticism and increasingly frequent modulations to distant keys tended to obscure the feeling of major and minor tonality. An extension of range and tessitura over the previous period was evident in some works. The prominence of a characteristic lyric, emotional melodic line was a significant feature of much Romantic music.

Contemporary. Impressionist composers achieve interesting effects in their music through the occasional use of pentatonic scales, whole-tone scales, archaic church modes, extensive chromaticism, and frequent modulations to distant keys. However, in this music, as in contemporary music in general, it is important to note that many compositions are still written in basically major and minor tonalities.

One of the most significant developments of the contemporary period in terms of tonal organizations is the twelve-tone system, which can be regarded as the logical outcome of the extended use of chromaticism and modulation in the late Romantic and Impressionist periods. The system may best be understood in terms in the words of Arnold Schoenberg, the pioneer composer in this type of music.

> I call this procedure *Method of Composing with Twelve Tones Which Are Related Only with One Another.*
>
> This method consists primarily of the constant and exclusive use of a set of twelve different tones. This means, of course, that no tone is repeated within the series and that it uses all twelve tones in the chromatic scale, though in a different order. It is in no way identical with the chromatic scale.[2]

The basic set referred to by Schoenberg is also called a *tone row* and it can be used in its original form, inversion (upside down), retrograde (backwards), or in retrograde inversion (upside down and backwards). Example 2–46 illustrates the four forms of the tone row used for Schoenberg's Third Quartet.

EXAMPLE 2–46. Four forms of the tone row of Schoenberg's *Quartet No. 3.* Reprinted by permission of Gertrud Schoenberg.

Original

1	2	3	4	5	6	7	8	9	10	11	12

2 Reprinted by permission of Gertrud Schoenberg.

EXAMPLE 2–46. continued.

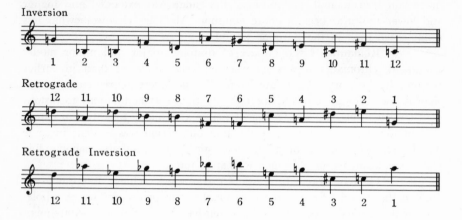

Another new development in the tonal element of contemporary music is the use of multiple divisions of the octave. Instead of the normal division of the octave into the 12 tones of the chromatic scale, the octave is divided into 19, 21, 36 or more tones. Compositions using this technique are extremely complex, requiring special instruments for performance. A simpler technique is the occasional use of quarter tones in compositions basically written in traditional octave division. Quarter tones may be indicated:

EXAMPLE 2–47.

= Quarter tone above c

= Quarter tone below c

A somewhat similar device in jazz is the use of so-called "blue" notes, which are produced by singing or playing certain tones, especially the third, fifth, or seventh degrees of the scale, slightly flat. On a keyboard instrument, this effect is approximated by striking the two tones of a minor second simultaneously.

EXAMPLE 2-48.

Tonal Element Summary

PROMINENCE
prominent, subordinate

TONALITY
major, minor, church modes, diatonic, moderately chromatic, extensively chromatic, pentatonic, whole-tone, twelve-tone, multiple octave division, other

CHANGE OF TONALITY
no modulation, moderate modulation, extensive modulation, modulation to related keys, modulation to distant keys

PITCH PROGRESSION
conjunct, disjunct, mixed

PITCH PATTERNS
prominent intervals or patterns

PITCH DIRECTION
ascending, descending, stationary, mixed

PITCH CONTOUR
climax at the beginning, climax in the middle, climax at the end, indefinite climax

RANGE
narrow, average, wide

TESSITURA
low, average, high

ORNAMENTATION
no ornamentation, moderate ornamentation, extensive ornamentation

Exercises

Preliminary (for students with little or no experience in music reading)

1. Example 2-49 and Example 2-50 are designed to facilitate the learning of pitch notation in the treble and bass clefs. Beginning with the note indicated by the clef sign, they move in a progressive pattern to more distant notes. The student should recite the proper letter name for each note as he reads, referring back to Example 2-1 and Example 2-2 if necessary. After completing these exercises he should practice naming the notes of other examples in Part II of this book before returning to the study of Chapter 2.

EXAMPLE 2–49.

Treble   Clef

EXAMPLE 2–50.

Bass   Clef

Analysis

1. Regard each note in Example 2–51 as tonic and write a major scale above it using accidentals as needed to achieve the proper interval structure for a major scale.

EXAMPLE 2–51.

2. Identify the melodic intervals between each of the notes in Example 2–52.

EXAMPLE 2–52.

They may be computed according to the table on page 47 or according to the following procedure: (a) Construct a major scale above the lower note of the interval. (b) Counting the lower note of the interval as "one," count up letter names or scale degrees from the lower to the higher note; this establishes the numerical name of the interval (for example, third, fifth, octave, etc.). (c) Observe the relationship of the higher note of the interval to the equivalent note in the major scale constructed above the lower note and follow the chart given below; this yields the descriptive name of the interval (for example, major, perfect, augmented).

For 2nds, 3rds, 6ths, and 7ths

If H and E* are identical, the interval is major.

If H is a chromatic half step lower than E, the interval is minor.

If H is two chromatic half steps lower than E, the interval is diminished.

If H is a chromatic half step higher than E, the interval is augmented.

For 4ths, 5ths, and octaves

If H and E are identical, the interval is perfect.

If H is a chromatic half step lower than E, the interval is diminished.

If H is a chromatic half step higher than E, the interval is augmented.

* H = higher note of the interval
   E = equivalent note in the major scale built above the lower note of the interval

The following examples should make this procedure clear.

EXAMPLE 2–53.

The higher note of the interval is the same as the equivalent note in the major scale built above the lower note; therefore, the interval is a *major* third.

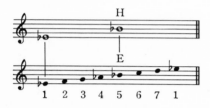

The higher note of the interval is the same as the equivalent note in the major scale built above the lower note; therefore, the interval is a *perfect* fifth.

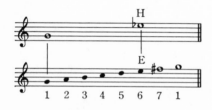

The higher note of the interval is a half step lower than the equivalent note in the major scale built above the lower note; therefore, the interval is a *minor* sixth.

3. Write the indicated scale above each note in Example 2–54.

EXAMPLE 2–54.

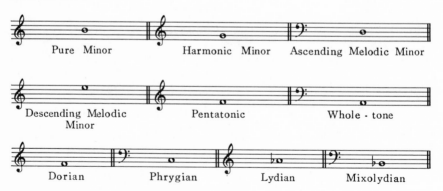

4. Refer to various examples given in other parts of the book, and analyze the melodies according to the tonal element summary.

Composition

1. Write examples according to the following specifications. Use any meter, tempo, or rhythms desired.

  a. Treble clef, F Major, diatonic, no modulation, mostly ascending, mostly conjunct, average range, average tessitura, no ornamentation, climax at the end, no particular melodic patterns, begin on f^1 and end on f^2.

  b. Bass clef, G Minor, moderate chromaticism, no modulation, mixed melodic direction, mixed melodic progression, fairly wide range, average tessitura, no ornamentation, climax in the middle, use the melodic interval of the third (major or minor) fairly frequently, begin and end on G.

  c. Treble clef, C Major, extensive chromaticism, modulate to E near the end of the piece, mixed melodic direction, mostly disjunct melodic progression, wide range, average tessitura, moderate ornamentation, climax in the middle, no particular melodic patterns.

  d. Write a tone row, being sure to use all of the twelve tones of a chromatic scale, but not in scale order. Write the inversion, retrograde, and retrograde-inversion forms of the row. Write a piece based on these four forms, using such contemporary aspects of the temporal element as syncopation, multimeter, complex rhythms, etc. Feature disjunct motion, wide range.

  e. Freely compose a melody to fit the words of a poem. Try to use both the tonal and temporal elements to bring out the natural inflection of the words.

Performance

1. One of the most challenging and rewarding of all musical experiences is the development of the ability to sing melodies at sight without the aid of a piano or other instrument. It is beyond the scope of this book to provide detailed exercises for the development of this skill; the following suggestions, however, may serve as a guide for those wishing to explore this technique.

  a. The student should first practice the major and minor scales in treble and bass clef, singing the notes on pitch names and on pitch numbers as shown in Example 2–55.

EXAMPLE 2–55.

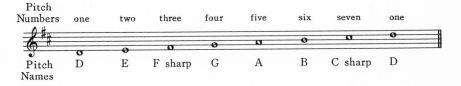

Pitch Numbers	one	two	three	four	five	six	seven	one
Pitch Names	D	E	F sharp	G	A	B	C sharp	D

  b. The student should then practice exercises and melodies that lie basically in in the range of the first five notes of the scale, always being conscious of the location of the tonic, the dominant, and (to distinguish major from minor) the mediant. Then he should practice exercises and melodies using the last four notes of the scale, being conscious always of the location of the dominant and

the tonic and paying particular attention to the various forms of the sixth and
seventh degrees of the minor scale. When one is thoroughly proficient in the
singing of these two scale segments, he can progress to melodies which use
both segments of the scale joined together so that the range of the melody
runs either from tonic to tonic or from dominant to dominant. Most folk songs
and many Baroque and Classical melodies can be shown to have this type
of tonal organization as can be seen from Example 2–56 and Example 2–57.

EXAMPLE 2–56. Haydn, *Quartet in D Minor*, Op. 76, No. 2, third movement.

**EXAMPLE 2–57. Beethoven, *Sonata No. 4 in C Major for Cello and Piano*,
Op. 102, No. 1, first movement.**

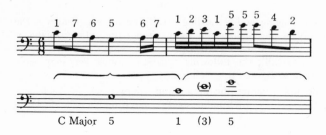

   c. Melodies involving chromatic tones or extended range can be sung by relating
     them to the basic tonal framework described above.

   d. At the same time the student is learning to sing melodies by the approach
     described above, he should also develop the ability to sing isolated melodic
     intervals. This can be facilitated by associating the interval with a particular
     melody using this interval. An ascending minor third, for example, can be
     learned by association with the opening of Brahms' "Lullaby." The student
     should also learn to recognize and sing chordal patterns, as described in
     Chapter 4.

2. Sing and play examples from this book such as the Schubert songs in Chapter 9.

3. Sing and play your own compositions.

Listening

1. Listen to the following examples and describe them according to the tonal
element summary, i.e., indicate if the piece is in major or minor, if the melody is

conjunct or disjunct, etc. Refer to previous sections in this chapter for suggestions on listening.

a. Gregorian chant, any example.
b. Bach, *Cantata No. 80,* "A Mighty Fortress Is Our God."
c. Mozart, *Marriage of Figaro,* excerpts.
d. Schumann, *Dichterliebe,* excerpts.
e. Gershwin, *Porgy and Bess,* excerpts.

2. Using both the tonal and temporal elements as criteria, identify the stylistic characteristics of unfamiliar compositions and make an "informed guess" as to the period in which they were written. See listening exercise no. 2 in Chapter 1 for suggestions for this type of listening.

chapter **3**

*The
Timbre –
Dynamic
Element*

A musical composition derives its basic shape or identity from tonal and temporal elements, its unique character or color from the timbre-dynamic element. To be included in a discussion of the timbre-dynamic element are dynamics, articulation, character, instruments, voices, instrumental ensembles, and vocal ensembles.

Dynamics

Loudness in music could be indicated scientifically in terms of decibels (db), the smallest degree of change in loudness perceivable by the human ear (see p. 6). Usually, however, loudness is indicated by special words or symbols called *dynamics* as given in the following tables. The Italian terms are used more than the English, French, or German.

English	Italian	Italian Abbreviations	German	French
very soft	*pianissimo*	*pp*	*sehr leise*	*très doux*
soft	*piano*	*p*	*leise*	*doux*
moderately soft	*mezzo piano*	*mp*	*mässig leise*	*modéré*
moderately loud	*mezzo forte*	*mf*	*mässig laut*	*modéré*
loud	*forte*	*f*	*laut*	*fort*
very loud	*fortissimo*	*ff*	*sehr laut*	*très fort*

Occasionally *ppp*, *pppp*, *fff*, or *ffff* are used for extremes of softness and loudness.

Changes in dynamics are indicated by the following terms or symbols:

English	Symbol	Italian	Italian Abbreviations	German	French
growing softer	>	*descrescendo* or *diminuendo*	*decresc.* or *dim.*	*leiser werden*	*diminuant*
growing louder	<	*crescendo*	*cresc.*	*lauter werden*	*augmenter*

The following indicate changes in both tempo and dynamics:

English	Italian	Italian Abbreviation	German	French
decrease in loudness	*calando*	*cal.*	*nachlassen*	*en diminuant*
dying away	*smorzando*	*smorz.*	*verlöschen*	*en s'effaçant*
dying down	*morendo*	*mor.*	*ersterben*	*en mourant*
becoming faster and more intense	*stringendo*	*string.*	*drängend*	*en pressant*

Articulation

Articulation refers to the manner in which the notes are performed. It can be considered in terms of three basic types: *legato* articulation in which notes are connected smoothly without intervening pauses or accent; *non-legato* or *portato* articulation in which there is no intervening pause between notes but there is a slight accent or articulation on each note; and *staccato* articulation in which there is both an intervening pause between notes and a slight articulation or accent on each note.

Legato articulation may be indicated by a slur (c.f. "tie," p. 24).

EXAMPLE 3–1. Brahms, *Clarinet Quintet in B Minor*, last movement.

Non-legato or portato articulation may be indicated by short lines.

EXAMPLE 3–2. Mendelssohn, *Concerto in E Minor for Violin and Orchestra*, first movement.

Staccato articulation may be indicated by dots.

EXAMPLE 3–3. Beethoven, *Symphony No. 3 in E-flat Major*, third movement.

In music of various style periods there is great variety in the interpretation of these articulation signs. Other more specific types of articulation will be discussed under the various instruments.

The following Italian abbreviations or terms are used for special types of accents:

English	Italian	Italian Abbreviations
loud and then immediately soft	forte piano	fp
strong accent (forced)	sforzando	sfz
strong accent (reinforced)	rinforzando	rfz

Character

In addition to signs and terms indicating tempo, dynamics, and articulation, composers may use terms indicating the general character, mood, or spirit with which the piece is to be interpreted. Here are some of the most commonly employed:

English	Italian	German	French
affectionate	affettuoso	innig	affectueux
agitated	agitato	lebhaft bewegt	agité
amiable	amabile	lieblich	aimable
animated	animato	belebt	animé
caressingly	lusingando	schmeichelnd	caressant
expressive	espressivo	ausdrucksvoll	expressiv
with fire	con fuoco	feurig	ardent
gracefully	grazioso	zierlich	gracieux
grieving	dolente	klagend	triste
held	tenuto	gehalten	tenu
impassioned	appassionato	leidenschaftlich	passionné
joyously	gioioso	freudig	joyeux
lightly	leggiero	leicht	léger
majestically	maestoso	feierlich	majestueux
martially	marziale	kriegerisch	martiale
mournfully	mesto	traurig	triste
mysteriously	misterioso	geheimnisvoll	mystérieux
with movement	con moto	bewegt	mouvementé
playfully, joking	giocoso, scherzando	scherzhaft, scherzend	en badinant
resolutely	risoluto	entschlossen	résolu
simple	semplice	einfach	simple
singing	cantabile	gesangvoll	chantant
smoothly	piacévole	gefällig	plaisant
with spirit	con anima	munter	avec verve
sustained	sostenuto	getragen	soutenu
sweet	dolce	zart	doucement, doux
tenderly	teneramente	zärtlich	tendre
with vigor	con brio	schwungvoll	avec force

These terms may be used alone or in combination with indications of tempo, dynamics, or articulation, e.g., *allegro con moto:* fast (cheerful) with movement.

Instruments

We may categorize instruments scientifically according to the source of vibration:

Type	Source of Vibration	Example
idiophones	the instrument itself	cymbals
membranophones	stretched membrane	drums
aerophones	column of air	flute
chordophones	stretched string	violin
electrophones	electronic generator	electronic organ

Usually, however, we divide instruments into the sections of the modern orchestra: woodwinds, brass, percussion, special instruments, and strings. The instruments are listed below in four languages in the order in which they appear in a conductor's full score.

English	Italian	German	French
WOODWIND INSTRUMENTS			
piccolo	*flauto piccolo* or *ottavino*	*kleine Flöte*	*petite flûte*
flute	*flauto*	*Flöte*	*flûte*
alto flute	*flautone*	*Altflöte*	*flûte alto*
oboe	*oboe*	*Oboe*	*hautbois*
English horn	*corno inghlese*	*Englisch Horn*	*cor anglais*
clarinet (in B♭ or A)	*clarinet*	*Klarinette*	*clarinette*
alto clarinet in E♭	*clarinetto alto*	*Altklarinette*	*clarinette alto*
bass clarinet in B♭	*clarone*	*Bassklarinette*	*clarinette basse*
contrabass clarinet in B♭	*clarino contrabasso*	*Kontrabassklarinette*	*clarinette contrebasse*
bassoon	*fagotto*	*Fagott*	*basson*
contra-bassoon	*contrafagotto*	*Kontrafagott*	*contrebasson*
BRASS INSTRUMENTS			
French horn	*corno* or *corno ventile*	*Horn* or *Ventilhorn*	*cor-à-pistons*
trumpet	*tromba*	*Trompete*	*trompette*
cornet	*cornetto*	*Kornett*	*cornet-à-pistons*
trombone	*trombone*	*Posaune*	*trombone*

English	Italian	German	French
baritone	flicorno tenore	Tenorhorn	bugle tenor
tuba	tuba	Tuba	tuba

PERCUSSION INSTRUMENTS

kettledrum or timpani	timpani	Pauken	timbale
snare drum	tamburo militaire	kleine Trommel	petite caisse
bass drum	gran cassa	grosse Trommel	grosse caisse
cymbals	piatti	Becken	cymbales

SPECIAL INSTRUMENTS

piano or pianoforte	pianoforte	Klavier or Pianoforte	piano
harpsichord	clavicembalo	Cembalo	clavecin
clavichord	clavicordo	Klavichord	clavichord
organ	organ	Orgel	orgue
harp	arpa	Harfe	harpe

English	Italian	German	French

STRINGED INSTRUMENTS

violin	violino	Violine or Geige	violon
viola	viola	Bratsche	alto
cello or violoncello	violoncello	Violoncello	violoncelle
bass or string bass	contrabasso	Kontrabass	contrebasse

The ranges of the standard orchestral instruments are given in Example 3–4.

EXAMPLE 3-4. Instrumental Ranges.

WOOD WIND INSTRUMENTS

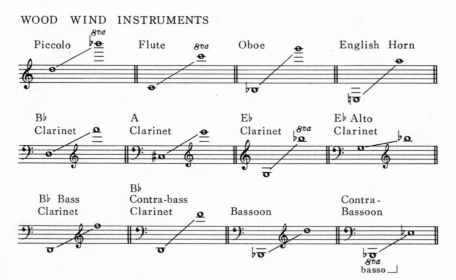

EXAMPLE 3-4 continued.

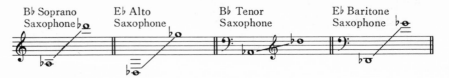

BRASS INSTRUMENTS

PERCUSSION INSTRUMENTS

STRINGED INSTRUMENTS

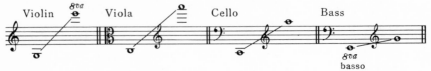

SPECIAL INSTRUMENTS

Transposition. Before discussing individual instruments, it is helpful to have some understanding of *transposition,* which is the moving of tones or melodies from one pitch level to another, preserving the original interval structure in doing so. Example 3–5 shows a melody in its original form and then transposed up a perfect fifth.

EXAMPLE 3–5.

Certain instruments are called transposing instruments because the tones they play sound at a different pitch level than the notes written for them. If a trumpet in B–flat would play these written notes,

EXAMPLE 3–6.

they would sound a major second lower:

EXAMPLE 3–7.

The designation "in B-flat" or "in F" indicates the tone that would sound if the note "C" were written. This formula is helpful in understanding transposition:

$$\frac{\text{written note}}{\text{sounding tone}} = \frac{C}{\text{transposition designation}}$$

What tone would a horn in F sound if the note B-flat were written? Inserting the known quantities into the formula we would have:

$$\frac{\text{B-flat}}{?} = \frac{C}{F}$$

Since the interval between C and F is a perfect fifth, then the interval between the written note and the sounding tone must also be a perfect fifth; therefore the sounding tone must be E-flat.

Clarinets, English horn, French horn, and trumpets are traditional transposing instruments. Some contemporary composers and editors, however, write for all instruments without transposition, except for the octave transposition for certain instruments such as the string bass and piccolo.

Stringed instruments. With stringed instruments, sound is produced by setting a string into vibration, either by plucking it with a finger (Italian: *pizzicato*) or by bowing it with a horse hair bow (Italian: *arco*).

Differences in pitch may be achieved in these ways:

Marc Bomse, photographer.

Thickness. The thicker the string is, the lower the pitch will be. Strings of varying thicknesses are used on each instrument.

Tension. The lower the tension is, the lower the pitch will be. Tension is adjusted by tuning pegs.

Length. The longer the string is, the lower the pitch will be. The length of the string may be determined by the instrument's basic construction (cello strings, for example, are longer than violin strings) or the length may be changed by placing a finger on the string (fingering or stopping), thereby shortening the vibrating length of the string.

In addition to *arco* (bowed) and *pizzicato* (plucked), these effects are possible on all string instruments:

Double stops—playing on two strings simultaneously. Triple and quadruple stops are also possible but are usually produced as "broken" chords, i.e., notes on the bottom two strings are sounded first, and then notes on the top two strings are played.

EXAMPLE 3–8.

Vibrato—a rapid sharping and flatting of the pitch, produced by rolling the stopping finger of the left hand back and forth. It gives warmth and expression to the tone.

Harmonics—flute-like sounds produced by touching the fingers lightly on certain parts of the string rather than stopping the string firmly against the finger board.

Glissando or *Portamento*—a sliding sound between tones, produced by gliding the same finger from one tone to another.

Con Sordino—(muted) a soft tone quality produced by placing a special device (mute) on the bridge to reduce the vibrations.

The next group of terms applies to bowing techniques:

Down bow—(⊓) moving the bow toward the tip.

Up bow—(∨) moving the bow toward the frog.

Legato—playing down and up bows with no pause or accent between notes, or playing several notes on one bow, as indicated by a slur.

Détaché—detached notes played with vigorous bow strokes.

Martelé—"hammered" or heavily accented bow strokes.

Spiccato—short, light notes played in the middle of the bow in such a manner that the bow bounces away from the string after each note.

Ricochet—several spiccato notes on one bow, usually played at the upper part of the bow.

Staccato—short accented notes; sometimes a virtuoso effect with several rapid, short notes played in one bow.

Tremolo—rapidly repeated notes, usually played at the tip of the bow.

Sul ponticello—unusually bright, "screeching" sound produced by bowing near the bridge.

Sul tasto or *sur la touche*—unusually soft sound produced by bowing slightly over the fingerboard.

Col legno—playing with the wood rather than the hair of the bow, usually spiccato.

The *violin* is one of the most versatile and flexible of all instruments, capable of executing all styles of music from difficult passage work to sustained lyric melodies. The lowest string (g) is rich and sonorous, the middle strings (d^1 and a^1) are more neutral, and the highest string (e^2) has a brilliant sound. The *viola* is about four inches larger in size and a perfect fifth lower in pitch than the violin. It is held and played in the same manner as the violin and has the same technical capabilities. It is frequently called upon to perform melodies which exploit its darker, more nasal tone quality.

The *cello* is more than twice as long as the violin and is pitched an octave plus fifth below it. Its characteristic tone quality is rich and full, and it frequently plays sonorous, lyric melodies. The *string bass* is the largest and lowest of the string instruments. It is the only transposing instrument in the strings; its notes sound one octave lower than written. The somewhat rough, husky timbre of the string bass and the difficulty of executing rapid passage work on it have caused it to be generally neglected as a solo instrument, but it adds strength and sonority to ensembles.

The immediate predecessors of the present day string instruments were the viols: treble viol, tenor viol, and bass viol or viola da gamba. The instruments of the viol family differ from present-day string instruments basically in that they have a slightly different shape, a softer sound, and six strings instead of four. Other early string instruments include the *cithara* and *lyre*, plucked string instruments from ancient Greece; the *lute*, a plucked string instrument popular in the Medieval and Renaissance periods; and the *rebec* and *vielle*, early predecessors of the violin. The *viola d'amore* and the *baryton* have sympathetic strings which are usually not played but are meant to reinforce and enrich the sound of the bowed or plucked strings through sympathetic vibration.

The *guitar* and *mandolin* are now used mostly for popular music, but they have been employed effectively in some "art" music. The *banjo* and *ukelele* are used only in popular and folk music.

Woodwind instruments. All woodwind instruments involve a vibrating column of air set into motion by the player's breath blowing

The Lipinski
Stradivarius
(violin).
Courtesy of
Rembert
Wurlitzer.

The Davidoff
Stradivarius (cello).
Courtesy of Rembert
Wurlitzer.

The Cassaveti
Stradivarius (viola).
Courtesy of Rembert
Wurlitzer.

against a mouth hole, a single reed, or a double reed. Different pitches are achieved by covering or uncovering finger holes on the body of the instrument; this, in effect, lengthens or shortens the vibrating column of air. The longer the column of air is, the lower the pitch will be. The pitch may also be raised an octave (or, for the clarinets, a twelfth) by "overblowing," or blowing with more force.

All woodwind instruments can execute various styles of legato and staccato articulation and can play with vibrato but they do not use mutes or unusual special effects. The flute, oboe, clarinet, and bassoon are the most frequently used woodwinds; the piccolo, English horn, bass clarinet and contra-bassoon are less frequently used. The instruments are listed here according to type of sound production.

Edge-tone instruments. These have a mouth hole or *embouchure* with a sharp edge; the player blows over this in such a manner that the column of the air inside the instrument is set into vibration. The same principle is involved when one blows over the edge of a bottle. The *flute* has a clear, bright tone quality in the upper register and a more covered, "breathy" tone quality in the lower register. It frequently plays light, rapid passage work or lyric melodies. The *piccolo* is one octave higher than the flute and has a brilliant, shrill quality which can be used to advantage in solo work or ensemble passages. The *alto flute* is pitched a fourth lower than the regular flute and, though rarely used, has a distinctively rich, sombre tone quality.

Single-reed instruments. These have a single cane reed placed against a mouthpiece in such a manner that the tip is free to vibrate when the player's breath is blown against it. The vibration of the reed sets the column of air into vibration. A somewhat similar principle is in operation when we blow

Wood Piccolo

Flute

B-flat Clarinet.

Courtesy Conn Corporation, Elkhart, Indiana.

| Bassoon | Oboe | Bass Clarinet |

Courtesy Conn Corporation, Elkhart, Indiana.

on a blade of grass held between the thumbs. The *clarinet* in *B-flat* or *A* is the most versatile of the woodwind instruments, capable of extremes of dynamics, range, articulation, and character. The low or *chalameau* register is dark and rich, the upper or *clarion* register is bright and clear, and the middle register is more neutral in tone quality. The *E-flat clarinet* has a shrill, piercing tone quality which is sometimes exploited for comic or grotesque effect. The *bass clarinet* has a hollow, breathy tone quality and can be used effectively for ensemble or solo passages. The *saxophone* family is not used as extensively in orchestral or chamber music as it is in concert band and popular music. The tone quality varies for the various types but is, in general, fuller, rounder, and more "reedy" than that of the clarinet. The family includes soprano, alto, tenor, baritone, and bass saxophones.

Double-reed instruments. These have two reeds placed back to back and inserted in the instrument so that the tips are free to vibrate when the player blows against them. The *oboe* has a distinctive, somewhat "oriental" or nasal quality which lends itself particularly to slow, minor-key melodies. It can also execute rapid passage work. The *English horn* is neither English nor a horn: it is an alto oboe with a tone quality somewhat richer and deeper than the regular oboe. The *bassoon* has a distinctive, rather "reedy" timbre and can be used effectively for humorous staccato passages, lyric melodies or as the bass in ensemble passages. The *contra-bassoon* is the lowest instrument in the woodwind section and indeed in the entire orchestra; it is used primarily for ensemble passages rather than solo passages.

Other woodwind instruments. The *bagpipe* is essentially a double-reed woodwind (with the air coming from a bag instead of the player's mouth), used primarily for Scottish marches and dances. The *recorder* is a Baroque and Renaissance transverse flute somewhat similar to the tonette used in public school music. *Shawm* is a general term for early predecessors of the oboe.

Brass instruments. All brass instruments have a vibrating column of air, set in motion by the "buzz" of the player's lips in the mouthpiece. Early, so-called "natural" or valveless trumpets, horns, and bugles can produce only the notes of the overtone series. Different pitches on these instruments are achieved by "overblowing." The lowest or fundamental tone is produced by applying the least possible amount of tension and pressure in the lip position and breath. As the player increases tension and pressure, the pitch jumps progressively up the notes of the series. Instruments in C and B-flat would have the series in Example 3–9.

EXAMPLE 3–9.

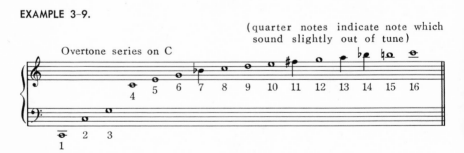

(quarter notes indicate note which sound slightly out of tune)

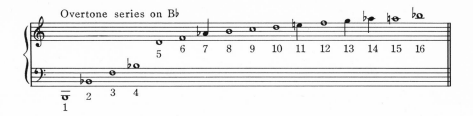

Note that the intervals in the series become smaller as they progress up the series. In order to play a melody with half and whole steps on a natural brass instrument, it is necessary to play in the upper part of the overtone series. This accounts for the high range of most Baroque brass parts. A valve mechanism is added to modern trumpets and horns which makes it possible to shorten or lengthen the column of air by depressing the proper valves; thus, half steps can be played in any part of the range. In the trombone, the length of the air column is adjusted by a slide mechanism.

Brass instruments can be played with various styles of staccato or legato. They can be played with vibrato, and they can be muted by placing various devices or the player's hand in the bell of the instrument. Other special effects include flutter tonguing, a type of brass tremolo, and glissando, used especially on the trombone.

The *trumpet* is the highest and most agile of the brass instruments with a clear, bright, powerful timbre. It often plays fanfare passages but can also play lyric melodies. Most trumpets are in B-flat, but other sizes and transpositions are occasionally used.

The *French horn* has a mellow timbre which blends well with other brasses, strings, or woodwinds. It is frequently employed for broad, noble themes, passages reminiscent of hunting calls, and other solo and ensemble passages. Horns use many transpositions but the most common is the transposition in F.

The *trombone* has a rich, full timbre and a wide range of dynamic possibilities. It is especially effective when used in chorale-like passages for three trombones and tuba.

The *tuba* has a rich, full sound suitable for ensemble passages, droll or grotesque solos (especially in the low register), or occasional lyric solos (especially in the high register).

Other brass instruments are used primarily in bands, infrequently in orchestras. These include the *cornet* and the *flugelhorn* (both similar to the trumpet), the *mellophone* or *altonium* (both similar to the French horn), the *baritone* and *euphonium* (both similar to the tuba in design but pitched like a trombone), and the *helicon* and *Sousaphone* (both similar in

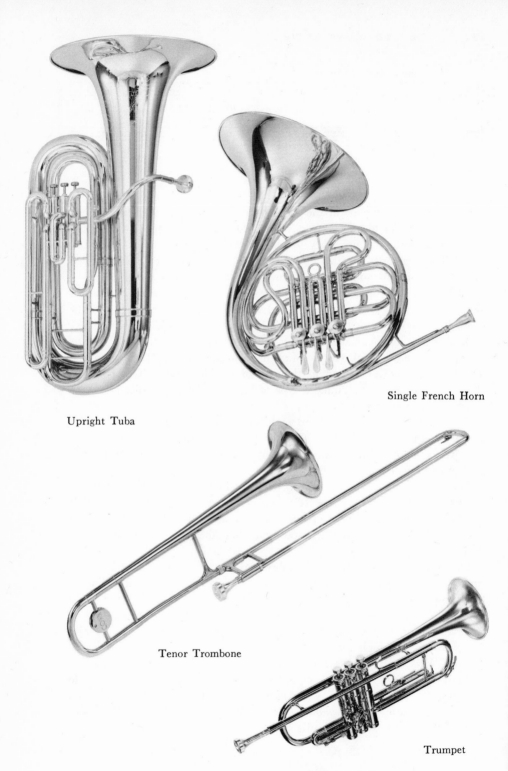

Upright Tuba

Single French Horn

Tenor Trombone

Trumpet

Courtesy Conn Corporation, Elkhart, Indiana.

pitch to the tuba but built in circular shape and carried over the shoulder). The *bugle* is a trumpet-like instrument without valves, and is used mainly in the military service.

Percussion instruments.   Percussion instruments may be either idiophones or membranophones; they may have definite or indefinite pitch.

Instruments with definite pitch. Timpani or *kettle drums* consist of a calfskin head stretched over a copper bowl. The tension of the head may be changed by hand screws or a pedal mechanism and this change of tension produces different pitches. The instruments are usually used in sets of three or four, are of varying sizes, and are struck by various types of sticks. Although limited in melodic possibilities, the timpani have the widest dynamic range in the orchestra.

The *xylophone* consists of a number of wooden bars which are of various lengths and pitches, arranged somewhat like a piano keyboard, and struck with mallets. The resulting sound is "dry," but lively and incisive. The *marimba* is similar except that the tone is amplified and prolonged by tubular resonators under the wooden or metal bars. The *vibraphone* or *vibra-harp* adds an electric device to the marimba, thereby prolonging the sound and adding a vibrato effect.

Chimes are a set of suspended metal tubes of various lengths that are struck with a wooden hammer. *Bells* or *glockenspiel* are a set of tuned metal bars arranged like a keyboard and struck with a mallet.

Instruments with indefinite pitch. The *snare drum* has two taut calfskin heads with a set of "snares" or wire springs in contact with the lower head. The top head is struck or rolled with two wooden sticks to produce a dry crackling sound. The *bass drum* is a large drum with two heads and no snares, and is struck with a covered stick to produce a low, booming sound. The *triangle* is a triangular shaped metal bar struck by a straight metal beater to produce a high, bright, tinkly sound.

Cymbals are concave metal plates, struck in pairs to produce a "crash." A single cymbal may be suspended and struck with a stick. Other instruments of indefinite pitch include *tenor drum, tambourines, gong, castanets, wood block, temple block, whip, cow bell, antique cymbals, rattles, claves, gourds, sandpaper,* and many others.

Special instruments.   Although these instruments are sometimes listed under one of the preceding categories, they are grouped here as a separate category.

The *piano* or *pianoforte* has a keyboard of 88 keys. These activate hammers which strike metal strings of various lengths, thus producing various pitches. The piano is capable of great variety of articulation, dynamics, range, and tone color.

The *clavichord* is somewhat like the piano except that the strings are struck by T-shaped pieces of metal called tangents and the intensity is always very soft. The *harpsichord* is also similar to the piano but the strings are plucked by quills set in a jack mechanism.

Concert Bass Drum

Snare Drum

Timpani

Xylophone

The *pipe organ* has a keyboard which activates various mechanisms to channel compressed air into pipes of various lengths fitted with reeds or edge-tone openings. For each pitch and tone quality there is a separate pipe. The *electronic organ* has a keyboard which activates various electronic resonators to produce sounds that approximate the pipe organ or other orchestral instruments. The *novachord* and *solovox* are simpler versions of the electronic organ.

The *harp* has 45 strings tuned according to a C-flat major scale and plucked by the fingers of both hands. By means of a set of pedals, each string can be raised two half steps (for example, the C-flat strings can be raised to C-natural and to C-sharp), thus making chromatic passages possible. The harp frequently plays broken chords, and these are in fact called *arpeggios* (Italian: *arpeggiare,* to play the harp). Another characteristic effect is the *glissando,* in which the player draws his finger rapidly over the strings producing a blurred row of tones with no one pitch heard clearly.

Instrumental Ensembles

Chamber music groups. Chamber music may be defined as music intended for performance in an intimate setting, involving between one and approximately eight players, each playing an independent part.

It is usually performed without a conductor. According to the number of players the following combinations are possible:

One player (solo). This is commonly written for keyboard instruments, such as the piano, organ, or harpsichord. When written for one orchestral instrument, the terms "unaccompanied" or "solo" are often added, for example, *Suite for Unaccompanied Cello, Solo Violin Sonata,* etc.

Two players (duo or duet). Technically this may be written for any two like or unlike instruments: two violins, violin and cello, flute and clarinet, etc. More commonly, duos consist of one keyboard instrument, especially piano, and one orchestral instrument. Music written for such combinations is referred to with such terms as *Sonata for Violin and Piano, Rhapsody for Clarinet and Piano,* etc. Occasionally, however, a more confusing terminology is used, and reference will be made, for example, to a *Violin Sonata* when actually a *Sonata for Violin and Piano* is understood.

Three players (trio). String trio is generally understood to mean violin, viola, and cello; piano trio generally implies piano, violin, and cello. A significant amount of literature has been written for both of these standard combinations. Other compositions for trio employ such diverse combinations as two violins and viola; piano, clarinet, and violin; piano, violin, and horn; three violins; flute, oboe, and clarinet; trumpet, horn, and trombone; and others. Here also, confusing terminology is sometimes used. Works written for the Baroque combination of harpsichord, cello (gamba, bass, or bassoon), and violin, for example, are often referred to as *Violin Sonatas* or *Sonatas for Violin and Continuo.*

Four players (quartet). The string quartet, consisting of first violin, second violin, viola, and cello, is the most common and, in many respects, the most satisfactory chamber ensemble. The piano quartet regularly consists of piano, violin, viola and cello. Combinations of one wind instrument and three strings are named after the wind instrument; a flute quartet consists of flute, violin, viola, and cello. Other possible combinations include the woodwind quartet (flute, oboe, clarinet, and bassoon), four cellos, etc. Works written for the Baroque combination of a keyboard instrument such as harpsichord, a bass instrument such as the cello or gamba, and two melody instruments such as two violins or flute and oboe, are called *Trio Sonatas.*

Five players (quintet). The woodwind quintet, regularly consisting of flute, oboe, clarinet, bassoon, and French horn (actually a brass instrument but used here because of its ability to blend well) is also a standard chamber music ensemble. The string quintet consists of the standard string quartet plus an extra viola or an extra cello. The piano quintet adds piano to the string quartet. Other quintets with a woodwind or brass instrument added to the standard string quartet are named according to the added instrument; for example, a clarinet quintet consists of clarinet, first violin, second violin, viola, and cello.

Six players (sextet). The string sextet consists of two violins, two violas, and two cellos. Numerous other combinations are possible.

Other ensembles. Septets, octets, nonettes, etc., can be made up of various combinations of instruments.

Larger ensembles. Instrumental groups with more than eight to ten players usually perform with a conductor.

The *string orchestra* consists of first violins, second violins, violas, cellos, and basses. The number of players on each part varies.

The *woodwind choir* is made up of flutes I,[1] II (III, piccolo) ; oboes I, II (III, English horn) ; clarinets I, II (III, bass clarinet) ; bassoons I, II (III, contra bassoon) ; and (saxophones). Instruments in parenthesis are less frequently used than others.

The *brass choir* usually has French horns I, II, III, IV; trumpets I, II, III; cornets I, II, III; trombones I, II, III; baritone; and tuba.

The *percussion ensemble* has from two to ten players playing various combinations of percussion instruments.

The *symphonic wind ensemble* is basically a combination of a woodwind choir, a brass choir and a percussion ensemble. The instrumentation varies with different compositions.

The *concert band* is similar in instrumentation to the symphonic wind ensemble, except that it usually has more than one player on each part.

Jazz ensembles vary from small ensembles such as piano, vibraphone, bass, and drums to large stage or concert jazz bands with five saxophones, (players may also double flute, clarinet, oboe, and bassoon), five trumpets, five trombones, piano, guitar, string bass, and drums.

The *chamber orchestra* consists basically of the string orchestra plus a small number of additional keyboard, woodwind, brass, or percussion instruments.

The *symphony orchestra* is composed of instruments from the string, woodwind, brass, and percussion sections, occasionally with special instruments added. See the literature section of this chapter for specific instruments used in various periods of history.

The term *orchestration* refers to the craft of writing effectively for the various instruments and instrumental combinations, taking account of technical limitations and possibilities. The term *instrumentation* can be used synonomously with *orchestration,* or in a more limited sense, referring only to the number and types of instruments used in a particular piece.

---

[1] Roman numerals indicate various parts; Flute I means first flute, Flute II means second flute, etc.

The Orchestral Score

In an orchestra or other ensemble, the individual players have parts which contain only the notes which they are to play. The conductor, however, has a *score* which shows what all the instruments are playing.

Example 3–10 shows a page of the orchestral score for the second movement of Beethoven's *Symphony No. 3 in E-flat Major*, measures 135–141. According to this, we see that the flutes play an eighth note in the first measure and then rest until the end of the page. The oboes play an eighth note and then rest for two measures, coming in again in the second half of measure 138. The sign "a2" indicates that both players play the same part here. In measure 140, the two oboes have different parts. The clarinets play a legato melody throughout. The bassoons play throughout except for occasional rests.

The first and second horns are silent until measure 140. Then they come in *fortissimo* with a written C octave, that sounds, however, as an E-flat octave, because the horns are written in the E-flat transposition. The third horn plays until measure 140. The trumpets enter at measure 140 with the first and second horns. The timpani begins one quarter note earlier in measure 139 with a roll (*tr*).

All the strings begin on the first eighth note of measure 135. The second violins, the cellos, and the basses continue a sixteenth-note scale in this measure while the first violins and violas rest for one and one-half beats. In measure 136 the parts are reversed; the first violins and violas have sixteenth-note scales while the second violins and the cellos and basses play one eighth note and then rest for one and one-half beats. This alternation continues for the next two measures (137 and 138). In measure 139, the first violins and the violas play throughout the measure; the second violins come in after an eighth rest; and the cellos and basses come in after a quarter rest. In measure 140, the first violins play an eighth note and then rest for one and one-half beats. The other strings play throughout the bar.

When two instruments are written on one staff, both players may play separate parts, they may play in unison (indicated *a2* or *a due*), or one player may rest while the other plays. Occasionally a single string instrument will play alone (solo). A return to the entire section is indicated by the word *tutti* (Italian: all).

The line connecting the staves is called a *brace* and the collection of staves is also called a *brace*. Sometimes only a few instruments are playing and the brace consists only of those instruments. Then it is possible to have several braces on each page.

In following a score, one should try not only to follow the important melodic lines but also to note which instruments have the secondary lines and the accompaniment. The effort necessary to develop even a rudimentary skill in this will be amply repaid with the increased understanding of the real structure of orchestral music thereby attained.

EXAMPLE 3-10. Beethoven, *Symphony, No. 3 in E-flat Major,* second movement.

Voices

The human voice is essentially an aerophone. Vibrations are originated by air passing from the lungs over the vocal chords. Pitch is altered by changing the tension of the vocal chords. The throat, mouth, and nose act as resonators, and timbre (vowel sound) is changed by varying the shape of the resonators, especially the mouth.

The voice is capable of a wide variety of articulation and can be used with or without pitch vibrato. Other special effects include *falsetto,* a light, artificial method of sound production used by some male singers to achieve high notes in the range of the female voice; *parlando,* a quasi-spoken method of singing; and *sprechstimme,* a type of singing declamation in which pitches are only approximated.

The ranges of the six basic vocal categories are given in Example 3–11. These are only the standard ranges; most professional singers exceed them.

EXAMPLE 3–11.

In addition to these basic categories, there are more specialized voice types. The *coloratura* is a soprano voice capable of executing rapid scales, arpeggios, trills, and other passage work. The *lyric soprano* has a light tone quality and sings lyric music usually requiring less vocal agility than needed by the coloratura. The *dramatic soprano* has a heavier and more powerful tone quality suitable for music of more emotional intensity. The *spinto* combines qualities of the dramatic and lyric soprano.

The *lyric tenor* and the *dramatic tenor* have characteristics similar to the lyric and dramatic sopranos, but, of course, in the tenor range. The *Heldentenor* (German: heroic tenor) is a special type of powerful dramatic tenor called for in the operas of Wagner and others. The *bass-baritone* has a combination of the characteristics and range of the baritone and the bass. The *basso* or *basso profundo* is an especially low voice capable of singing several notes below the customary bass range.

The *boy soprano* is the high, unchanged voice of a young boy. The *countertenor* is an adult male voice which sings in approximately the alto range using a type of falsetto. The *castrato* was the high soprano voice of a castrated adult male. Castrati were popular and influential in the seventeenth and eighteenth centuries, but the practice was then discontinued.

Vocal Ensembles

Chamber ensembles. Vocal chamber music ensembles may range from one to eight or more voices, with or without accompaniment. The terms solo, duo, trio, quartet, etc., refer to the number of voices, regardless of the accompaniment. Groups of five to fifteen singers, specializing in the performance of unaccompanied vocal music, are called *madrigal singers* or *chamber singers.*

Large vocal ensembles. *Women's choruses* usually include soprano I, II and alto I, II. *Men's choruses* include tenor I, II and bass I, II. The *mixed chorus* (or *choir,* or simply *chorus*) usually has a four-part grouping of soprano, alto, tenor, and bass. It may also have fuller groupings such as soprano I, soprano II, alto, tenor, bass I, and bass II. An *a cappella* choir performs music without instrumental accompaniment. *Glee clubs* were originally male groups performing *glees,* or light, humorous songs; later the term was extended to denote other vocal ensembles, usually connected with colleges or universities.

The Timbre-Dynamic Element in Music Literature

Pre-Baroque. Dynamics were not indicated in most music of this period, and it is assumed that little use was made of dynamic extremes or changes. Articulation and character were also not indicated. The majority of the works preserved from the period are sacred works indicated for *a cappella* performance; however, it is probable that the voices were often doubled or replaced by instruments. Independent instrumental music for organ, harpsichord, and various instrumental combinations was also written, especially in the Rennaissance period. Instruments employed in this period included the recorder, viol, cornetto, organ, and lute.

Baroque. Dynamic indications such as *piano* and *forte* were used in this period. "Terraced dynamics," or sudden changes from one dynamic level to another without *crescendo* or *decrescendo,* were characteristic. Often, however, only one dynamic level was indicated for an entire movement. Although articulation marks were generally not indicated in this music, most present-day interpreters tend to perform the slow sections of Baroque music with legato articulation and the fast sections with staccato or semi-staccato articulation.

Violin, viola, and cello gradually replaced the viol family, except for the bass viol. Flutes, oboes, bassoons, natural horns, natural trumpets, trombones, and timpani were also used. Organ, harpsichord, and clavichord were used as solo instruments and in ensembles. The most identifiable and characteristic timbre of the Baroque period was that of the *continuo* consisting of one keyboard instrument, such as harpsichord or organ, plus one or occasionally more bass instruments, such as the cello, viola da gamba, string bass, or bassoon. The *continuo* was part of almost all Baroque chamber ensembles and orchestral combinations.

Baroque instrumentation was not standardized but usually consisted of *continuo,* strings, and various wind instruments. In the *concerto grosso* type of composition, a small group of soloists, called the *concertino,* was contrasted with the rest of the orchestra, called the *ripieno* or *tutti.* This not only provided a typical Baroque contrast of timbre and dynamics, but also enabled the composer to write more difficult passages for the soloists of the *concertino* group. Another characteristic of the Baroque period was a tendency to have the bass and the soprano instruments prominent with a rather thin sound in the middle range, producing a phenomenon usually called "polarity of outer voices." This was brought about partly by the predominance in the Baroque orchestra of high-pitched instruments, such as natural trumpets, oboes, flutes, violins, and low-pitched instruments, such as bass, cello, bassoon, and the pedal notes of the organ.

Some idea of the variety of Baroque instrumentation can be seen in Bach's *Brandenburg Concerti:*

Concerto No. 1 in F Major
> Concertino—2 horns, 3 oboes, bassoon, violino piccolo (small violin—this part is now usually played on a regular violin)
> Ripieno— violin I, violin II, viola, cello, bass, continuo

Concerto No. 2 in F Major
> Concertino—trumpet, flute, oboe, violin
> Ripieno— violin I, violin II, viola, cello, bass, continuo

Concerto No. 3 in G Major
> violin I, violin II, violin III, viola I, viola II, viola III, cello I, cello II, cello III, bass, continuo

Concerto No. 4 in G Major
> Concertino—violin, flute I and II
> Ripieno— violin I, violin II, viola, cello, bass, continuo

Concerto No, 5 in D Major
> Concertino—klavier (harpsichord), flute, violin
> Ripieno— violin I, viola, cello, bass, continuo

Concerto No. 6 in B-flat Major
> viola I, viola II, gamba I, gamba II, cello, bass, continuo

Although such effects as tremolo and pizzicato were used as early as 1607 in Monteverdi's *Orfeo,* composers of the Baroque period in general did not use many special instrumental effects. However, instrumental music of the period was usually very idiomatic or well-suited to the instruments. Vocal music, from solos to large choruses, was important in the Baroque period and was written with specific instrumental accompaniment.

Classical. Classical composers made more use of such dynamic indications as *p*, *pp*, *f*, and made use of the *crescendo* and *diminuendo*. Articulation was more varied than in the Baroque period. Special instrumental effects were generally not used but idiomatic instrumental writing continued to be developed. The instrumentation of the Classical orchestra was relatively standardized; the *Symphony No. 39* (K.543) of Mozart is representative: flute I, II; oboe I, II; clarinet I, II; bassoon I, II; horn I, II; trumpet I, II; timpani; violin I; violin II; viola; cello; bass.

Clarinets were not scored in early Classical compositions; trombones, third and fourth horns, and other percussion instruments were added in some later works. The basses usually played the same part as the cellos, one octave lower.

Polarity of the outer voices was replaced in the Classical period by a more equally distributed orchestral tone color. Strings continued to play the leading role in orchestral compositions, but wind instruments were now employed with increasing frequency to play important passages.

In chamber music the string quartet and the piano trio were the favored ensembles. The piano replaced the harpsichord as the principal keyboard instrument; the organ was not as frequently used. The use of the continuo was discontinued except for operatic recitative.

Romantic. Composers of this period made effective and extensive use of all dynamic possibilities, with special emphasis on *crescendo* and *diminuendo*. Great variety in articulation and frequent use of special instrumental effects added color to the orchestral palette. Gradually the "related" woodwind instruments and extra brass and percussion instruments were added until the expanded orchestra of the late Romantic period called for instrumentations such as this used in Wagner's *Die Götterdämmerung:*

flute I, II, III, piccolo
oboe I, II, III, English horn
clarinet I, II, III, bass clarinet
bassoon I, II, III, contra bassoon

horns I, II, III, IV, V, VI, VII, VIII
Wagner-tuben I, II, III, IV (special brass instruments designed for Wagner's music-dramas.)
trumpet I, II, III, bass trumpet
trombone I, II, III, contrabass trombone

timpani
cymbals, triangle, side drum, glockenspiel

harps (6)

violin I (16 players)
violin II (16 players)
viola (12 players)
cello (12 players)
bass (8 players)

Wind, brass, and percussion instruments assumed increased importance in the orchestration of Romantic composers; the unique tone colors of the woodwind instruments and the rich sound of the full brass section were effectively used. Cello and bass played independent parts and the string sections were frequently divided into many parts.

Chamber music was somewhat less important in the total picture of Romantic music, but many works were written for solo piano, the favored instrument for many Romantic composers because of its intimate character and large scope of expressive possibilities. Some of the best known operas and songs for solo voice and pianos are products of the Romantic period.

Contemporary. Contemporary composers continue to make highly interesting use of all dynamic and articulation possibilities. Some twentieth-century writers use the expanded orchestra, adding to it novel percussion instruments and unusual instrumental effects. Others stress economy of musical means in such unusual chamber music combinations as these:

Stravinsky: *L'Histoire du Soldat*	Schoenberg: *Pierrot Lunaire*
clarinet	flute (piccolo)
bassoon	clarinet (bass clarinet)
trumpet	violin (viola)
trombone	cello
violin	piano
bass	female reciter
percussion	

Other interesting developments in the contemporary period include electronic "instruments" and tape-recorder music. The use of these makes possible the performance of highly complex and unusual music, which could never be realized with conventional instruments.

Timbre-Dynamic Element Summary

DYNAMICS

basic level *pp, p, mp, mf, f, ff*

CHANGE OF DYNAMICS

no changes, moderate changes, extensive changes, "terraced dynamics," crescendo and decrescendo

ARTICULATION

legato, portato, staccato, special accents

CHARACTER

giocoso, dolce, etc.

INSTRUMENTS OR VOICES USED

special instrumental effects, doublings, combinations, etc.

Exercises

Analysis

1. Study the various examples of full scores given in this book as well as individual scores to other works. Describe the works according to the timbre-dynamic summary.

2. Transpose a given melody up a fifth and then down a major second.

Composition

1. Compose new pieces and rearrange some already composed for instruments. Indicate carefully dynamics, articulation, and character.

Performance

1. Sing or play on the piano various examples, paying particular attention to dynamics, articulation, and character.

2. If possible, have some introductory experience with orchestral instruments.

Listening

1. Listen to any of the many special recordings designed to introduce the instruments of the orchestra—*The Young Person's Guide to the Orchestra* by Britten, *The Complete Orchestra* by Wheeler Beckett (research, narration, conducting), and others.

2. Listen to representative concertos for various instruments:

Mozart, *Concerto No. 1 in G Major for Flute and Orchestra,* K. 313
Handel, *Concerto in G Minor for Oboe and Strings*
Copland, *Concerto for Clarinet and String Orchestra with Harp and Piano*
Mozart, *Concerto No. 1 in B-flat Major for Bassoon and Orchestra,* K. 470
Strauss, *Concerto No. 1 in E-Flat Major for Horn and Orchestra*
Haydn, *Concerto in E-Flat Major for Trumpet and Orchestra*
Rimsky-Korsakov, *Concerto for Trombone and Military Band*
Paganini, *Concerto in D Major for Violin and Orchestra*
Hindemith, *Concerto for Viola and Small Orchestra Based on Old German Folk Tunes (Der Schwanendreher)*
Dvořák, *Concerto in B Minor for Cello and Orchestra*
Koussevitsky, *Concerto in F Minor for Double Bass and Orchestra*

3. Listen to the following works and describe them according to the timbre-dynamic element summary:

des Prez, "Ave Maria"
Bach, *Suite in D Major for Orchestra*
Haydn, *Symphony No. 94 in G Major*
Wagner, *Die Götterdämmerung,* final scene
Stravinsky, *Le Sacre du Printemps*

4. Listen to compositions from various periods and try to determine the period, using aspects of the timbre-dynamic element as well as the temporal and tonal elements. See Chapter 1 for suggested methods.

chapter 4

The Textural Element

T he term *texture* in its widest sense refers to relationships between any simultaneously sounding elements in music such as tones, melodies, rhythms, etc. The three basic textures used in music are *monophonic* (one melody alone), *homophonic* (one main melody with accompaniment), and *polyphonic* (two or more independent melodies sounded simultaneously). Chapters 1 and 2, with their consideration of the temporal and tonal aspects of a single line, were, in effect, devoted to a study of monophonic texture; this chapter is concerned primarily with aspects of homophonic and polyphonic textures. Before beginning this, however, we must first have some background in *harmony,* the study of relationships between simultaneously sounded tones in music.

Harmonic Intervals

Two tones sounded simultaneously form a *harmonic interval.* The terminology used to describe these is the same as that given on page 47 for *melodic intervals.*

EXAMPLE 4-1.

Classification of intervals.   Harmonic intervals may be classified according to their characteristic sound.

Perfect consonances. These intervals are called *perfect* because their ratios are simple; they are called *consonant* because they sound well together. Perfect consonances have a pure or "hollow" sound. Octaves sound like a duplication or reinforcement of the single tone; fifths and fourths have a somewhat "oriental" sound.

EXAMPLE 4-2.

Interval name	perfect octave	perfect fifth	perfect fourth
Interval ratio	2 : 1	3 : 2	4 : 3

111

EXAMPLE 4–2 continued.

| Interval name | perfect unison |
| Interval ratio | 1 : 1 |

Imperfect consonances. These intervals are called *imperfect* because their ratios are more complex. They have a pleasant, euphonious sound.

EXAMPLE 4–3.

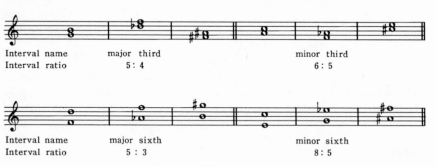

| Interval name | major third | | minor third |
| Interval ratio | 5 : 4 | | 6 : 5 |

| Interval name | major sixth | | minor sixth |
| Interval ratio | 5 : 3 | | 8 : 5 |

Dissonances. These intervals are called *dissonant* because they do not sound as well together as the consonant intervals. The minor second and the major seventh have the most harsh or jarring quality; the major second and the minor seventh are not quite as harsh. The augmented fourth or diminished fifth has a unique, unstable quality which led Medieval theorists to refer to it as "the devil in music."

EXAMPLE 4–4.

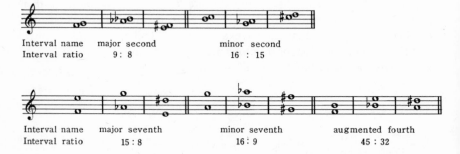

| Interval name | major second | minor second |
| Interval ratio | 9 : 8 | 16 : 15 |

| Interval name | major seventh | minor seventh | augmented fourth |
| Interval ratio | 15 : 8 | 16 : 9 | 45 : 32 |

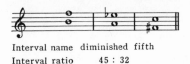

Interval name diminished fifth
Interval ratio   45 : 32

The definition of consonance and dissonance, which we have treated superficially here, is one of the oldest and most controversial problems of music theory. Numerous definitions, categories, and explanations of this phenomenon have been advanced at various times. Our categorization, based on euphony, is a useful one which is accepted by many practicing musicians.

Compound intervals. Intervals larger than an octave are called *compound intervals* and have generally the same characteristics as the equivalent intervals within an octave. Tenths, for example, are similar in quality to thirds.

Chords

A musical sonority consisting of three or more tones sounded simultaneously is called a *chord.*

Triad.   The term *triad* refers to a three-tone chord, based upon the harmonic interval of the third. The following are the most commonly used triads:

EXAMPLE 4–5.

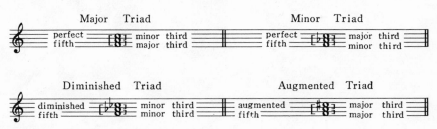

Seventh chords.   If an additional third is added to a triad, the resulting four-tone chord is called a *seventh chord.* A few of the more commonly used seventh chords are given in Example 4–6. The chords are designated according to the basic triad and the seventh; *major-minor seventh chord,* for example, indicates that the basis of the chord is a *major* triad and that the added tone is a *minor* seventh above the root of the chord.

EXAMPLE 4–6.

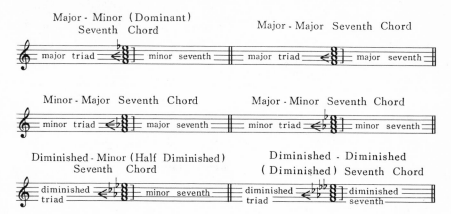

Other chords. The addition of still more thirds to the basic triad produces ninth, eleventh, and thirteenth chords.

EXAMPLE 4–7.

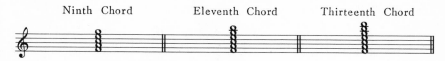

Chords such as triads, seventh chords, ninth chords, etc. are called *tertian* because they are based on thirds. It is also possible to construct *non-tertian* chords, that is, chords based on harmonic intervals other than the third.

EXAMPLE 4–8.

Chords built from the tones of a major or minor scale are called *diatonic;* chords with one or more chromatic tones are called *chromatic* or *altered*

chords. In a composition written in F Major, for example, the F major triad, the D minor triad, and the E diminished triad would be called diatonic chords because they use only tones present in the F major scale; in the same key, the F minor triad, the D major triad, and the E-flat major triad would be called chromatic or altered chords because they contain at least one chromatic tone, not present in the F major scale.

EXAMPLE 4-9.

F Major:

Doubling. Any tone of a chord may be doubled or replaced by a tone one or more octaves higher or lower. Although this will change the sonority of the chord slightly, the basic character and the terminology of the chord will remain the same. The following, for example, are all F major chords:

EXAMPLE 4-10.

Inversion. The lowest tone of a chord constructed in thirds is called the root. The other tones are named according to the interval they form with the root (third, fifth, seventh, etc.). A chord is said to be in root position when the root of the chord is the lowest tone sounded. When a tone other than the root is sounded as the lowest tone, the chord is said to be inverted.

EXAMPLE 4-11.

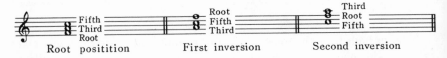

Harmonic tension. Chords may be classified as follows in terms of harmonic tension, or relative degree of consonance and dissonance:

Consonant chords—major and minor triads and inversions

Mildly dissonant chords—diminished and augmented triads, seventh and ninth chords, and their inversions

Strongly dissonant chords—eleventh chords, thirteenth chords, non-tertian chords based on seconds, fourths, etc.

Figured bass. *Figured bass* is a musical "shorthand" used for practical and theoretical purposes. In its earliest usage, figures were placed under a bass part to indicate the chords to be sounded above each bass tone.

EXAMPLE 4-12.

A later adaptation of this system is used as an aid in harmonic analysis, especially for music based on major or minor tonalities. Roman numerals are used to indicate the position of the root tone of each chord in the scale. Arabic numerals indicate inversions, alterations, and seventh chords, etc. by designating the intervals above the bass tone. Large roman numerals indicate major chords; small roman numerals indicate minor chords.

EXAMPLE 4-13.

Harmonic progression. The relationship between successive chords is called *harmonic progression* and is usually thought of in terms of

the relationship between the roots of the chords. There are three basic types of harmonic progression: by seconds (or sevenths), by thirds (or sixths), and by fourths (or fifths).

EXAMPLE 4-14.

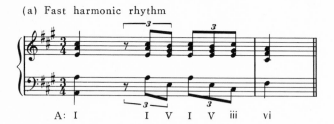

| Harmonic progression by seconds (sevenths) | Harmonic progression by thirds (sixths) | Harmonic progression by fourths (fifths) |

C: I   ii   iii   I   iii   V   I   V   ii

Harmonic rhythm.   *Harmonic rhythm* refers to the rate at which harmonic progression occurs. Harmonic rhythm is fast if chord changes occur several times per beat, moderate if changes occur every beat or every measure, or slow if changes occur every other measure or even less often. These are arbitrary categorizations and would have to be adjusted for various tempi. Repetitions or inversions of chords do not critically affect considerations of harmonic rhythm.

EXAMPLE 4-15a.   Brahms, *Piano Quartet in A Major*, Op. 26, first movement.

(a) Fast harmonic rhythm

A: I   I   V   I   V   iii   vi

EXAMPLE 4-15b.   Beethoven, *Quartet in A Major*, Op. 18, No. 5, last movement.

(b) Moderate harmonic rhythm

E: I   iv $\begin{smallmatrix}7\natural\\1\natural\end{smallmatrix}$ vii $\begin{smallmatrix}6\\4\natural\\3\natural\end{smallmatrix}$ iii $7\natural$

EXAMPLE 4–15c.   Beethoven, *Symphony No. 3 in E-flat Major*, Op. 55, first movement.

(c) Slow harmonic rhythm

E♭:   V⁷ ——————————————————   I ————————————————

Harmonization

The technique of adding tones or chords to a melodic line is known as *harmonization*. The development of this technique is one of the unique and most fascinating aspects of Western music. It is impractical to list here all of the various procedures of this technique, but we shall consider some of the most basic principles.

There are two approaches to the subject of harmonization: an *additive* approach, which begins with a melody and then adds other melodic lines or chords to it, and a *derivative* approach, which begins with a series of chords and then derives a melody from this. Although it can be shown historically that music began with what might be called an additive approach (see the literature section of this chapter), we can more easily begin with the derivative approach.

Derivative approach.   Let us begin with a C major chord and derive a melody from this by moving from one note of the chord to another. Most bugle calls can be derived in this manner.

EXAMPLE 4–16.

It is also possible to derive a melody from a single chord by using **not** only notes in the chord, but also some notes *not* in the chord. These are called *non-chord tones* or *non-harmonic tones*. We can classify them as follows:

EXAMPLE 4-17.

Using some of these non-harmonic tones we could derive another melody from the same chord.

EXAMPLE 4-18.

Our next step would be to derive a melody from a series of two or more chords. To do this we must know something about the procedures for writing chord progressions. These can best be learned in terms of traditional four-part writing, which involves three basic concepts—chord distribution, harmonic progression, and voice leading.

1. Distribution of tones in a single chord. Four-part harmonizations may be written in close position (i.e., with no more than an octave between the tenor and soprano part) or in open position (i.e., with more than an octave between the tenor and soprano part).

EXAMPLE 4-19.

In traditional writing the bass often has the root of the chord; that is the chord is in root position. Inversions, however, are used fairly frequently to provide harmonic variety and a more interesting bass line.

In four-part writing of triads it is necessary to double one note of the chord and this is usually the root of the chord. One exception to this is that the leading tone is rarely doubled, even if it is the root of a chord.

EXAMPLE 4-20.

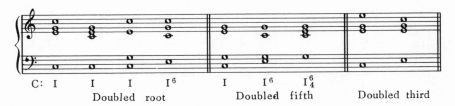

Sometimes it is necessary to omit a tone in four-part writing, especially with seventh chords or more extended structures. In such cases it is customary to omit the fifth of the chord.

EXAMPLE 4-21.

C: V⁷   V⁹   I⁹

2. Harmonic progression. Some general principles of harmonic progression were discussed on pp. 117–118. At this point it is helpful to consider some more specific procedures which can provide a basis for writing traditional harmonic progressions. To do this we shall first classify diatonic triads according to functional tendencies as shown in Example 4–22.

EXAMPLE 4-22.

Inversions, seventh chords, and most chromatically altered chords based on the chords listed above remain generally in the same category as the original chords. These, for example, are all *class 2 chords:*

EXAMPLE 4-23.

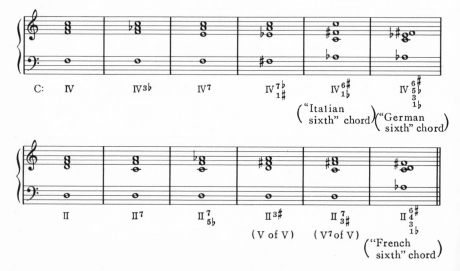

The tonic triad stands outside this categorization. It is usually the first, last, and most frequently used chord in a progression or composition. It can be used before or after chords of any of the four classes.

Class 1 chords, especially the V or V⁷ chords, are the second most frequently used chords. Many folk songs and other simple melodies can be harmonized exclusively with the tonic and dominant chords. Class 1 chords usually progress directly to the tonic.

Class 2 chords are the next most frequently used. They tend to move to class 1 chords and then on to the tonic chord, or, especially in the case of the subdominant chord, they may progress directly to the tonic chord.

Class 3 chords are less frequently used. They generally progress to chords of class 2, class 1, and then to tonic. The tonic seventh chord is sometimes regarded as a member of this class.

Class 4 chords are the least frequently used. They tend to move to chords of class 3, then to class 2, class 1, and then to tonic.

This functional classification of chords only indicates tendencies, not strict rules. Many pieces of music do follow the tendencies given here; many others, however, do not. The beginner will be more likely to write smooth progressions if he follows these tendencies at first. Later, he can experiment with other possibilities.

3. Voice leading. A general rule in traditional practice is that the individual voices or parts, especially the upper voices, should move in conjunct motion whenever possible. This makes the parts easier to sing and makes the harmonic progression smoother. If some tones are common to two chords in a progression, it is advisable to have these remain in the same voice.

EXAMPLE 4-24.

Another rule of traditional practice is to avoid having two or more voices move in parallel fifths or octaves. The use of parallel fifths or octaves reduces the effectiveness of a progression, since the upper tones of such parallel intervals (especially octaves) act, in effect, as mere reinforcements of the lower tones.

EXAMPLE 4–25.

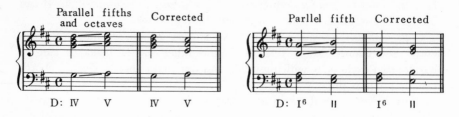

With these procedures in mind, let us now write some chord progressions and derive melodies from them. The following chord progression is especially common in folk songs and popular music. The student is encouraged to learn to play this progression in various keys on the piano.

EXAMPLE 4–26.

Here are some melodies derived from the three chords of this progression (I, IV, V). Non-harmonic tones are indicated by letter.

EXAMPLE 4–27a. Foster, "Old Folks at Home."

EXAMPLE 4-27b. Dvořák, "Humoresque."

EXAMPLE 4-27c. -Scottish folk song, "Auld Lang Syne."

Example 4-28. is based on another common chord progression by fifths; interestingly enough, the same progression is also used in the song, "Autumn Leaves."

EXAMPLE 4-28. Vivaldi, *The Seasons*, "Winter."

Additive approach. With this background in the derivative approach we can now proceed to the problem of adding a harmonization to an existing melody. For very slow-moving melodies we can harmonize each note of the melody with a chord. The melody note can be regarded as the root, third, or fifth of the chord (or the seventh, ninth, etc. in more complex chords.) The choice of chord can best be made according to the functional classifications given previously; i.e., the tonic chord should generally be used as first, last, and most frequently used chord, and the chords of the other classifications should be used according to their tendencies. In writing the harmonization, care must also be taken to follow the procedures described under chord distribution and voice leading. To illustrate this, we shall use the melody of "Frère Jacques" in long notes and provide two harmonizations for it, the first using only chords I, IV, and V⁷ and the second using other chords.

EXAMPLE 4–29.

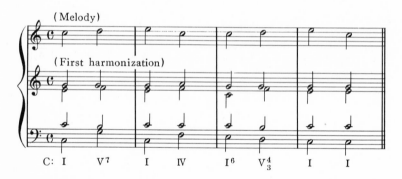

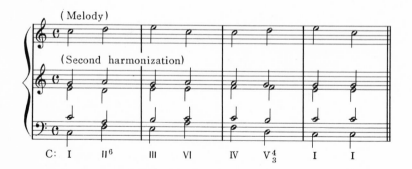

We may also regard the melody as the top part, or soprano, of a four-part setting, in which case, we must take care that the soprano also follows the suggested procedures of good chord distribution and voice leading.

EXAMPLE 4–30.

It is not necessary or advisable to have a change of chord on each note. Often the melody itself will contain notes that outline a chord, and these notes may be harmonized with the chord outlined, as in Example 4–31.

EXAMPLE 4–31.   Haydn, *Symphony No. 94 in G Major,* second movement (adapted).

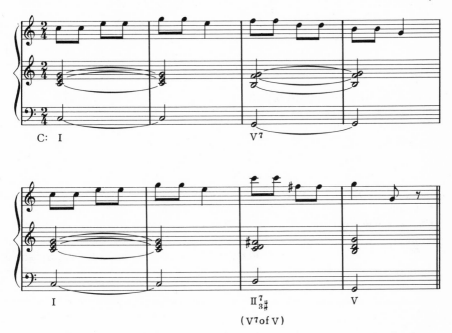

Other melodies, in fact most melodies, may best be harmonized by regarding some notes, especially the more prominent notes of the melody, as chord tones and other notes of the melody as non-harmonic tones. Here are two melodies harmonized in this manner.

EXAMPLE 4–32a. Dvořák, *Symphony No. 5 in E Minor,* second movement.

Db: I   V⁷   I   I⁶   II⁶₅ V⁷ I

EXAMPLE 4–32b. Tchaikowsky, *Symphony No. 5 in E Minor,* second movement.

D: I   V⁷⁻⁶₄   V⁴₂   I⁷⁻⁶   I   II⁴₃   V⁷₄₋₃   I⁴⁻³

Homophonic Texture

With this background on harmony we can proceed to a discussion of homophonic texture, i.e., one main melody with accompaniment. We shall be concerned with various types of accompaniment and with the location of the melody in relation to this accompaniment.

Types of accompaniment. Accompaniments may vary from single notes to complex harmonic expressions, but they are always subordinate to the melodic line. The following are only a few of the more commonly employed types:

Block chord accompaniment has a chord in the accompaniment for each note in the melody.

EXAMPLE 4–33.

Sustained chord accompaniment has one chord sustained in the accompaniment while several notes of the melody are played.

EXAMPLE 4–34.

Repeated chord accompaniment is just the reverse. Several chords of the accompaniment are sounded against one note of the melody.

EXAMPLE 4–35.

Broken chord accompaniment, or *arpeggio accompaniment,* has the notes of the accompanying chords sounded successively instead of simultaneously.

EXAMPLE 4–36.

Bass afterbeat accompaniment involves sounding one note of the chord (usually the root tone) alone and then following this with one or more soundings of the chord.

EXAMPLE 4–37.

Mixed accompaniments involve combinations of the previously discussed accompaniment types. Many composers prefer changing accompaniment types rather than consistent use of one type only.

EXAMPLE 4–38.

Location of the melody. In the examples given above, the melody is always *above* the accompaniment; it is also possible to have the melody *below* the accompaniment, or in the *middle* of the accompaniment.

EXAMPLE 4–39.

Melody below accompaniment

Melody in the middle of accompaniment

Polyphonic Texture

Polyphonic texture involves the simultaneous sounding of two or more independent, clearly recognizable melodies. The analysis of polyphonic texture is concerned with the rhythmic activity, pitch motion, and melodic relationship of the various melodies, and with the number and spacing of the melodies.

Rhythmic activity. Regarding only the temporal element of two or more polyphonic lines, we may describe the rhythmic activity as identical, equal, unequal, or complimentary.

Identical. Both lines have exactly the same rhythmic patterns.

EXAMPLE 4-40.

Equal. The two lines have equivalent but not identical rhythmic activity.

EXAMPLE 4-41.

Unequal. The rhythm of one line is more active, varied, or prominent than that of the other line.

EXAMPLE 4–42.

Complimentary. Rhythmic prominence alternates between the two lines.

EXAMPLE 4–43.

      Pitch motion. The relationship of the pitch pattern of one line to another can be described as parallel motion, similar motion, oblique motion, contrary motion, or mixed motion.

Parallel motion. The two lines move in the same direction and maintain the same distance from one another.

EXAMPLE 4-44.

Similar motion. The two lines move in the same direction, but do not maintain the same distance from one another.

EXAMPLE 4-45.

Oblique motion. One part stays on the same pitch while the other part moves.

EXAMPLE 4-46.

Contrary motion. The two parts move in opposite directions.

EXAMPLE 4-47.

Mixed motion. This involves some combination of the four types described above.

EXAMPLE 4-48.

Melodic relationship.   Regarding both the tonal and temporal elements of polyphonic lines, their melodic relationship may be described as imitative or non-imitative.

Imitative. Polyphonic lines are said to be imitative when they have the same melody (or melodic fragment), beginning at different times in different parts."Frère Jacques"can be used effectively to illustrate this since it is a *round* or *canon,* a type of composition based on imitative polyphony. In Example 4-49, the second part imitates the first part two measures later and one octave higher.

EXAMPLE 4-49.

It is also possible to have imitation at other temporal and tonal distances; in Example 4-50, for example, the second part imitates the first part two beats later and an octave and a fifth (twelfth) higher.

EXAMPLE 4-50.

Imitation may be strict or free, depending upon the fidelity with which the second part imitates the first part. Example 4–49 and Example 4–50 are in strict imitation; Example 4–51 illustrates free imitation.

EXAMPLE 4–51.

Non-imitative. When polyphonic lines are based on contrasting melodies, their relationship may be described as non-imitative. In imitative polyphony the parts cannot begin simultaneously or one part would merely be heard as a duplication or reinforcement of the other; in non-imitative polyphony the parts may or may not begin simultaneously.

EXAMPLE 4–52.

Number of parts.   The examples given above have been written for only two parts; however, it is possible to have three, four, or more parts in a polyphonic texture. In the following three-part example, the original melody is in the lowest part; the middle part is written in imitative polyphony; the upper part is in non-imitative polyphony.

EXAMPLE 4–53.

Spacing of parts. In polyphonic as well as in homophonic texture we speak of the spacing between the various lines. The limits given below are arbitrarily chosen.

Close spacing. The parts are less than an octave apart.

EXAMPLE 4–54.

Average spacing. The parts remain approximately an octave to a double octave apart.

EXAMPLE 4–55.

Wide spacing. The parts are over a double octave apart.

EXAMPLE 4–56.

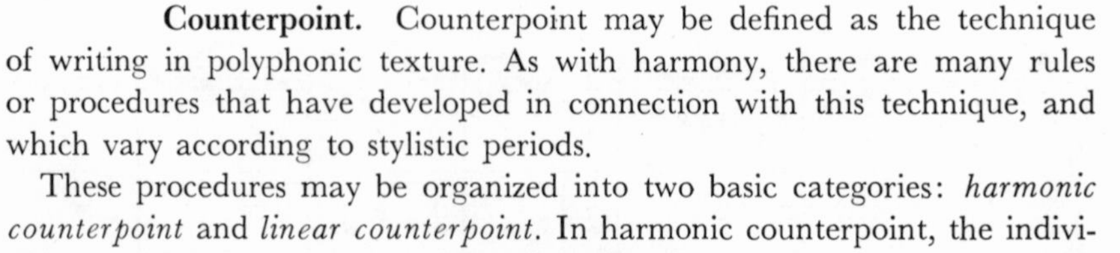

Counterpoint. Counterpoint may be defined as the technique of writing in polyphonic texture. As with harmony, there are many rules or procedures that have developed in connection with this technique, and which vary according to stylistic periods.

These procedures may be organized into two basic categories: *harmonic counterpoint* and *linear counterpoint*. In harmonic counterpoint, the individual melodic lines are governed by a harmonic progression. The contrapuntal lines are woven through the chords of the harmonic progression in a manner that might be represented as in Example 4–57.

EXAMPLE 4–57.   Schubert, *Quintet in A Major for Piano and Strings,*
fourth movement.

In linear counterpoint, the individual melodic lines are thought of primarily in relation to each other, and the resulting vertical structures or chords are only products of the momentary relationships between the contrapuntal lines. Linear counterpoint may be represented as in Example 4–58.

EXAMPLE 4–58.   Josquin des Prez, Motet, *Ave Maria*.

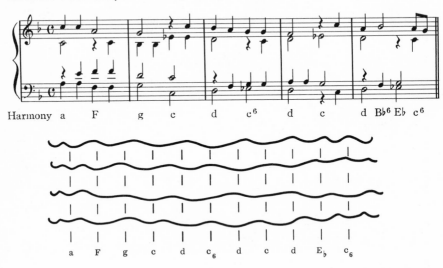

The term *contrapuntal* is used as a synonym for polyphonic. Other more specific terms implying *imitative* polyphony are *canonic* and *fugal*. *Canonic* refers to musical sections written in strict, continuous, imitative polyphony; *fugal* refers to sections with more free and less continuous use of imitative counterpoint.

   Hybrid texture.   Often music will display elements of both polyphonic and homophonic textures as in Example 4–59.

EXAMPLE 4–59.

Another type of texture that may be regarded as a hybrid between
homophonic and polyphonic writing is *antiphonal* writing. In antiphonal
writing, a portion of music is stated in one voice or section; then another

voice or section answers with the same musical material in identical or slightly varied form, or with new musical material.

EXAMPLE 4–60.

The Textural Element in Music Literature

The development of polyphonic and homophonic textures is one of the unique features of the music of Western civilization. The music of non-Western cultures often shows great sophistication and refinement in the temporal and tonal elements, but relatively little development in the textural element. In Western music, aspects of the textural element are particularly significant in the stylistic identification of compositions from various periods.

Pre-Baroque. Gregorian chant, or plainsong, was written in monophonic texture. The first tentative experiments in early polyphony, or *organum,* were begun in about the ninth century. To trace the historical development of polyphonic writing, we shall take a plainsong melody and see how it was, or might have been, treated in various styles. Most pre-Baroque polyphonic compositions are based on a pre-existing melody which may be designated as a *cantus firmus* or a *tenor.* These cantus firmus melodies are usually drawn from the repertoire of plainsong or from secular songs. We shall use the plainsong melody, *Te Deum Laudamus.* This melody is sometimes called the "Ambrosian Hymn" because it was formerly thought to have been written by Ambrose of Milan (c.400 A.D.); actually it was probably written at a later time. Here is a portion of the chant in its original monophonic version.

EXAMPLE 4–61. *Te Deum Laudamus.*

We have no preserved music showing how this particular melody was treated in polyphonic settings up to the sixteenth century, but by referring to theoretical and musical sources from the Ancient and Medieval periods, we can approximate the manner in which it might have been set in various polyphonic styles. In the earliest and simplest type of *parallel organum* at the fifth, as described in the *Musica Enchiriadis* of the ninth century, it could have been written thus:

EXAMPLE 4–62.

In *composite organum,* the *vox principalis* and *vox organalis* are doubled at the octave.

EXAMPLE 4–63.

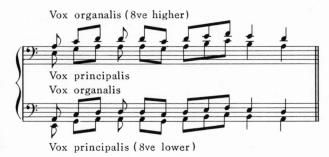

In free organum (c. tenth century) contrary motion is introduced.

EXAMPLE 4–64.

In *melismatic organum,* the notes of the original plainsong are held for a long time while the other parts have moving notes.

EXAMPLE 4–65.

etc.

In the *clausula* of the twelfth and thirteenth centuries, the cantus firmus, or tenor, is based on a melisma from chant, i.e., a section in which several notes are sung on the same syllable. These notes are sung as long, even notes in the lowest part and the two parts above have free contrapuntal parts which can be represented in modern ⅜ meter. Since the *Te Deum* has no extended melisma, we shall instead use the first few notes of the chant to illustrate this type of music.

EXAMPLE 4–66.

The *thirteenth-century motet* is somewhat similar to the clausula, except that it has a poetic text, often in the vernacular, added to the two upper parts.

In the fourteenth-century *isorhythmic* (Greek: iso, equal or same) *motet,* the tenor is based on a short melodic pattern or *color* taken from a chant. Example 4–67 is a *color* taken from the *Te Deum.*

EXAMPLE 4–67.

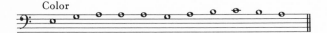

This *color* is organized according to a predetermined rhythmic pattern, known as a *talea.* Example 4–68 is one possible *talea.*

EXAMPLE 4–68.

Talea

Since the *color* has more notes than the *talea,* an interesting "overlapping" effect results when these are repeated, causing each successive presentation of the *color* to have a slightly different rhythmic organization.

EXAMPLE 4–69.

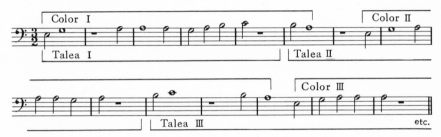

Upper parts are added in a manner similar to the clausula or thirteenth-century motet, as can be seen from Example 4–70. In this example, the rhythmic organization of the upper parts is free. In some isorhythmic motets, all the parts are organized according to isorhythmic procedures.

EXAMPLE 4–70.

Tentative experiments in imitation can be found even before the fourteenth century, and by the time of the Renaissance, imitative polyphony was established as the predominant type of texture. Phrases from plainsong were used as the basis of polyphonic imitative compositions such as Example 4–71 by Palestrina, which is based on the *Te Deum* melody. The notes of the *Te Deum* are marked with X's.

EXAMPLE 4–71.   Palestrina, *Missa, Te Deum.*

As can be seen from the examples given above, the earliest polyphony was based harmonically upon the perfect consonance; then there was a period of harmonic experimentation in which a variety of harmonic intervals was used, often with some striking dissonances; and finally, in the Renaissance period, harmony was based mostly on consonant triads with controlled usage of non-harmonic tones, especially passing tones and suspensions. In both Medieval and Renaissance music, composers frequently ended a piece on an incomplete chord with root and fifth but no third. In general, harmonic rhythm was moderately slow, and harmonic progression by seconds was more common than in the Baroque or Classical periods.

Secular music shows a similar, though less complex and extensive, development from the monophonic troubadour and trouvère songs of the twelfth and thirteenth centuries through the polyphonic chansons of the fourteenth and fifteenth centuries to the madrigals of the sixteenth century. Unlike most sacred compositions, however, secular polyphonic compositions were usually not based on a pre-existing melody.

Baroque.   Baroque composers continued the development of imitative and non-imitative polyphony and also continued to use the cantus firmus technique in some works. At the same time, homophonic textures were developed in such forms as the opera and the Lutheran chorale. The *Te Deum,* which we traced through the pre-Baroque period, was adapted as a Lutheran chorale and appeared in such settings as the following:

EXAMPLE 4–72.   Bach, " Herr Gott, dich loben wir."

This chorale was also used as the basis for several Bach cantatas.

EXAMPLE 4–73.   Bach, *Cantata No. 16.*

EX 4–73 continued.

EXAMPLE 4–74. Bach, *Cantata No. 190.*

There are many sacred and secular works that have no reference to pre-existing melodies; the *Te Deums* of Handel, for example, are freely composed, as are many of Bach's other cantatas.

In the early part of the Baroque period there was a considerable amount of harmonic experimentation especially in terms of unusual chord progression, as is shown in Ex. 4–75.

EXAMPLE 4–75. Monteverdi, *Orfeo.*

Later in the Baroque period, harmonic progression became more standardized, with progression by fourths or fifths predominant. Harmonic rhythm varied from a change per beat in a chorale to a change every four or more measures in some instrumental works. Major and minor triads or seventh chords with controlled usage of non-harmonic tones made up the harmonic vocabulary of the period.

Classical.   In reaction to the complex polyphony of much Baroque music, composers of the Rococo period stressed simple homophonic textures, featuring attractive ornamented melodies set against stereotyped accompaniments.

EXAMPLE 4–76. J. C. Bach, *Sonata in C Minor.*

One of the unique achievements of the Classical period was the synthesis of Baroque polyphony and Rococo homophony, as can be seen, for example, in the finale to Mozart's *Symphony No. 41 in C Major,* K. 551. Many works, however, stress either homophonic or polyphonic texture. In homophonic works, a greater variety of accompaniment types is manifest.

Classical composers continued to base their harmonic usage upon major and minor triads and seventh chords and harmonic progression by fourths or fifths. Harmonic rhythm tended to be more standardized and regular; many works showed harmonic change on every measure or every other measure.

Romantic. Though the synthesis of homophony and polyphony continued in many Romantic works, renewed emphasis on homophony is apparent in most works of the period. A large variety of effective accompaniment patterns were used, some of which were adaptations of Classical patterns. For example, the broken-chord accompaniment, which usually remained in the compass of an octave in the Classical period, was stretched to two or more octaves in a characteristic Romantic piano accompaniment, such as in Example 4–77.

EXAMPLE 4–77. Chopin, *Nocturne in C-sharp Minor.*

In terms of harmonic usage the Romantic period displayed considerable variety and experimentation. In addition to major and minor triads and seventh chords, composers used ninth chords and altered chords.

EXAMPLE 4–78. Wagner, *Lohengrin.*

EXAMPLE 4–79. Wagner, *Die Meistersinger.*

Non-harmonic tones were used more freely and often with effective emotional intensity.

EXAMPLE 4–80. Wagner, *The Flying Dutchman.*

Harmonic progression by fourths and fifths was continued, but often composers used other progressions with telling effectiveness. (In Example 4–81, some of the notation has been changed enharmonically for greater ease in reading.)

EXAMPLE 4–81. Dvořák, *Symphony No. 5 in E Minor,* second movement.

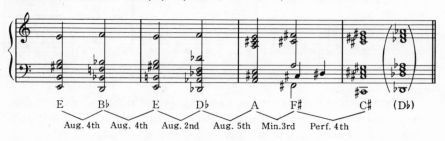

There is a great variety in harmonic rhythm, ranging from two or more changes per beat to sections of over 100 measures based on one harmony as, for example, the opening of Wagner's *Das Rheingold.*

Contemporary. Though the homophony-polyphony synthesis is evident is some contemporary music, there is, in general, an increased emphasis on polyphony, perhaps in reaction to the Romantic emphasis on homophony. One striking aspect of the textural element in contemporary music is the introduction of unusual chordal structures such as those in Example 4–82.

EXAMPLE 4–82.

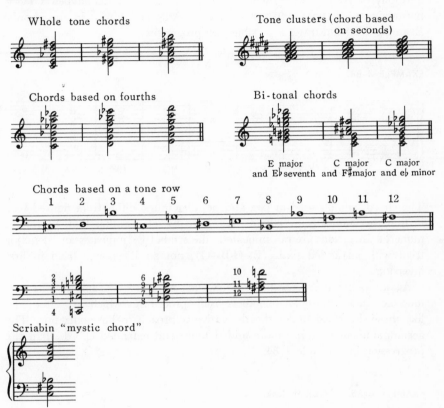

Another characteristic of the textural element in contemporary music is the frequent disregard of traditional procedures in harmonization, as described on pages 119 to 128. Unusual chord distribution, harmonic progression, and voice leading are frequently encountered, as can be seen in Example 4–83, where harmonic progression by seconds and parallel voice leading are obvious.

EXAMPLE 4–83.

Other textural characteristics of the contemporary period would include free treatment of non-harmonic tones, wide variety in harmonic rhythm, increased harmonic tension, and the use of varied accompaniments. The textural element in jazz ranges from the homophonic texture and triadic harmony of early jazz styles to the more polyphonic texture and dissonant harmony of later styles. Much jazz music is based on stereotyped I-IV-V harmonic progressions, often with added sixths and ninths in the chords. Example 4–84 illustrates a possible jazz progression.

EXAMPLE 4–84.

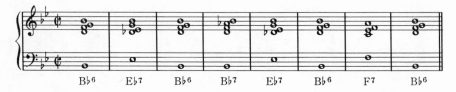

The chord symbols used in jazz and popular music differ from figured bass in that they indicate the root of the chord by letter rather than by roman numeral. Inversions are not indicated; the symbol E♭⁶ indicates an E♭ major triad with an added sixth (E♭-G-B♭-C), not an E♭ major triad in first inversion.

Against a set harmonic progression such as that of Example 4–84 jazz musicians may improvise melodies, using procedures which are essentially like those described under the derivative approach to harmonization. The accompaniment here has more added tones and extended chords than the progression in Example 4–84.

EXAMPLE 4–85.   "Brother Jack."

Textural Element Summary

HARMONY
 harmonic intervals:
  perfect consonances, imperfect consonances, dissonances
 chords:
  triads, seventh chords, ninth chords, eleventh chords, thirteenth chords, non-tertian chords, altered chords
 harmonic tension:
  consonant, mildly dissonant, dissonant
 harmonic progression:
  by seconds or sevenths, by thirds or sixths, by fourths or fifths
 harmonic rhythm:
  slow, moderate, fast

TEXTURE
 monophonic
 homophonic:
  accompaniment:
   block chord, sustained chord, repeated chord, broken chord, bass afterbeat, mixed, etc.
  location of melody:
   above the accompaniment, in the middle of the accompaniment, below the accompaniment
 polyphonic:
  rhythmic activity:
   identical, equal, unequal, complimentary
  pitch motion:
   parallel, similar, oblique, contrary, mixed
  melodic relationship:
   strict imitative, free imitative, non-imitative
  number of parts:
   two, three, four, five, etc.
  spacing of parts:
   close, average, wide
 hybrid or antiphonal

Exercises

Analysis

1. Identify the harmonic intervals indicated in Ex. 4–86.

EXAMPLE 4–86.

2. Write the indicated intervals above or below the given note.

EXAMPLE 4–87.

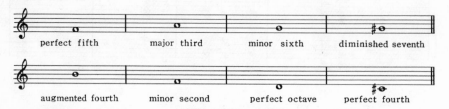

perfect fifth   major third   minor sixth   diminished seventh

augmented fourth   minor second   perfect octave   perfect fourth

3. Identify the chords according to the descriptions given on pp. 113–116.

EXAMPLE 4–88.

4. Write the indicated chords above the notes.

EXAMPLE 4–89.

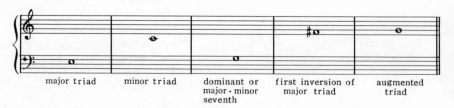

major triad   minor triad   dominant or   first inversion of   augmented

major - minor   major triad   triad

seventh

5. According to the textural element summary, analyze a selected work, such as a Schubert song or a piece from Bartók's *Mikrokosmos,* from the printed score.

Composition

1. Using the derivative approach (p 119) derive two melodies from the chord progression in Example 4–90. Change the chords to the following accompaniment types: (1) block chord, (2) repeated chord, (3) arpeggio.

EXAMPLE 4–90.

2. Same as Number 1., but first create your own chord progression.

3. Using the additive approach, write the following types of accompaniment to the melody given in Example 4–91: (1) block chord, (2) bass afterbeat.

EXAMPLE 4–91.

4. Same as Number 3., but begin with your own melody.

5. The following melody can effectively be imitated; see if you can discover at which interval and in which measure it can be done.

EXAMPLE 4–92.

6. To the melody in Example 4–93, add a second melody which (1) will be non-imitative, (2) will use different rhythms from the given melody, and (3) will usually form perfect or imperfect consonant harmonic intervals (i.e., unison, octave,

fifth, fourth, thirds, or sixths) with the given melody, especially on the first beat of each measure.

EXAMPLE 4-93.

7. Compose a piece using a hybrid texture of polyphony and homophony for piano, violin, and cello.

Performance

1. On the piano, practice finding and playing all the harmonic intervals above and below various notes.

2. Play the C major chord in as many different positions as you can. Repeat with various major, minor, and seventh chords.

3. Play this chord progression in various major and minor keys.

EXAMPLE 4-94.

I   IV   V⁷

Use these chords to accompany the following melodies in a sustained chord style and in other accompaniment styles.

EXAMPLE 4-95.

EXAMPLE 4-96.

Listening

1. Listen to the following works and analyze aurally according to the textural element summary.

Machaut, *Notre Dame Mass*

Handel, *Messiah* (excerpts)

Beethoven, *Symphony No. 3 in E flat Major, Op. 55*

Wagner, Overture to *Tannhäuser*

Debussy, Piano pieces such as "Gardens in the Rain," "The Sunken Cathedral"

Bartók, *String Quartet No. 3*

2. Listen to other works to determine what period they are from according to texture and other elements. (See Chapter 1 for suggested procedures.)

chapter 5

The Formal Element

The term form, as it is applied to music, denotes both general structural principles (repetition, contrast, variation, etc.) and specific schematic designs (binary form, rondo form, sonata form, etc.). In this chapter we shall consider general principles of form; in Part II we shall discuss specific forms as they occur in music literature.

In the preceding four chapters we have examined the temporal, tonal, timbre-dynamic, and textural elements of music. The formal element constitutes a synthesis of these four elements. It derives from the relationships between the structural units of a musical composition, relationships that are made apparent by the manner in which the musical elements are treated in each structural unit. We shall investigate the nature of these musical units, the types of cadences which may be used to delineate them, and the principles of repetition, contrast, and variation involved in their interrelationships. We shall also discuss thematic and transitional units, analysis of music, categories of specific formal structures, and functional and emotional types of music.

The perception and understanding of the formal element presents a greater challenge in music than in the visual arts. In painting or sculpture, the component units are presented in space and it is possible to shift attention back and forth among them to determine their relationships. In music, the component units are presented in time and must be compared to one another in the memory of the listener. The listener who has developed the ability to perceive the basic elements of music should be well prepared to meet this challenge and to understand the general principles of form presented in this chapter and the specific forms of music presented in Part II.

Musical Units

The basic units of music are often compared to the basic units of written language as follows:

Language	Music
letter	note
syllable or word	motive or figure
phrase	phrase
sentence	period, double period, or phrase group
paragraph	section
chapter	movement
book	composition

In written language there is considerable variety in the manner in which the basic units are treated, ranging from a simple folk story, consisting of one paragraph with short sentences and monosyllabic words, to a lengthy novel with a complex structure of chapters, sections, paragraphs, sentences, etc. In music there is a similar variety in the treatment of the basic units, ranging from a simple folk song, consisting of one repeated phrase based on a single motive, to a full length symphony with extended movements, sections, periods, etc.

Motive.   The motive is the smallest coherent, self-contained unit in music. It consists of two or more successive notes which form a distinctive rhythmic pattern, pitch pattern, or melodic pattern. The decision as to what constitutes a motive must often be an arbitrary one, but generally we can identify a motive by the fact that it is clear and separable from other surrounding notes, and that it plays an important role in the subsequent development of the music through repetition and variation. Often a composition will be non-motivic, that is, the composer will combine single notes into larger units, such as phrases or periods, without the intermediate stage of motivic development. The difference between motivic and non-motivic construction can be seen in the following examples.

EXAMPLE 5–1a.   Brahms, *Symphony No. 4 in E Minor,* first movement.

Motivic Construction

EXAMPLE 5–1b.   Brahms, *Symphony No. 4 in E Minor,* last movement.

Non-motivic Construction

Figure.   A figure is a unit similar to the motive; however, it appears in the accompanying or secondary voices rather than in the principal melody.

EXAMPLE 5–2. Brahms, *Symphony No. 4 in E Minor*, first movement.

Phrase.   The phrase is a more complete and comprehensive musical utterance than the motive. Four measures is a regular length for phrases in moderate tempos; other phrase lengths, however, are frequently used. The ending of a phrase is marked by a *cadence*. (See p. 162.)

EXAMPLE 5–3. Brahms, *Symphony No. 4 in E Minor*, first movement.

Period.   A period is composed of two related phrases, an *antecedent* and a *consequent* phrase. Often the effect of the two phrases is that of question and answer, or statement and restatement. The regular period length is eight measures, that is, two four-measure phrases.

Double period, phrase group.   A double period consists of two periods. A phrase group consists of a more irregular grouping of three, five, or more phrases.

EXAMPLE 5–4. Mozart, *Quartet in B-flat Major, K. 458 (Hunt)*, first movement.

EXAMPLE 5-4 continued.

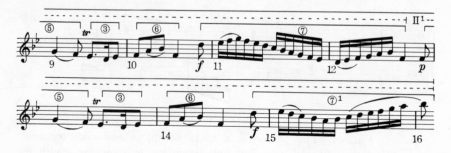

Section.   A section is a musical unit that may be made up of one or more periods, phrase groups, or other, more irregular structures.

Movement.   A movement is a complete, self-contained, and independent musical unit. Its length can vary from a period to several sections.

Cadence

A cadence is a more or less definite conclusion in music, occurring at the ends of phrases or larger musical units. It is generally considered to consist of the final two chords and the concurrent melodic material. It may, however, involve more chords, or, in some instances, it may be a purely melodic phenomenon.

Harmonic cadences.   The following cadences are classified according to the harmonic progression involved:

Full cadence. A cadence ending on the tonic chord.

EXAMPLE 5-5.

C: V   I

Half cadence. A cadence ending on a chord other than tonic, usually dominant.

EXAMPLE 5–6.

C: I   V

Authentic cadence. A cadence involving the harmonic progression of dominant to tonic (**V-I**).

EXAMPLE 5–7.

C: V   I

Plagal cadence. A cadence involving the harmonic progression of subdominant to tonic (**IV-I**), often used for the concluding amen in hymns.

EXAMPLE 5–8.

C: IV   I

Deceptive cadence. A cadence involving the harmonic progression of dominant to a chord other than tonic. The following is a common pattern.

EXAMPLE 5–9.

C: V⁷   VI

Melodic cadences. The following cadences are classified according to aspects of the temporal or tonal elements:

Masculine cadence. A cadence ending on a strong beat.

EXAMPLE 5–10.

Feminine cadence. A cadence ending on a weak beat.

EXAMPLE 5–11.

Perfect cadence. A cadence ending on the tonic note.

EXAMPLE 5–12.

Imperfect cadence. A cadence ending on a note other than tonic.

EXAMPLE 5–13.

Modal cadences. Cadences based on the church modes are sometimes used in the framework of major-minor tonality. The *phrygian cadence,* with a descending half step in the bass, is the most frequently used.

Combined cadences. In describing cadences in homophonic or polyphonic music, it is helpful to mention both harmonic and melodic characteristics. A perfect authentic cadence, for example, would indicate that the harmonic progression is V to I and that the melody ends on tonic. Occasionally, as in Example 5–14, harmonic and melodic aspects of a cadence are in conflict. Here the accompanying harmony makes an obvious half cadence on the first beat of measure 8, while the melodic line continues its forward motion.

EXAMPLE 5–14.   Mozart, *Symphony No. 41 in C Major, K. 551,* last movement.

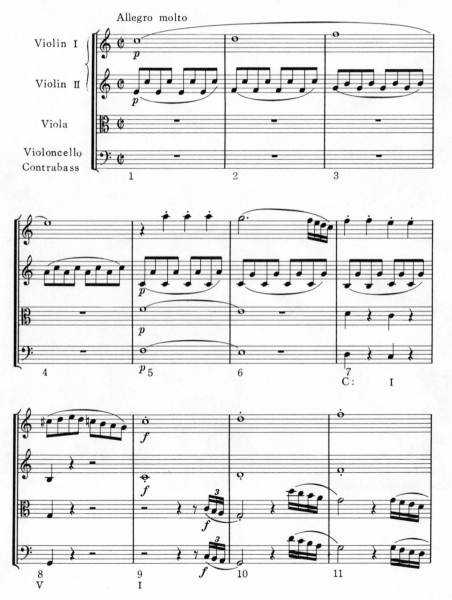

Marc Bomse, photographer.

Sometimes, as in Example 5–15, the reverse situation appears. Here the melody reaches a point of momentary conclusion on the half note (e^2) in measure 4, while the harmony continues its forward impetus.

EXAMPLE 5–15. Mozart, *String Quartet in D Major*, K. 499, second movement.

The use of cadence patterns such as those in Example 5–14 and 5–15 avoids the obvious, monotonous, and over-sectionalized effect that would result if the melodic and harmonic aspects of cadences would always coincide.

Repetition, Contrast, and Variation

It is possible to reduce all the manifold operations involved in the construction of an extended musical composition to three basic principles—repetition, contrast, and variation. Repetition, the presentation of the same musical material in two or more structural units of a composition, and contrast, the presentation of different musical material, may be readily perceived and understood. Variation, a compositional process in which some musical elements remain the same while others are more or less changed, is somewhat more complicated. The following examples, based on "Frère Jacques," illustrate some of the many possible applications of variation technique.

Temporal variations.
Original.

EXAMPLE 5–16.

Change of meter.

EXAMPLE 5–17.

Change of tempo (allegro to adagio, etc.).
Change of rhythm.

EXAMPLE 5–18.

Augmentation (doubling the value of each note).

EXAMPLE 5–19.

Diminution (halving the value of each note).

EXAMPLE 5–20.

Change of beat division (duplets to triplets).

EXAMPLE 5–21.

Extension.

EXAMPLE 5–22.

Abbreviation.

EXAMPLE 5–23.

Tonal variations.

Inversion (proceeding by the same intervals but in the opposite direction).

EXAMPLE 5-24.

Retrograde (playing the melody backwards).

EXAMPLE 5-25.

Retrograde inversion.

EXAMPLE 5-26.

Sequence (repetition of the same motive or phrase on different pitch levels).

EXAMPLE 5-27.

Ornamentation.

EXAMPLE 5-28.

Transposition.

EXAMPLE 5–29.

Added notes (the notes of the original melody are marked **X**.).

EXAMPLE 5–30.

Deleted notes.

EXAMPLE 5–31.

Change of tonality (major to minor, etc.).

EXAMPLE 5–32.

> **Timbre-dynamic variations.**
> *Change of dynamics* (*forte* to *piano*, etc.).
> *Change of articulation* (legato to staccato, etc.).
> *Change of instrumentation* (strings to woodwinds, etc.).
> **Texture variations.**
> *Change of accompaniment.*

EXAMPLE 5-33.

Change of texture (homophonic to polyphonic).

EXAMPLE 5-34.

Change of harmony

EXAMPLE 5-35.

Combined variations.
Change of tonality, texture, and melody.

EXAMPLE 5-36.

Change of texture, meter, rhythm, and melody.
Soprano, theme in retrograde.
Alto, theme in free inversion and sequence.
Tenor, theme in augmentation (twice as slow), and a third higher.
Bass, theme in augmentation (three times as slow).

EXAMPLE 5–37.

The distinctions between repetition, contrast, and variation are not always clear-cut. For example, minor changes in dynamics, articulation, melody, and harmony etc., though technically aspects of variation technique, do not necessarily destroy the effect of repetition. On the other hand, the extensive use of combined variation techniques may produce the effect of contrast.

Satisfactory form in music may be achieved in part through a balance of unity and variety in the presentation of the structural units of a composition. The repetition of musical material contributes to the unity and coherence of a composition; the presentation of contrasting material adds variety and interest. Variation provides both unity and variety.

Theme and Transition

Not all parts of a musical composition have the same purpose or significance. Some units, especially those with clearly identifiable melodic material, are called themes or thematic sections; these are usually repeated at some time during the composition and therefore they become the most significant parts of the composition. Other units, with less cogent musical material, are called transitions; though they may be written with great beauty and skill, their main purpose is to connect thematic sections. Transitions have a feeling of motion, incompleteness, instability, and tension; thematic sections have a feeling of arrival, completeness, stability, and release. Themes usually remain in one basic tonality; transitions often modulate.

The Analysis of Music

Just as a travel guide can increase the enjoyment of a trip, an analysis of a musical composition can add to the listener's enjoyment by sharpening the sense of direction and anticipation. Musical analysis, however, is not as exact and universally understood as a road map. Some analyses of music are so vague and subjective as to be practically useless for any purpose, except perhaps to give some idea of the emotions the analyst felt when hearing a particular composition—emotions that might not be shared by other listeners.

To avoid this we have attempted in this book to provide a simple, objective, uniform system of analysis, supplemented by musical examples and verbal description when needed. The following symbols are used:

Motives: ①, ②, ③, etc.
Phrases: I, II, II, etc.
Periods: a, b, c, etc.
Double periods or phrase groups: A, B, C, etc.
Sections: verbal descriptions such as trio, development, coda, etc.

The first appearance of a motive is labeled ①. Subsequent repetitions of this same motive are also labeled ①. Variations of this motive would be labeled $①^1$, $①^2$, etc. Contrasting motives are labeled ②, ③, etc. The designation of phrases, periods, and double periods is similarly handled. Immediate repetition is indicated as follows:

A:‖:BA^1:‖   indicates AA BA^1BA^1

In analyzing a musical composition all elements (temporal, tonal, timbre-dynamic, textural, and formal) must be considered. Often, however, tonality is the most decisive factor in determining the analysis. For this reason the tonality is usually indicated below the analysis; capital letters denote major keys and small letters denote minor keys.

Thematic sections are indicated with a solid line thus: ——————
Transitions sections or secondary parts are indicated with a wavy line thus: ～～～～～～～

Specific Forms of Music

Although extensive discussion of specific forms is reserved for the second part of this text, it is possible here to provide an over-all picture of the various formal organizations.

Sectional forms. Sectional forms are always characterized by more or less clear divisions between the formal units and usually by a balance between the principles of repetition and contrast. Typical forms include the following:

Binary: AA^1 or AB
Ternary: ABA or ABA^1
Rondo: ABACABA
Minuet and trio: a:‖:a^{1}a:‖:b:‖:b^{1}b:‖aa^{1}a

In sectional forms, immediate repetition does not change the basic formal structure. For example, AA BB (A:‖:B:‖) would still be considered a binary form.

Variation forms. Variation forms consist of an opening statement of a theme, followed by several sections in which certain elements, such as the melody or harmony of the original theme, are repeated substantially without change, while other elements, such as texture, rhythm, etc., are varied. Included in this category are such forms as *theme and variations, passacaglia, chaconne,* and others.

Fugal forms. The most distinctive characteristic of the various forms in this category is that they are based upon the use of imitative polyphonic texture. For this reason, some writers regard the *fugue, motet,* and other similar works as being written in a specific technique, rather than in a specific form. It can be shown, however, that these works do share certain structural characteristics. (See p. 211.)

Sonata-allegro form. The sonata-allegro form may be regarded as a separate form based on both sectional and variation principles. It is sectional in its general division into three large units (exposition, development, and recapitulation) and in the division of the exposition and recapitulation into first and second themes or theme groups. It uses the variation principle in the development section. However, the developmental technique differs from the theme and variations technique in that the former involves manipulation and alteration of fragments, motives, or phrases from the main themes; the theme and variations technique involves manipulation and alteration of the entire theme.

Free forms. Formal structures that do not fit conveniently in any of the above categories are called free forms.

In addition to the single movement structures described above, there are many types of multi-movement forms that will be discussed in Part II.

Types of Music

All music may be divided into three general types: *abstract* music, which *does not* refer or relate to anything outside the music itself; *program* music, which *does* refer or relate to something outside the music such as a poem, story, drama, character, or emotion; and *textual* music, which involves a poetic or prose text sung by a vocal solo or ensemble.

These three types are not rigidly separated or mutually exclusive. An abstract composition may have some programmatic implication, referring, for example, to a general emotion or mood of tension and excitement. Such a reference is, however, not as explicit and unequivocal in an abstract composition as it might be in a programmatic composition. All program music has some abstract implications; even the most vividly descriptive piece will have a certain strictly musical form. Textual music has both abstract and programmatic characteristics.

We may also divide music into two other general categories: subjective music, in which the expression of personal feelings and emotions is emphasized; and objective music, in which impersonal, purely musical elements and forms are emphasized. Program music tends to be subjective; abstract music tends to be objective. However, the two sets of terms are not synonymous. Chopin *Etudes,* for example, are abstract, but they are intensely personal and subjective. We sometimes refer to subjectivity in music as *pathos;* to objectivity as *ethos.*

Formal Element Summary

MOTIVES
motivic or non-motivic treatment

PHRASES
regular or irregular

PERIODS
regular or irregular

CADENCES
full, half, authentic, plagal, deceptive, etc.

COMPOSITIONAL PRINCIPLES EMPHASIZED
repetition, contrast, variation

FORM
sectional, variation, fugal, sonata-allegro, free

TYPE
abstract, program, textual

CHARACTER
subjective, objective

FORM GRAPH
(label component musical units)

Exercises

Analysis

1. Analyze the motive, phrase, and period structure of the melody of Example

5–38, using the proper symbols. Describe the cadences and discuss the uses of the compositional principles of repetition, contrast, and variation.

EXAMPLE 5–38.   Beethoven, Sonata No. 12 in A-flat Major for Piano, Op. 26, first movement.

2. Write similar analyses of other examples from this text and from other sources.

Composition

1. Write a composition for piano in F major, $\frac{3}{4}$ meter, andante tempo. Use homophonic texture with the melody written above a simple sustained chord accompaniment. Write according to the formal outline given in Example 5–39.

EXAMPLE 5–39.

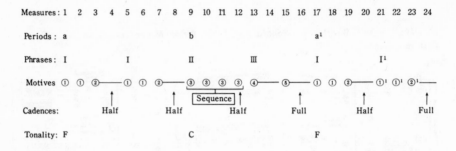

2. Write a set of variations on a folk song or on one of your own compositions. Refer to the variation techniques described on pp. 168–173.

3. Advanced students may wish to write one of the more complex forms, such as sonata-allegro or fugue, especially after studying examples of these in Part II.

Performance

No specific exercises in performance are given at this time. The student is encouraged to perform as many of the examples from Part II as possible.

Listening

No specific listening exercises are given here, since aspects of the formal element will be covered in more detail in Part II. We might consider here how the form graphs given in Part II may best be used.

a. Listen first to the composition without looking at the themes or graphs and try to grasp the over-all structure of the work, its sectional divisions, the main themes, the use of repetition, variation, contrast, the points of maximum and minimum tension in the composition, and the general character of the work.

b. Then study the themes thoroughly. Sing and play them until you know them from memory.

c. Next listen to the work with the form graph and notice how the thematic elements are used to create a formal structure. Ideally each work should be heard and studied enough so that you know the formal structure by memory and can anticipate each new musical event without referring to the graph.

d. As soon as possible listen for other elements besides the themes. Observe how dynamics, texture, instrumentation, tempo, meter, tonality, and melodic and rhythmic characteristics serve to underline and enhance the essential formal structure.

e. Although it is helpful to study some works with full score, the goal for intelligent listening is to develop the ability to grasp the basic structure and characteristics of a composition from listening only.

PART II

The Periods of Music Literature

chapter **6**

The Pre-Baroque Period

Until recently, music written before 1600 was little known, seldom performed, and poorly understood. However, musicological research and the development of ensembles and musical societies specializing in early music have done much to make this rich treasury of music available to the present-day listener.

Though there is a wealth of preserved material from the ancient civilizations in sculpture, architecture, poetry, and drama, there are but a few extant fragments of actual music dating before the birth of Christ. Philosophical and theoretical writings from ancient Greece, Egypt, China, and other countries give us some insight into the highly significant role music played in these societies but provide little understanding of the music itself.

The early Christian Church developed a body of monophonic liturgical music that eventually was called Gregorian chant, after Pope Gregory (reigned 590–604), even though the bulk of the extant manuscripts of the music dates from a later period. In the Romanesque period, extending roughly from the ninth to the twelfth century, polyphonic lines of increasing independence and complexity were added to portions of the Gregorian chant. These developments reached a peak in the School of St. Martial (early twelfth century) and the School of Notre Dame (late twelfth and early thirteenth centuries).

Among the earliest extant examples of secular music are a few songs of the *goliards* and *jongleurs,* traveling students and minstrels from the early Middle Ages. Many songs of the *troubadours* and *trouvères,* courtly poet-musicians in France in the twelfth and thirteenth centuries, are preserved in beautifully illuminated manuscripts called *chansonniers*. Roughly contemporary to these and similar in style are the songs of the *Minnesinger* in Germany.

Around the year 1300 a significant change occurred in the development of music. The thirteenth-century *ars antiqua* (Latin: old art), with its emphasis on sacred music was replaced by the fourteenth century *ars nova* (Latin: new art), with its increased emphasis on secular music and its innovations in harmony, rhythm, form, and notation.

In the Burgundian School of the early fifteenth century, composers showed a preference for melodic and harmonic thirds and sixths, and for higher tessitura. Motets of this period are in free polyphonic texture.

The Renaissance period in music extends roughly from 1450 to 1600 and includes the Flemish, Venetian, Roman, Spanish, and English schools. The sixteenth century, one of the most fertile periods of all music literature, saw the culmination of sacred polyphonic vocal writing, the development of the secular madrigal, and the beginnings of independent instrumental writing.

The Formal Element in the Pre-Baroque Period

The greater part of the music written before 1600 is vocal and the formal element in this music is largely governed by considerations of the text. Much of the music is irregular in motive and phrase construction. Repetition and contrast were the dominant principles in the early part of the period; later, especially in the Renaissance, the variation principle also became important. Textual music of an objective character comprised the bulk of the early music of the period; later, abstract music and some program music were introduced and subjectivity became more apparent in such works as Renaissance madrigals. With the exception of the Mass, most compositions were written as single movements in sectional, variation, fugal, or free forms.

Example 6–1 illustrates some characteristic cadential formulae which were used at various times in the pre-Baroque period. The dates given for each cadence are approximate.

EXAMPLE 6–1.

Occursus (ninth - twelfth centuries)

II   I Cadence (twelfth - fourteenth centuries)

Double leading tone cadence (fourteenth and fifteenth centuries)

"Landini" (7–6 –1) cadence (fourteenth century)

Ornamented "Landini" cadence with double leading tone (fifteenth century)

Authentic cadence with crossed voices (fifteenth century)

Sacred Vocal Forms

Gregorian chant or plainsong. These are terms applied to early monophonic settings of the words of the two main liturgies or services of the Roman Catholic Church,—the Office and the Mass. The text for both services is mostly in Latin and is largely drawn from the Bible, especially from the Psalms.

The *Office* involves a variety of texts for the various hours: *Matins, Lauds, Prime, Terce, Sext, None, Vespers,* and *Compline.* The Service for Vespers is the most interesting musically because it includes the *Magnificat* (the song of the Blessed Virgin) and it is the only service at which "non-Gregorian" music, such as organ music or motets, may be performed.

The *Mass* is the commemoration of the sacrifice of Christ on the cross. It consists of some texts to be sung and others to be recited. It can also be divided according to texts that remain the same throughout the liturgical year (*Ordinary*), and texts that change according to the day of the Church year on which the Mass is sung (*Proper*). The name Mass is derived from the last item of the Ordinary—"Ite missa est."

The sung portions of the Ordinary and Proper of the *Missa Solemnis* or High Mass are listed below.

Ordinary	*Proper*
(Texts remain the same throughout the liturgical year.)	(Texts vary for each day of the liturgical year)
	Introitus (sung during the entrance of the priest)
Kyrie (Lord, have mercy on us)	
Gloria (Glory to God)	
	Graduale (name derived from the fact that it was sung from the *gradus* [Latin: step] of the altar)
	Alleluia (Hebrew: Praise the Lord) or
	Tractus (more sombre texts replacing the Alleluia for Requiem Mass or during Lent and Ember Days)
	Sequence (see below)
Credo (I believe in God)	
	Offertorium (sung during the offering of gifts)
Sanctus (Holy, Holy, Holy)	

Agnus Dei (Lamb of God)

Communio (sung during the distribution of communion)

Ite missa est (Depart, you are dismissed)

Gregorian chant may be in free form, strophic form (i.e., the same music repeated for different verses), or in a quasi-rondo form (i.e., one section recurring over and over with varying material between these recurrences. The text may be set in *syllabic* style (one note per syllable), *neumatic* style (roughly two to four notes per syllable), or in *melismatic* style (more than four notes per syllable). Some Gregorian chants are to be sung *responsorially* (alternating between soloist and chorus) and others are to be sung *antiphonally* (alternating between two choruses).

Trope.   A trope is an addition of text, music, or both to an existing chant. The most common procedure was to add words to the notes of a *melisma,* that is, to a section where one syllable is set to many notes. These words not only made the melisma easier to perform, but also served to amplify and illuminate the original text.

Sequence.   The sequence is a specific type of trope based musically upon the melisma of an Alleluia and textually upon a poetic text with extended paired lines. The *Dies Irae* (Latin: day of wrath) from the Requiem Mass is one of five sequences remaining in the Gregorian repertory. It has been used by many Romantic and Contemporary composers in various works to represent the idea of death (see page 289). The first section of the chant is given in Example 6–2 in an early notation using a four-line staff and early musical symbols called *neumes,* which were the predecessors of our modern notes.

EXAMPLE 6–2.

Example 6–3 shows the same section in modern notation and a form graph of the entire sequence showing the division of the chant into a series of paired lines.

EXAMPLE 6-3.

Music: A

Text: 1 Di - es ir - ae, di - es il - la, sol - vet saec - lum in fa - vil - la
(Day of wrath, day of judgement. The earth dissolves in ashes)

Tes - te Da - vid cum Si - byl - la
(Testify David and Sibylla)

Music : A A B B C C A A B B C C A A B B C D E F
Text : 1 2 3 4 5 6 7 8 9 10 11 12 13 14 15 16 17 18 19 20
(Amen)

Conductus. The conductus is a twelfth- and thirteenth-century Latin, non-liturgical processional song set in syllabic style in monophonic or polyphonic texture. The polyphonic conductus is one of the earliest examples of a polyphonic composition that is not based on a pre-existing melody.

Organum. Early sacred, polyphonic, vocal writing is known as organum and involves adding one or more melodic lines to a given Gregorian chant or portion of chant. The original chant melody is called variously the *cantus firmus,* the *tenor,* or the *vox principalis.* For various types of organum see pp. 141–142.

Clausula. The clausula is a specific type of organum in which all voices are rhythmically organized. For an example see p. 142.

The thirteenth-century or Paris motet. This is similar to the clausula, but the upper parts have texts, sometimes in two different languages.

The fourteenth-century isorhythmic motet. This is a complex, polyphonic form based on a cantus firmus taken from Gregorian chant. A repeated melodic pattern from chant, called the *color,* is set to a repeated rhythmic pattern, called the *talea.* See pp. 142–143.

The sixteenth-century motet. The motet of the sixteenth century is written for four to six voices and consists of a series of overlapping *points of imitation*. In a point of imitation, a short phrase of the text is set to a melody in one voice, and this is then imitated in other voices. As these voices are finishing their imitating parts, another voice enters with the next portion of the text to begin another point of imitation. "Word painting," or the expressive use of musical devices to bring out the meaning of the text, is an important aspect of many motets. This is indicated on the themes in Example 6–4.

EXAMPLE 6–4. Byrd, Motet: *Ego Sum Panis Vivus.*

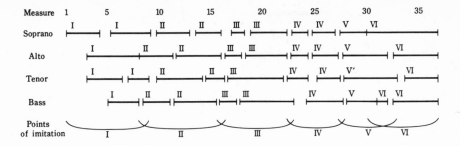

Anthems. The anthem is the motet of the Anglican Church. It may be written for full chorus throughout (full anthem) or for alternations of full chorus with solo voice and instruments (verse anthem).

Hymn. Renaissance hymns are strophic settings of Latin texts. The Catholic Church developed polyphonic settings of these, while the Lutheran Church later tended toward homophonic, block-chord settings known as *chorales*. The French Protestants also developed a homophonic setting with somewhat more interesting rhythms than those of the Germans.

Polyphonic Mass settings. Until 1300, composers made polyphonic settings of portions of the Proper of the Mass. After 1300 they concentrated on polyphonic settings of the Ordinary, except for the closing *Ite missa est*. In the Renaissance, composers often used one pre-existing melody as a cantus firmus for all movements. The pre-existing melody was taken from Gregorian chant, folk songs, motets, or other sources. In a *Parody Mass,* whole polyphonic sections from other works are borrowed.

Secular Vocal Forms

Troubadour, trouvère, and Minnesinger songs. These included various musical and poetic forms, usually sectional in nature. Some typical forms are illustrated in these examples:

EXAMPLE 6–5. Trouvère ballade form. (The same form is used for the troubadour canzo and the Minnesinger *bar*.)

Music: a a b
Text : 1 2 3

EXAMPLE 6–6. Trouvère rondeau form.

Music: a   b   a   a   a   b   a   b
Text: 1   2   3   1   4   5   1   2

EXAMPLE 6–7. Trouvère virelai form. (The same form is used for the fourteenth-century Italian *ballata*.)

Music: a   b   b   a   a
Text: 1   2   3   4   1

Caccia.   The caccia is a fourteenth-century Italian hunting song, written as a two-voice canon with a free instrumental tenor part.

EXAMPLE 6–8.

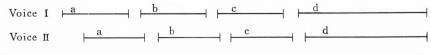

Madrigal.   The fourteenth-century madrigal is a fixed secular form with two or three verses with the same music followed by a stanza with contrasting music (AAB). The sixteenth-century madrigal is a free secular form somewhat similar to the *motet,* but having more sections in homophonic texture and more definite cadence points. Madrigal texts may be concerned with love, philosophy, the beauties of nature, or similar themes. Like the motet, they are written with effective "word painting."

EXAMPLE 6–9. Morley, " Hard by a Crystal Fountain."

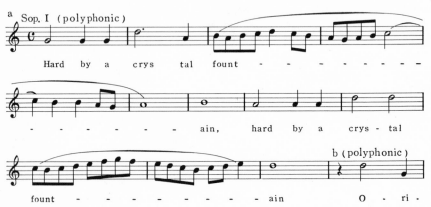

EXAMPLE 6–9 continued.

long live fair   O - ri - a - na,   Long live fair   O - ri   a - -

- - - na, fair   O - ri - a - - - na,   Long   live fair O - ri - - -

Long live fair   O - ri - a - - - - na,   long live fair

O - ri - a - - - na, long live fair   O - ri - a - - na,

long live fair O - ri - a - - - - - - - - - na.

The French chanson. The French chanson is more clearly sectional than the madrigal. It can often be identified by a characteristic dactylic opening rhythm (♩ ♪♪).

The polyphonic Lied. The German equivalent of the madrigal, the polyphonic *Lied* is often based on a folk melody.

Instrumental Forms

Dance forms. The development of independent instrumental music grew out of two sources: the use of instruments to double or replace parts of a vocal composition and the use of instruments for dance music. One of the earliest dance forms was the *estampie* which resembled the vocal sequence in having a number of repeated sections, or *puncta*.

In the Renaissance, many so-called "dance pairs" were written, each consisting of a slow dance in duple or quadruple meter, followed by a fast dance in triple meter, often related melodically and harmonically to the first dance. Some of the most common dance pairs were the *pavanne* and *galliard* in France, the *passamezzo* and *saltarello* in Italy, and the *Tanz* and *Nachtanz* in Germany. The relationship between these dances can easily be seen and heard:

EXAMPLE 6–10.   Gervaise (sixteenth century), Pavanne and Gaillarde.

Theme and variations.   This form has had a longer continuous history than any other musical form and was especially popular with lute and keyboard composers of the sixteenth century. Pre-existing secular or sacred songs were frequently used as themes, and the variations were based on the addition of melodic figurations and embellishments or upon changes in texture. The ground bass was frequently used.

Canzona.   The canzona is a sixteenth-century form based upon the vocal chanson. At first it was merely a transcription of the vocal work; later it developed into an original composition for instruments in the same style.

Ricercare.   The ricercare is a sixteenth-century instrumental form similar to the motet in that it consists of several polyphonic imitative sections, each based on a different theme. It is a predecessor of the Baroque fugue.

Free forms.   A wide variety of instrumental compositions in the fifteenth and sixteenth centuries are in a free, irregular, or improvisatory form. These include the *prelude, fantasia, toccata* (Italian: touch piece), and *intonazione* (Italian: tuning piece).

Representative Composers of the Pre-Baroque Period

Notre Dame School

> Leonin (French, twelfth century)
> Perotin (French, twelfth century)

Ars Nova

> Guillaume de Machaut (French, 1300–1377)
> Francesco Landini (Italian, 1325–1397)

Burgundian School

> John Dunstable (1370–1453)
> Guillaume Dufay (1400–1474)

Flemish School

Johannes Ockeghem (1430–1495)
Jakob Obrecht (1430–1505)
Josquin des Prez (1450–1521)

Giovanni Pierluigi da Palestrina (Italian, 1525–1594). Generally regarded as the greatest master of Renaissance sacred vocal polyphony, Palestrina has been more studied than performed, more idealized than understood. His creative output was limited almost entirely to masses, motets, hymns, and other works written for the Catholic church. In these works he shows a high degree of technical skill in writing conjunct, diatonic melodies in a narrow range, set in a continuous polyphonic imitative texture, interrupted occasionally by passages in "familiar" or homophonic style. His music is characterized more by objectivity and lucidity than by drama and passion. His *Missa Papae Marcelli* is often taken as a model of pure religious choral writing.

Orlando di Lasso (Flemish, 1532–1594). In contrast to Palestrina, Lasso wrote in a variety of sacred and secular forms, and his works are marked by more subjectivity and passion. Palestrina spent most of his life in Rome; Lasso travelled extensively and wrote over two thousand compositions, including Latin masses and motets, French chansons, Italian madrigals, and German lieder. One of his most celebrated works is the *Penitential Psalms of David.*

William Byrd (English, 1543–1623). Byrd wrote not only sacred and secular choral music but also many significant works for organ, virginal, and instrumental combinations. His music is somewhat more experimental than that of his contemporaries in terms of formal treatment and the handling of dissonance and chromaticism; and his vocal compositions, such as the *Psalmes, Sonnets, and Songs of Sadness and Pietie,* are remarkable for their expressive "word painting." In the preface to this work, Byrd writes the following eloquent plea to the listener:

> ...Only this I desire; that you will be but as careful to heare them well expressed as I have been both in the Composing and Correcting of them. Otherwise the best song that ever was made will seeme harsh and unpleasant, for that the well expressing of them, either by Voyces, or Instruments, is the life of our labours, which is seldome or never well performed at the first singing or playing. Besides a song that is well and artificially made cannot be well perceived nor understood at the first hearing, but the oftner you shall heare it the better cause of liking you will discover; and commonly that Song is best esteemed with which our eares are most acquainted. As I have done my best endeavour to give you content, so I beseech you satisfie my desire in hearing them well expressed, and then I doubt not, for Art and Ayre both of skillful and ignorant they will deserve liking.

Giovanni Gabrieli (Italian, 1557–1612). The leader of the sixteenth-century Venetian School, Gabrieli is credited with several important innovations in music. His *Sonata pian' e forte* is one of the earliest works with specifically indicated instrumentation and dynamics. His *symphoniae sacrae* are among the earliest examples of works for a specified combination of voices and instruments. His polychoral works could be effectively performed in St. Marks Cathedral in Venice, the principal church he served, because the architecture of that cathedral made it possible to place the various choruses at a proper distance from each other.

chapter 7

The Baroque Period

The word *Baroque* (Portuguese: irregularly-shaped pearl) was originally a derogatory term implying poor taste and excessive elaboration and ornamentation. Later, in both art and musical criticism, it was used without such connotations to apply to works created in the seventeenth and early eighteenth centuries.

Demarcations of stylistic periods in music literature are seldom precise and unequivocal; however, the beginning and end of the Baroque period are relatively clear and obvious. The period began with the early experiments in *monody* (recitative style), opera, and oratorio of the camerata in Italy around 1600; it ended with the death of the two great figures of the Baroque period, Bach (d. 1750), and Handel (d. 1759). In contrast to the stylistic and functional unity of Renaissance music, Baroque music had at least two different styles and three principal functions. The two main styles were the *Stile Antico* (the old polyphonic style of the sixteenth century) and the *Stile Moderno* (the new homophonic style of the seventeenth century). The music was intended for at least three main functional categories: religious music for the churches, chamber music for the courts of the nobility, and theatrical music, especially opera, for the general public.

The Baroque period may also be divided chronologically and geographically. The early Baroque period (c. 1600–1650), was marked by extensive use of homophonic texture, expressive use of recitative style, and experimentation in harmony and instrumentation. One of the main achievements of the middle Baroque period (c. 1650–1700) was the development of *bel canto* (Italian, beautiful song), which emphasized brilliant rendition of highly ornamented melodies. The experimental harmonic techniques of the early Baroque period were largely discarded in favor of major and minor tonalities. Major-minor tonality was fully established in the late Baroque period (c. 1700–1750) and provided the framework for extended instrumental compositions. Most Baroque music performed today comes from the late Baroque period; however, we are also witnessing a long overdue appreciation of music from the early and middle Baroque. Valid stylistic distinctions in the Baroque period can also be made between the lyric, vocally oriented Italian school and the polyphonic, instrumentally oriented German school, as well as between the national schools of France, England, and other countries.

The Formal Element in the Baroque Period

In our discussions of the other musical elements of the Baroque period, we characterized the period as one of strong contrasts; the same holds true for the formal element. This varies from the irregular structure of a recitative to the regular structure of a dance movement; from the objectivity of a fugue to the subjectivity of an oratorio chorus.

The most notable aspect of the formal element in the Baroque period is the number and variety of new formal structures that were crystallized during this period. No other period shows such an abundant development of new vocal and instrumental forms. Three factors account for this: 1) the establishment of major-minor tonality; 2) the increased importance of secular music; 3) the development of new instruments, instrumental techniques, and instrumental combinations.

In contrast to the variety of cadential formulae written in pre-Baroque music, Baroque music has relatively standardized cadential types. Perfect authentic cadences are regularly used at the ends of sections and movements; imperfect authentic cadences, plagal cadences, and half cadences may be written at the ends of interior phrases. Phrygian cadences and deceptive cadences, though not frequently employed, may sometimes be found at significant structural points in the music.

Single Movement Vocal Forms

Recitative. The recitative is a free form for solo voice with accompaniment in which the vocal melody approximates the natural rhythm and pitch inflection of the text. It is performed in a free, rubato style. Recitative may be categorized as *recitativo secco* (Italian: dry recitative) in which the voice part is relatively unexpressive and the accompaniment is limited to the *continuo*, or as *recitativo accompagnato* or *stromentato* (Italian: accompanied recitative), in which the voice part is more expressive and the accompaniment may include parts for other instruments. The recitative style is used for narrative or dramatic portions of operas, oratorios, and cantatas.

EXAMPLE 7-1. Handel, Alto recitative from *Messiah.*

and shall call His name Em - man - u - el ,   "God   with us ".

Aria. The aria is a song for solo voice and accompaniment in which the vocal part is written in a fairly complex style, often with several notes to each syllable of the text. Unlike the recitative, the Baroque aria is to be performed in strict tempo. Arias of the middle and late Baroque periods are often written in *da capo* form, consisting of a main section (A), followed by a contrasting section (B), and ending with a repeat of the first section (A). The repeated A section is frequently not written out; instead, the words *da capo* (Italian: from the head or beginning) are written at the end of the B section. In operas, oratorios, and cantatas, the aria usually follows a recitative and allows opportunity for expressive commentary on the preceding action. For an example, see p. 202.

Arioso. The arioso, often used at the conclusion of a recitative, is a work for solo voice and accompaniment written in a style between that of recitative and aria. For an example, see p. 205.

Chorale. The chorale is a hymn of the Lutheran Church. It may be sung in unison or in four-part block-chord style. Melodies for chorales are derived from Gregorian chants, early hymns, folk songs, or they may be original compositions. Chorales are usually strophic, with several stanzas, each containing short phrases ending with *fermatas* or holds. For an example, see p. 204.

Solo song (Lied or chanson). These terms all apply to works for voice and accompaniment, usually in a fairly simple, homophonic style, and in binary or ternary form.

Chorus. Choral sections of operas, oratorios, or other large works may be written in a variety of forms and textures, ranging from short, declamatory passages in homophonic texture to extended motet-like compositions in polyphonic texture. For an example see p. 201.

Motet and anthem. Baroque motets differ from those of the Renaissance period in that they often have instrumental accompaniment. Baroque anthems incorporate elements of recitative and arioso style, especially in the verse anthem.

Multi-Movement Vocal Forms

Opera. The opera (Italian, *opera in musica*: works in music) is a drama sung with instrumental accompaniment and presented with appropriate scenery, costumes, and staging. The text or *libretto* (Italian: little book) of most operas is secular. Baroque opera is presented in a series of independent sections or "numbers"—arias, recitatives, ariosos, choruses, duets, trios, other ensemble numbers, ballets or dance numbers, and independent instrumental numbers.

Baroque opera may be categorized according to various types and schools:

Opera seria (Italian: serious opera) is usually based on plots from Greek and Roman history, legend, or mythology. *Opera buffa* (Italian: comic opera) developed late in the Baroque period out of the short, humorous *intermezzos* presented between the acts of an *opera seria*.

Early *Florentine opera* (c. 1600–1630) is set almost entirely in recitative style. *Roman opera* (c. 1630–1650) introduces choral sections and comic episodes. *Venetian opera* (c. 1637–1667) is characterized by expressive musical content and lavish staging. *French opera* (c. 1671–1750) emphasizes ballet, chorus, and dramatic spectacle. *German opera* is based largely on Italian models.

English opera may be divided into two main types; complete operas in the Italian tradition and *masques,* lavish theatrical spectacles including acting, dancing, and incidental vocal and instrumental numbers. *Neapolitan opera* (1710–1750) has clear distinction between sections of dramatic action, usually set to *recitativo secco,* and sections of reflective commentary, usually set to *da capo* arias. Virtuoso, *bel canto* singing is the most prominent feature of these operas; the chorus is rarely used, and the orchestra is used primarily for accompaniment.

Cantata. The cantata (Latin: sung piece) is a composite vocal form in several movements for solo voice and instrumental accompaniment or for solo voices, chorus, and instrumental accompaniment. Sacred cantatas, written for specific holy days in the Lutheran Church calendar, often have an appropriate Lutheran chorale as the concluding movement or, less frequently, as a cantus firmus for other movements. Bach's *Cantata No. 80,* "Ein' feste Burg ist unser Gott" (German: "A Mighty Fortress Is Our God") is an impressive example of this form. Note the temporal, tonal, and textural variations applied to the chorale melody in movements I, II, and V. Note also such subtle examples of word-painting as the architectonic grandeur of the first movement, depicting the "mighty fortress." In the second movement, the orchestra (motive ①) depicts tumult, the bass (theme a) sings a message of hope, and the chorale melody (I^3) in the sopranos soars over the other lines. The fifth movement vividly presents the struggle between the fiends of evil (theme I^4) and the faithful (theme I^5, sung in powerful unison). It studying this work, it is best to begin with the chorale (No. 8) and then proceed to the other movements.

EXAMPLE 7–2. Bach, Cantata No. 80, "Ein' feste Burg ist unser Gott."

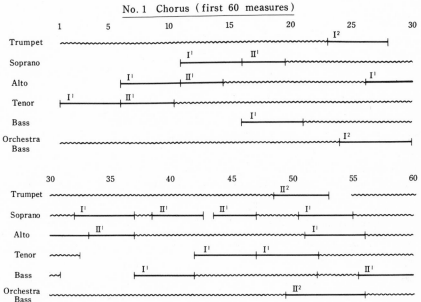

The entire number is treated similarly, that is, the chorus begins with a fugal statement of a variation of one phrase of the chorale; then the trumpets and bass instruments of the orchestra enter in canon with the same chorale phrase in augmentation.

	1	60	119	143	163	180	199	228
Chorus	I¹ and II¹	I¹ and II¹	III¹	IV¹	V¹	VI¹	VIII¹	
Trumpet and Bass	I² II²	I² II²	III²	IV²	V²	VI²	VIII²	

EXAMPLE 7-2 continued.

No. 2 Aria (duet) for Bass and Soprano
(often Sung soprano section)

No. 2   Aria (duet) for Bass and Soprano   (often sung by soprano section)

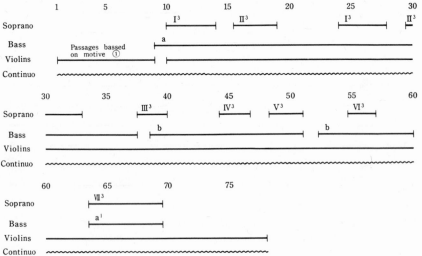

No.4 Aria for Soprano
(not based on chorale melody)

b

Treib Welt   und   Sa -   tan   aus.———
(Drive   the   world   and   Satan   out)

c

Weg, schnö - der Sünd - en   Graus! ———
(Away,   horror   of   vile   sins)

No. 4 Aria for Soprano
not based on chorale melody

1	5	10	15	20	25	30	35
(a)	a		(a)	b	(a)	c	(a)	a	(a)

Intro.   Interlude   Interlude   Interlude   Coda

No.5 Chorus

I⁴ (Orchestra)

No. 5 Chorus

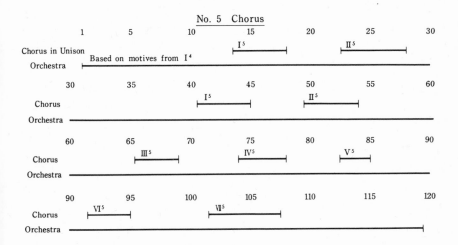

	1	5	10	15	20	25	30

Chorus in Unison   I⁵   II⁵
Orchestra   Based on motives from I⁴

| 30 | 35 | 40 | 45 | 50 | 55 | 60 |

Chorus   I⁵   II⁵
Orchestra

| 60 | 65 | 70 | 75 | 80 | 85 | 90 |

Chorus   III⁵   IV⁵   V⁵
Orchestra

| 90 | 95 | 100 | 105 | 110 | 115 | 120 |

Chorus   VI⁵   VII⁵
Orchestra

No.6 Recitativo for Tenor
(Free form based or chorale melody)

I⁵ (Chorus)

Und   wenn   die   Welt——voll   Teu —fel   wär
(And   if   the   world   were full of   devils)

EXAMPLE 7–2 continued.

No. 7 Duet for Alto and Tenor
(not based or chorale melody)

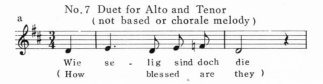

Wie se - lig sind doch   die
(How   blessed are they)

Es blei - bet un - be - siegt und kann die Fein - de schlag -
(It   remains   unvanquished and can slay the   foe.)

No. 7 Duet for Alto and Tenor
not based on chorale melody

	1	5	10	15	20	25	30
Alto					a	a	
Tenor					a	a	
Orchestra	a				a	a	

	30	35	40	45	50	55	60
Alto			a	a			
Tenor			a	a			
Orchestra	a		a			a	

	60	65	70	75	80	85	90
Alto		Pedal tone b	b				
Tenor		b	Pedal tone	b			
Orchestra							a

*Dal segno
al ⌒*
⌜Repeat from the sign⌝
⌊ (𝄋) to the fermata (⌒) ⌋

No. 8 Chorale

No. 8   Chorale

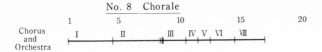

Secular cantatas were written for festive occasions, such as marriages, birthdays, or for state ceremonies. Other terms for works similar in form to cantatas are *concerti ecclesiastici* and *geistliche Konzerte*.

Oratorio. The oratorio is a composite vocal work for soloists, chorus, and orchestra, based on a sacred or secular text. It is similar to the opera except that it does not involve staging and allots more importance to the chorus. It is also like the cantata except that it is longer and more dramatic in nature. Some oratorios have a narrator, or *historicus,* who provides the narrative framework of the oratorio through recitatives. The *Passion* is an oratorio based on the last days of Christ as told in one of the four Gospel texts.

Handel's *Messiah* can be taken as an example of the oratorio form. The first nine numbers are discussed below.

No. 1, *Sinfonia:* Written in French overture form. Theme A is treated homophonically; theme B is treated fugally. The closing return of A is abbreviated.

EXAMPLE 7–3a.

No. 2, *Arioso* for tenor: The accompaniment motive ① dominates the first part; the second part is a short secco recitative.

EXAMPLE 7–3b.

No. 3, *Air* for tenor: Written in da capo aria form. The A theme is played by the orchestra as introduction. Then tenor and orchestra present the theme antiphonally, after which the tenor has long melismatic passages. The B theme is also presented antiphonally. The A theme returns first in the subdominant key and then in the tonic key. A brief recitative passage and a coda for orchestra based on theme A end the movement.

EXAMPLE 7–3c.

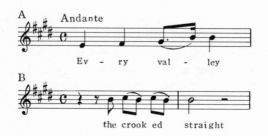

No. 4, *Chorus*: The text is set in alternate homophonic and polyphonic sections with orchestral introduction and interludes.

EXAMPLE 7–3d.

No. 5, *Recitative* for bass: Dotted note figures and even sixteenth-note patterns are used.

EXAMPLE 7–3e.

No. 6, *Air* for bass: Formally, the air is organized as follows: ABA[1]B[1].

EXAMPLE 7–3f.

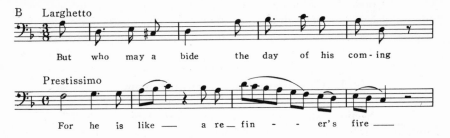

But who may a bide the day of his com-ing

For he is like — a re— fin - - er's fire —

No. 7, *Chorus*: Mostly set in polyphonic texture with some homophonic sections.

EXAMPLE 7–3g.

And he shall pu - ri - fy, and he shall pu-ri - fy———

No. 8, *Recitative* for alto: Brief secco recitative passage.

EXAMPLE 7–3h.

Be - hold a vir gin shall con - ceive.

No. 9, *Air* and *Chorus*: The same melody is sung first by the alto and then in a shortened version by the chorus.

EXAMPLE 7–3i.

O thou that tell est good tid - ings to Zi - on

Mass. Baroque Masses differ from Renaissance Masses in that they have orchestral accompaniment, sections for vocal solos or ensembles, and in general a more dramatic, almost operatic character. Often the original Mass movements are subdivided into several musical sections.

Single Movement Instrumental Forms

Sectional dance forms. Baroque dances, such as the allemande, courante, saraband, gigue, bouree, gavotte, were almost invariably written in rounded binary form. The following example illustrates some of the characteristics of this form. The first section, based on motive ①, modulates from the tonic to the dominant; the second section begins in the dominant with an inversion of motive ① and then returns to the tonic and to the original form of motive ① in measure 20. Many binary forms do not use the inversion device.

EXAMPLE 7–4. *French Suite in G Major, Gavotte.*

Binary form is called "closed" or "rounded" if the second section brings back material from the first section; it is called "open" if the second section does not bring back material from the first section.

Ternary design was not as commonly used in the Baroque period as in later periods, but it can be seen, for example, in the structure formed by the combination of two dance movements (Minuet I—Minuet II—Minuet I). Rondeau form consists of a recurring section or couplet, alternating with new material (ABACABA).

Orchestral overture. An instrumental composition which serves as an introductory movement for an opera, oratorio, or cantata, or as the first movement of a composite instrumental piece is called an *overture* or *sinfonia*. In Baroque music two main types appear, both written in ternary form. The *Italian* overture consists of a fast opening section, a slow middle section, and a fast concluding section, sometimes based on the first fast section. The *French* overture consists of a slow opening section usually based on dotted rhythms and rapid scale passages, a fast middle section in polyphonic imitative or fugal style, and a slow concluding section similar to the opening section. For an example of French overture form, see p. 205.

Ritornello form. This is a term used by many modern writers to describe a type of instrumental composition in which sections for the entire orchestral ensemble (*tutti*) alternate with sections for a solo instrument or a group of solo instruments (*concertino*). In Example 7–5 this alternation can be seen clearly since thematic sections are indicated with solid lines and accompanying sections with wavy lines.

EXAMPLE 7–5. Bach, *Brandenburg Concerto No. 2 in F Major*, first movement.

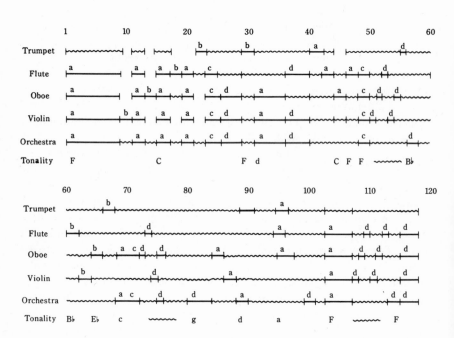

Variation forms. Baroque theme and variations forms are usually based on pre-existing melodies. Three main types of variations were used in the Baroque period; a *cantus firmus* type of variation in which the theme is maintained intact and moved from voice to voice while varying contrapuntal lines are written against it; an *ornamented* type in which the melody, remaining in the top part, has extra notes, trills, appoggiaturas, and other ornaments added to it; and a *harmonic* type in which the variations are not based on the melody but rather on the harmonic progression of the original theme.

The terms *chaconne* and *passacaglia* were used interchangeably in the Baroque period to refer to variation forms in which the repeated element is either a harmonic progression or a theme with simple, consistent rhythmic patterns in moderately slow triple meter. Though Baroque composers used the terms interchangeably, modern writers refer to the chaconne as being based on a repeated harmonic progression, and the passacaglia as being based on a repeated theme heard usually in the bass but sometimes moving to upper parts. The *ground bass* is similar to the passacaglia except that the repeated theme is shorter (often four measures), and remains in the bass part while different harmonies and melodies are played over it.

Chorale prelude. The chorale prelude is a sacred organ composition based on a Lutheran chorale. The chorale melody may be treated in theme and variations style, motet style, fugal style, or free improvisatory style.

Fugue. The fugue is a composition based on polyphonic imitative treatment of a short theme known as the *subject*. Present-day writers often assert that the fugue is a technique rather than a form. This assertion would seem to be a reaction against that mythical, musical monstrosity, the "textbook fugue," a pedagogical device with little or no relationship to actual music. However, it can be shown that the fugues of the Baroque period, though they do not follow as rigid a pattern as, for example, the binary dance form, do nevertheless have certain formal characteristics in common.

In general, fugues consist of alternations of *statements* and *episodes,* culminating in sections in which the principles of *stretto* and *pedal point* are often used. In fugal statements, the subject is announced in one voice and then imitated in the others while the first voice plays a secondary theme or countersubject. In fugal episodes, motivic material drawn from the subject is handled in free contrapuntal fashion. In stretto (Italian: close) sections, the entries of the imitating voices come in close succession. In pedal point sections, one voice (usually the bass) sustains a long note, while the other voices continue melodic motion and harmonic change against it.

Fugues are written for a specified number of parts. All parts normally enter one at a time in the opening statement; fewer parts may participate in subsequent statements. Tonally, fugues begin with a statement based on the tonic and dominant, then move in subsequent statements to related keys, and return at the end to the tonic.

EXAMPLE 7–6.   Bach, Fugue in C Minor from *The Well-tempered Clavier,* Book I.

EXAMPLE 7-6 continued.

Ricercare. In Baroque music, the term *ricercare* may be used for fugues of a more solemn and learned character, often employing such devices as augmentation and diminution. Ricercare is also applied to fugues based on more than one subject.

Invention. The term *invention* is occasionally used in the Baroque period (notably in Bach's two-part inventions) for compositions written in a polyphonic, imitative style similar to the fugue.

Fantasia. In the Baroque period, the term *fantasia* was applied either to compositions in fugal form or to works in free form. The term *fancy* was applied to English Baroque compositions in fugal form, written especially for *consorts* (ensembles) of viols.

Prelude, toccata. These terms are used to describe pieces in free, improvisatory form. Occasionally, however, the terms are used to describe pieces in definite binary, ternary, or other forms.

Multi-Movement Instrumental Forms

Sonata da chiesa (Italian: church sonata). The *sonata da chiesa* is a composition in several movements in alternating slow and fast tempos. It is serious in character and basically polyphonic in texture. Works in this form may be written for solo instruments, solo instruments with accompaniment, trio sonata (two melody instruments with continuo), or other combinations.

EXAMPLE 7–7. Corelli, *Sonata da Chiesa in E Minor.*

EXAMPLE 7–7 continued.

Sonata da camera (Italian: chamber sonata). The *sonata da camera* is a composite instrumental work based on dance forms. It is lighter in character than the *sonata da chiesa* with more emphasis on homophonic texture. The term is sometimes used synonymously with suite.

Suite. An important Baroque instrumental form for solo harpsichord, clavichord, or orchestral instruments, the suite has the following basic set of dance movements: allemande, courante, sarabande and gigue. Often this collection of dances is preceded by a prelude; occasionally optional dances, such as the gavotte, minuet, bourrée, loure, and others, are inserted between the sarabande and the gigue. Other terms used for this composite form are *partita* and *ordre*.

EXAMPLE 7–8. Bach, *French Suite in G Major.*

Sarabande

Gavotte

Bourrée

Gigue

Solo concerto. The solo concerto is a work for one solo instrument, such as harpsichord, violin, or flute, with orchestral accompaniment, usually strings and continuo. It is customarily in three movements of varying tempos: fast–slow–fast. The fast movements are written in sectional, fugal, or ritornello form; the slow movement may be written in binary or ternary form with a continuous solo melody and orchestral accompaniment, or in ritornello form.

Concerto grosso. The *concerto grosso* is similar to the solo concerto except that the single soloist is replaced by a small group of soloists known as the *concertino*. The concertino may consist of two violins and cello, violin and two flutes, or other combinations. The remaining strings are called the *tutti* or *ripieno*.

Representative Composers of the Baroque Period

Giulio Caccini (Italian, c. 1546–1618). Caccini was a member of the *camerata,* a group of Florentine composers and poets who sought to re-create Greek music-drama, but created instead a new form—opera. Caccini's *Eurydice,* written in 1600, is the earliest extant opera. An earlier opera, *Dafne,* was written in 1597 by another member of the *camerata* group, Jacopo Peri (Italian, 1561–1633) ; however, the music for this has been lost.

Jan Pieterszoon Sweelinck (Dutch, 1562–1621). Sweelinck, the founder of the North German organ school, is important in the development of the ricercare and the chorale prelude.

Claudio Monteverdi (Italian, 1567–1643). Some of Monteverdi's madrigals and religious choral music are in the polyphonic style of the late

Renaissance; other works, especially his operatic compositions, were written in the new homophonic style of the early Baroque. His *Orfeo* (1607), generally regarded as the first opera of genuine musical significance, is notable for its use of orchestra with specified instrumentation, its use of special instrumental effects such as tremolo, and its use of aria and dance forms instead of the continuous recitative of the early Florentine opera. Other important operatic works by Monteverdi include *Il Ritorno di Ulisse* (*The Return of Ulysses*) and *L'Incoronazione di Poppea* (*The Coronation of Poppea*). In these works and in his other vocal works, Monteverdi was faithful to his own dictum: "The words should be the master and not the servant of the music."

Girolamo Frescobaldi (Italian, 1583–1643). His organ works, such as the liturgical collection *Fiori Musicali* (*Musical Flowers*), are important in the development of the fugue.

Heinrich Schütz (German, 1585–1672). Born one hundred years before J. S. Bach, Schütz is generally regarded as the most significant composer of the German middle Baroque period. His *Sinfonia sacrae* are predecessors of the Bach cantatas; his *Historia der Geburt Jesu Christi* (*Story of the Birth of Jesus Christ*) is not only a predecessor of later Baroque oratorios but also a significant work in its own right.

Samuel Scheidt (German, 1587–1654). Scheidt is noted for organ works, including the collection, *Tablatura Nova.*

Piero Francesco Cavalli (Italian, 1602–1676). Cavalli's 41 operas, including *Egisto* and *Jason,* are written in the lavish Venetian style.

Jacques Champion Chambonnières (French, c. 1602–1672). Chambonnières was the founder of the French *clavecin* (harpsichord) school.

Giacomo Carissimi (Italian, 1605–1674). His oratorio, *Jepthe,* is regarded as the first great masterpiece in this genre.

Johann Jakob Froberger (German, 1616–1667). His keyboard works established the order of dances in the dance suite (allemande, courante, sarabande, gigue).

Marc' Antonio Cesti (Italian, 1623–1669). *Il Pomo d'Oro* (*The Golden Apple*) is the most famous of his Venetian style operas.

Jean-Baptiste Lully (French, 1632–1687). Lully's operas, such as *Cadmus et Hermione* and *Alceste* are notable for their effective use of recitative and their emphasis on ballet. He also wrote ballets for plays of Molière, independent instrumental music, and religious works.

Dietrich Buxtehude (German, 1637–1707). His organ music and religious choral music were important influences on J. S. Bach.

Johann Pachelbel (German, 1653–1706). Pachelbel's major works are for organ and keyboard instruments.

Archangelo Corelli (Italian, 1653–1713). As a composer, Corelli wrote four volumes of trio sonatas, one volume of sonatas for violin and keyboard, including the famous *La Folia,* and one volume of *Concerti grossi,* including the well-known *Christmas Concerto.* As a performer, he is regarded as the founder of modern violin playing.

Henry Purcell (English, 1659–1695). Purcell is noted for his incidental music to such plays as the *Fairy Queen, King Arthur,* and *The Tempest,* and especially for his complete opera, *Dido and Aeneas.* He also wrote chamber music and church music. Unusual harmonies and chromatic melodies are sometimes cited as characteristic of Purcell's style, but these appear only rarely; the majority of his works are consonant and diatonic. Purcell has a special affinity for the *ground bass;* several of his important works, such as the lament from *Dido and Aeneas,* are in this form.

Alessandro Scarlatti (Italian, 1659–1725). Scarlatti composed over 100 operas in the Neapolitan opera style and established the *da capo* aria form.

Johann Kuhnau (German, 1660–1722). Kuhnau is remembered especially for his programmatic harpsichord pieces entitled *Biblical Sonatas.*

François Couperin (French, 1668–1733). Couperin is noted primarily for his *clavecin* (harpsichord) compositions, which feature *gallant* style ornamentation.

Antonio Vivaldi (Italian, 1669–1741). His instrumental works, solo concerti, and concerti grossi have recently enjoyed a revival of interest and performance.

Georg Philipp Telemann (German, 1681–1767). Telemann was perhaps the most prolific composer of the Baroque period, with an output including 40 operas, 3,000 cantatas and motets, 600 overtures, 44 passions, and numerous other works.

Jean Phillipe Rameau (French, 1683–1764). Though his operas, ballets, and other works are important in the development of music, Rameau is best known today as a music theorist. He maintained that "to enjoy fully the effects of music, we must completely lose ourselves in it; to judge it, we must relate it to the source through which it affects us. This source is nature....Harmony alone can stir the passions. It is the one source from which melody directly emerges and draws its power."[1]

Johann Sebastian Bach (German, 1685–1750). The scope of Bach's professional musical activity was limited to various positions in German churches and courts; the breadth of his musical style embraced every aspect of Baroque musical thought except opera. The main positions he held were as organist at Arnstadt (1703–1707) and Mühlhausen (1707–1708), organist and chamber musician for the Duke of Weimar (1708–1717), chapel master and director of chamber music for the Prince of Anhalt-Cöthen (1717–1723), and finally as organist and director of music at the Thomaskirche and the Nicolaikirche and cantor at the Thomasschule in

[1] Jean Philippe Rameau, *Observations sur notre instinct pour la musique et son principe,* trans. A.W., (Paris, 1726) p. 3.

Leipzig (1723–1750). During his lifetime, Bach was probably as well known as an organist and an expert on organ construction as he was a composer. After his death, his works were virtually forgotten until Mendelssohn's performance of the *St. Matthew Passion* in 1829 brought them again to public attention.

It is sometimes said that Bach's music is primarily a form of religious expression. He once wrote that even an exercise in figured bass should be written to the glory of God. That he was a man of his time, however, not above interest in secular achievements can be seen from this excerpt from the dedication to the *Musical Offering:*

> Dedication—Most Gracious King in deepest humility I dedicate herewith to Your Majesty as a musical offering, the noblest part which is derived from Your Majesty's Own August Hand, with awesome pleasure I still remember the very special Royal Grace when, sometime ago, during my visit in Potsdam Your Majesty's Self deemed to play to me a theme for a fugue upon the Clavier, and at the same time charged me most gracious to carry it out in Your Majesty's Most August Presence. . .[2]

Secular compositions form a large and significant part of Bach's output. Some, like the delightful *Capriccio on the Departure of a Beloved Brother* or the *Coffee Cantata,* are far from religious in subject or character.

Mastery in polyphonic writing is cited as a hallmark of Bach's style. Works such as the fugues from the *Well-tempered Clavier* or the polyphonic choruses from his cantatas give evidence of his skill in writing in various contrapuntal styles. Even in his four-part harmonizations of chorales, which are basically homophonic in texture, each part has a vital melodic line of its own. But not all of Bach's works are polyphonic. The preludes from the *Well-tempered Clavier* and the arias from the cantatas show a wealth of different homophonic or hybrid textures. Monophonic movements of the *Partitas for Solo Violin* or the *Suites for Solo Cello* show Bach's skill in writing a single line of great beauty. Harmony in Bach's music is basically consonant but often the interplay of contrapuntal lines produces striking dissonances.

Many volumes have been written on Bach's harmony and counterpoint, but fewer works have been devoted to a study of Bach's melody. His own contemporaries and even some present day music students have been able to imitate his basic contrapuntal procedures more easily than they have been able to emulate his melodic style. Many of his melodies grow out of an initial "germ" motive in a manner that is somehow inevitable but not obvious. Albert Schweitzer and other commentators have pointed to the emotional or programmatic significance of many of Bach's melodic motives. Motives involving a diminished seventh, for example, are often associated

---

[2] Johann Sebastian Bach, dedication from "The Musical Offering," trans. Hans. T. David (New York: G. Schirmer, Inc., 1945). Used by permission.

with death or sorrow. Although most of Bach's melodies are based on the major or minor scales, some, such as the *Chromatic Fantasy and Fugue,* display a remarkable degree of chromaticism. Bach's rhythms are vital and varied, ranging from the consistent use of even sixteenth notes throughout some of his preludes and toccatas to the use of complex rhythms in some of his cantata arias and instrumental slow movements.

Bach's forms are based on traditional patterns, but his consummate mastery allows him to treat these with the greatest freedom. Even in such simple structures as binary form, his music often has unusual phrase lengths, irregular harmonic progressions, and free treatment of melodic material.

He thoroughly understood the limitations and possibilities of the various instruments; his instrumental writing is highly idiomatic and effective. Though some of his works, for example, the *Art of the Fugue,* are not written for any particular instrument, most of his works emphasize the unique timbre of specified instruments or instrumental combinations. His vocal writing, though often instrumental in nature, is also highly effective.

He studied the music of his German, Italian, and French predecessors and contemporaries, incorporating elements of their styles in his own uniquely personal musical utterance. German polyphony, Italian melody, and French orchestration and forms are among the important influences on his musical development.

Bach wrote five sets of cantatas for every Sunday and feast day of the liturgical year. Of these, approximately 190 cantatas still survive, including *Cantata No. 4, Christ Lag in Todesbanden* (*Christ Lay in the Bonds of Death*); *Cantata No. 80, Ein' Feste Burg ist Unser Gott* (*A Mighty Fortress Is Our God*); and *Cantata No. 140, Wachet Auf* (*Sleepers, Wake*).

Of his other vocal works the following are among the best known: *Mass in B Minor, St. Matthew Passion, St. John Passion, Magnificat in D Major,* and *The Christmas Oratorio.*

Bach wrote many works for organ including fugues (some with introductory preludes, or toccatas), sonatas, trios, toccatas, preludes, chorale preludes, fantasias, and other works. He also wrote many compositions for harpsichord or clavichord including *The Well-tempered Clavier* (2 books, 48 preludes and fugues in all 24 keys, written to advance the cause of equal temperament), 6 *French Suites,* 6 *English Suites,* 15 *Two-part Inventions,* 15 *Tree-part Inventions, Goldberg Variations, Italian Concerto,* and *Chromatic Fantasy and Fugue.*

His instrumental works include 6 *Brandenburg Concerti* (pp. 106, 210), 4 *Overtures* or *Orchestral Suites* (No. 2 contains the famous *Air.*), 2 *Violin Concerti, Double Concerto for Two Violins,* 6 *Suites for Solo Cello,* and 6 *Sonatas and Partitas for Solo Violin.*

Bach is regarded as one of the greatest composers of all time; however, critical opinion of his works has not always been unanimous. An eighteenth-century critic, Johann Adolf Scheibe, once wrote:

> This great man would be the admiration of whole nations if he had more amenity (*Annehmlichkeit*), if he did not take away the natural element in his pieces by giving them a turgid (*schwülstig*) and confused style, and if he did not darken their beauty by an excess of art.[3]

Replying to this, another writer of the time, Johann Abraham Birnbaum, defended Bach with these words:

> I will invoke the testimony of some impartial connoisseurs of music who on their journeys have also had the good fortune of hearing this great man, and have praised his ability uncommonly, but nevertheless have frankly stated that *there was only one Bach in the world, and no one could equal him*.[4]

Claude Debussy, who edited some of Bach's works, wrote his publisher the following:

> Never edit the Sonatas for violin and piano of J. S. Bach on a rainy Sunday. I've just finished revising the above, and I feel the rain inside.
> When the old Saxon cantor has no ideas, he sets off on anything and is truly merciless. In short, he is unbearable except when he is admirable. That's really something, you'll say.[5]

Richard Wagner expressed an opinion which most musicians would share when he called Bach the "most stupendous miracle in all music." The student who wishes to understand and appreciate this "miracle" is urged to study first Bach's harmonization of Lutheran chorales, then some of the cantatas and *Passions* based on these, and then the instrumental music.

Domenico Scarlatti (Italian, 1685–1757). Scarlatti is noted primarily for his over 600 *Esercizi* (Sonatas) for harpsichord. These highly idiomatic works are mostly in rounded binary form.

George Frederick Handel (German, 1685–1759). Handel and Bach were both born in the same year and together brought Baroque music to its culmination; however, their lives and their musical works show significant contrasts. Bach was part of a long family tradition in music that stretched from his great-great-great-grandfather, Hans Bach, who lived in the sixteenth century, to his grandson Wilhelm Friedrich Ernst Bach, who died in the middle of the nineteenth century; Handel had neither musical ancestors nor progeny. Bach spent his entire life, except for some brief trips,

---

[3] Johann Adolf Scheibe, *Critischer Musikus* (Leipzig, 1745), in *The Bach Reader*, trans. Hans T. David and Arthur Mendel (New York: W. W. Norton & Company, Inc., 1945), p. 238. Used by permission.

[4] Johann Abraham Birnbaum, separate publication reprinted in Mizler's *Neu Eröffnete Musikalische Bibliothek* (Leipzig, 1738), in *The Bach Reader,* trans. Hans T. David and Arthur Mendel, eds. (New York: W. W. Norton & Company, Inc. 1945), p. 239. Reprinted by permission.

[5] Claude Debussy, *Lettres à son éditeur* (Paris, Durand, 1927) p. 179, in *Composers on Music*, trans. Sam Morgenstern, ed., (New York, Pantheon Books, A Division of Random House, Inc., 1956), pp. 324–325. Reprinted by permission of Mme. Gaston de Tinan.

in his native Germany; Handel traveled extensively and spent the major part of his adult life in England.

Bach absorbed various national styles into his own unique musical style; Handel mastered several different national styles in turn, writing opera in Neapolitan style, instrumental music in German and Italian style, and religious choral music incorporating aspects of English style.

Bach's music is described as introverted, restrained, and reflective; Handel's music is characterized as extroverted, grandiose, and dramatic. However, any such generalizations ignore the great breadth of musical expression found in the music of both composers.

Oratorio and opera are the most important forms in Handel's music. Of his 32 oratorios, the most famous is the *Messiah*. Other important oratorios are: *Acis and Galatea; Saul; Israel in Egypt; Samson; Semele; Belshazzar; Judas Macabeus; Joshua;* and *Jeptha.*

It is unfortunate that Handel's operas are infrequently performed today, for they contain some of his most characteristic and effective music. Of his 46 operas, some of the most important are: *Rinaldo; Giulio Cesare; Tamerlano; Rodelinda;* and *Serse.*

Handel's church music includes the *Utrecht Te Deum, Dettinger Te Deum, Eleven Chandos Anthems,* and other works. His instrumental works include the *Water Music, Fireworks Music,* orchestral concerti, concerti grossi, organ concerti, and trio sonatas. He also wrote Italian solo cantatas and chamber duets.

chapter **8**

*The
Classical
Period*

The term *classical* has several connotations when applied to music. In its most specific sense, *Classical* refers to the period of music literature extending roughly from the death of Bach in 1750 to the death of Beethoven in 1827 and centering primarily in the works of the so-called Viennese Classicists: Haydn, Mozart, Beethoven, and, to a certain extent, Schubert. In a more general sense, the term *classical* may be applied to any composition, composer, or period that is marked by the characteristics of objectivity, restraint, traditionalism, stability, simplicity, clarity, balance, and symmetry. In this sense, it can be used in contrast to the general meaning of the term *romantic* (see p. 277).

The term *classical* is also used, less legitimately, to refer to any music that is not popular music or folk music. Though most writers on music regret its use in this latter sense, they are seldom able to provide a satisfactory substitute. The term *good* music is sometimes suggested, but this implies a value judgement which is not always valid. The term *serious* music is often used, but it seems inappropriate when applied, for example, to a gay work such as Haydn's *Quartet Op. 33, No. 2, (The Joke)*. Perhaps the most satisfactory term for music which is not folk or popular music is *art* music.

Between the Baroque and Classical periods there is a transitional period, extending roughly from 1725 to 1775, designated as the Rococo period (French: *rocaille,* shell) or the period of the *gallant* style. Both of these terms indicate a type of music that can be characterized as superficial, frivolous, mannered, and elegant. Although no major composer wrote entirely in this style, Rococo traits appear in the works of such Baroque composers as Francois Couperin, Telemann, and the sons of J. S. Bach; they also appear in the early works of such Classical composers as Haydn and Mozart.

The Classical period proper shows more stylistic unity than the Baroque period because it is relatively limited both in terms of time and place. Toward the end of the period, however, there is less unity of style; the later works of Beethoven and Schubert display traits that are characteristic of the Romantic period.

The Formal Element in the Classical Period

Much of the music of the Classical period is constructed from short motives, which lend themselves readily to developmental treatment. Phrases and periods tend to be cast in regular four- or eight-bar lengths, ending with full or half cadences.

In contrast to the Baroque period, with its emphasis upon repetition as a principle of expansion, the Classical period is marked by a balance of repetition, variation, and contrast. This balance is particularly evident in sonata-allegro form, the most significant single-movement form of the period. The distinction between thematic sections and transition sections is, in general, more clearly drawn in the Classical period, but, in some of the works of Mozart and Beethoven, transition sections are so skillfully written that it is difficult to distinguish them from thematic sections, except by their general feeling of movement.

In terms of the type of music written, the Classical period shows a definite emphasis on abstract instrumental music. Programmatic titles, such as the *Surprise Symphony* or the *Moonlight Sonata*, often represent the imaginative responses of listeners rather than the programmatic intentions of the composer. Though composers of the Classical period continued to write sacred vocal music, they were more concerned with the composition of orchestral music for the public concert halls, operas and ballets for the theater, and chamber music and solo literature for professional performance in aristocratic salons or for amateur performance in the home.

Single Movement Instrumental Forms

Binary form.   The binary form of the Baroque period developed into the sonata-allegro form of the Classical period, but as a form itself, the binary structure was less often used in the Classical period than in the Baroque period.

Ternary form.   In the Classical period, ternary form is frequently employed, especially for slow movements where the form is often called *three-part song form*. Each section is a complete, harmonically closed entity in itself; that is, each section begins and ends in the same tonality. Example 8–1 is especially clear, because the middle section is in a different meter and tempo. Most Classical movements in this form, however, remain in one meter and tempo throughout. Note the unifying use of motive ① in the codetta, B section, and coda.

EXAMPLE 8–1. Beethoven, *Quartet in G Major*, Op. 18, No. 2, second movement.

A   Adagio cantabile

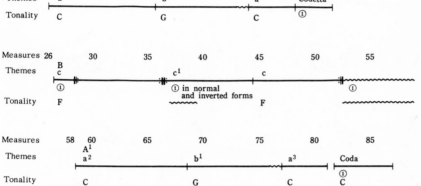

Compound ternary form.   This form is almost invariably used for the dance-like third movements of Classical symphonies and other instrumental works, where it is referred to either as *Minuet and Trio* form or *Scherzo and Trio* form. The *minuet* is a graceful, triple meter dance in moderate tempo, used occasionally as an optional dance in the Baroque suite. The term *trio* refers to the fact that in early examples of the form this section was played by only three instruments. The *scherzo* (Italian: joke) is a lively triple meter movement, usually in fast tempo and often, as the name implies, in a humorous style. The distinction between these two is often not clearly drawn. The scherzos in the six quartets of Haydn's Op. 33, for example, are more like minuets in style; other Haydn minuets have definite scherzo characteristics. As can be seen from Example 8–2 and Example 8–3, both the scherzo and minuet have the same basic form: three main sections, each of which can usually be analyzed as a rounded binary form.

EXAMPLE 8–2. Mozart, *Symphony No. 41 in C Major, K. 551*, third movement.

EXAMPLE 8–3. Beethoven, *Symphony No. 3 in E-flat Major*, third movement.

The return of the minuet or trio is usually not written out but instead indicated by the following words at the close of the trio: *Minuet* (or *Scherzo*) *da capo, senza repetizione* (Italian: minuet from the start, without repetitions).

Occasionally the compound ternary form is expanded to a five-part structure by the addition of a second trio section, followed by another return of the minuet or scherzo.

EXAMPLE 8–4. Beethoven, *Symphony No. 7 in A Major,* third movement.

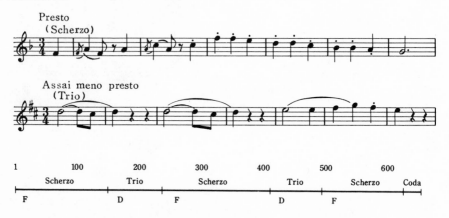

Rondo form. Like the Baroque *rondeau,* the Classical rondo is based on the recurrence of a principal theme with contrasting material appearing between these recurrences. It differs from the rondeau in that it usually has transition passages between the thematic sections and fewer contrasting sections or episodes. Example 8–5 illustrates a common pattern.

EXAMPLE 8–5. Beethoven, *Sonata in C Minor,* Op. 13, last movement.

Variation forms. Classical composers, like their Renaissance and Baroque predecessors, continued to be fascinated by the challenges and opportunities afforded by the variation form. Specialized variation forms such as the *chaconne, passacaglia,* and *ground bass* were largely neglected by Classical composers, but the *theme and variations* form was treated in a variety of techniques, ranging from a simple "cantus firmus" treatment to complex double variations.

EXAMPLE 8–6. Haydn, *Quartet in C Major, Op. 76, No. 3,* second movement.

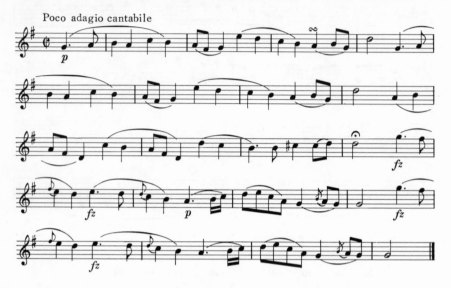

Theme (1–20)	Theme in violin I, simple block-chord accompaniment in other parts.
Variation I (20–40)	Theme in violin II, sixteenth-note figures in violin I.
Variation II (40–60)	Theme in cello, countermelody in violin I, accompanying lines in violin II and viola.
Variation III (60–80)	Theme in viola, countermelodies in other parts.
Variation IV (80–100)	Theme in violin I, accompaniment in other parts using some altered chords.
Coda (100–104)	Cadential harmonies over a pedal g in the cello.

EXAMPLE 8–7. Beethoven, *Symphony No. 3 in E-flat Major,* fourth movement.

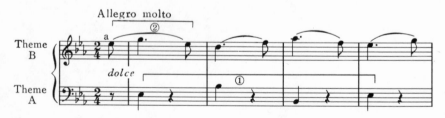

Countermelody I

Countermelody II

Transition T

Theme C

motive ① inverted

Rhythmic variant of Theme B

Introduction (1–11)	Rapid scale passages leading to a repeated dominant seventh chord. The theme and Variations I–III are in E♭ major.
Theme (A) (12–43)	Presented by pizzicato strings in octaves, winds have answering afterbeats in the repeat of the a and b sections.
Variation I (44–59)	Theme A in violin II, countermelody I played alternately by cello and violin I.
Variation II (60–75)	Theme A in violin I, countermelody II in other strings.
Variation III (76–107)	Theme A in cello, bass, bassoon II and horns. Theme B in oboe, accompanying parts in other instruments.
Transition (107–116)	Transition ③ in violin I. Modulation to c minor.
Variation IV (117–174)	C minor. Fugal passage based on motive ① from Theme A. Countermelody I and transition motive ③ appear as counterpoint. Ends on dominant seventh of c minor, which is deceptively resolved to D major at beginning of Variation V.
Variation V (175–210)	D major. Theme B in flute, first legato and then staccato, Transition section leads to next variation.
Variation VI (211–256)	G minor. Theme C in violin I, flute, oboe, and bassoon. Motive ① of theme A repeated in cello and bass. Later, theme C played by clarinet and viola, and motive ① of theme A played by flute and violin I.
Variation VII (258–277)	C major. Theme B in violin I and flute. Motive ① of Theme A in cello and bass, followed by modulatory passage in which theme B is played by violin II, viola, and cello and bass.
Variation VIII (277–348)	E-flat major. Fugato based on motive ①, first in inverted form, later in original form. The transition motive ③ and a rhythmic variant of Theme B are heard as counterpoint. Leads to a climax on the dominant chord.
Variation IX (349–380)	E-flat major. Tempo changes to poco andante. Simple block-chord harmoniaztion of theme B, heard first in the woodwinds and then in the strings. Followed by a syncopated figure based on the harmony of the section of the original themes (A and B).
Variation X (381–430)	E-flat major. Tempo remains poco andante. Theme B heard powerfully in the horns, cellos, basses, clarinets, and bassoons, against accompaniment figures in the other instruments. Ending modulates to g minor and makes a diminuendo.
Coda. (431–473)	E-flat major. Presto tempo. Based on scale passages from introduction and motives from theme B.

Fugal forms.   Although some movements in the form of the Baroque fugue were written in the Classical period, it was more common for Classical composers to use fugal techniques in the framework of another form such as the sonata-allegro form. (See pp. 239–240).

Sonata-allegro form.   The most significant single movement form of the Classical period, the sonata-allegro form can be regarded as one of the most satisfying forms of all music because of its balance of repetition, variation, and contrast. Although it can be shown to have evolved from the rounded binary form of the Baroque period, it may be regarded as a ternary form, consisting of *exposition, development,* and *recapitulation* sections.

The *exposition* section emphasizes the compositional principle of contrast. It regularly consists of a first theme (or theme group) and a second theme (or theme group). A third theme (or theme group) and a codetta may be used to end the section and transition passages serve to link the thematic passages. The essential contrast in the exposition is in terms of tonality. The first theme group is presented in the tonic key; the remaining parts of the exposition are presented in a different key, such as the dominant or the relative major. The themes themselves often have contrasting musical characteristics and moods. In some sonata-allegro movements, however, the themes are similar in character and occasionally, as in some works by Haydn, the same thematic material will appear in the first and second theme groups.

The *development* section is based on the compositional principle of variation. In this section, motives and phrases from the exposition section are treated according to many of the variation techniques described in Chapter 5. It should be borne in mind that the essential difference between a theme and variations form and a developmental form is that the whole theme is treated in a variation, but only motives and phrases are treated in a development. The development section features frequent modulations to distant keys and frequent changes in instrumentation, dynamics, texture, and character. In general, it has a feeling of motion and tension. Usually the last few measures of the development section center on the dominant tonality and effectively prepare for the beginning of the recapitulation section.

The *recapitulation* section shows the influence of the principle of repetition, in that it regularly consists of a recapitulation or return of the material of the exposition section. Although the exposition material is brought back basically in its original form, there may be slight changes in instrumentation, texture, and other elements. One change that is virtually mandatory is that in the recapitulation the second and third theme groups and the codetta are presented in the tonic key, instead of in a related key as in the exposition.

To these three main sections (exposition, development, and recapitulation), Classical composers often added a prefatory *introduction* and a concluding *coda*. The introduction is generally in a slow tempo, and though it may contain references to motives from the exposition, it is more often based on independent thematic material. The coda is either in the same tempo as or a faster tempo than the body of the movement. It is regularly based on material from the three main sections of the movement. The term coda (Italian: tail or end) is used for the conclusion of an entire movement; the term codetta (Italian: little tail or end) is used for the conclusion of sections within a movement. Both terms are also used·in forms other than sonata-allegro.

The following examples illustrate the basic concepts of this important form as well as some of the changes and expansions possible within its general framework. The first movement of Beethoven's Symphony No. 1 in C Major is a typical structure.

EXAMPLE 8-8. Beethoven, *Symphony No. 1 in C Major*, first movement.

Example 8–9 illustrates Beethoven's powerful expansion and development of the sonata-allegro form in his later works. The exposition has more thematic material than usual; even the transition sections have nearly thematic significance. The development section is greatly extended and contains a new theme of its own. The lengthy coda is, in effect, a second development section. In contrast, the introduction to the movement is startlingly brief— just two short chords, which capture our attention for the breathtaking movement that follows.

EXAMPLE 8–9. Beethoven, *Symphony No. 3 in E-flat Major,* first movement.

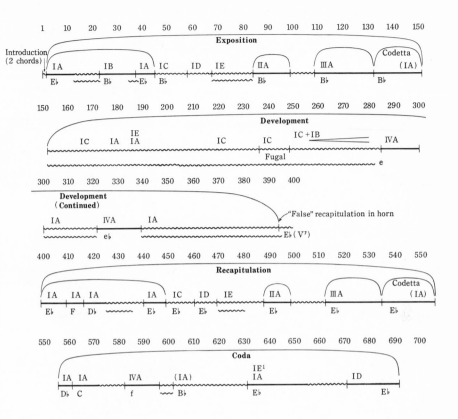

Example 8–10 is not written in "fugal form," as is sometimes stated; it is written in sonata-allegro form with extensive use of fugal or imitative techniques.

EXAMPLE 8-10. Mozart, *Symphony No. 41 in C Major, K. 551,* first movement.

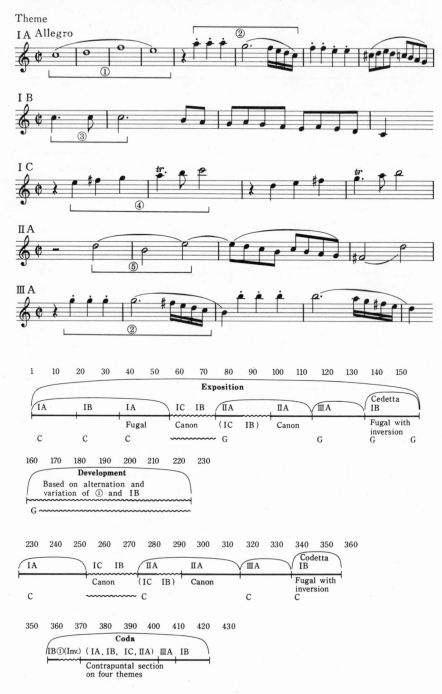

Sonatina form. Sonatina form is, in essence, a miniature version of sonata-allegro form, but with shorter themes, an abbreviated or occasionally omitted development section, and a generally lighter character.

EXAMPLE 8–11. Mozart, *The Marriage of Figaro*, Overture, K. 492.

Concerto-allegro form. The concerto-allegro form, used for the first movements of concertos, differs from the sonata-allegro form in that it has a double exposition, first for the orchestra alone and then for the soloist with orchestral accompaniment. The Classical concerto usually has a *cadenza* for the soloist alone near the end of the movement. This cadenza may be improvised (especially when the composer himself is the soloist), but it is more often written out by either the composer or the performer. The cadenza is somewhat like a development section, containing passages designed to show the technical skill of the soloist, and performed with great freedom or rubato.

EXAMPLE 8–12.   Mozart, Concerto in A Major for Piano and Orchestra, K. 488, first movement.

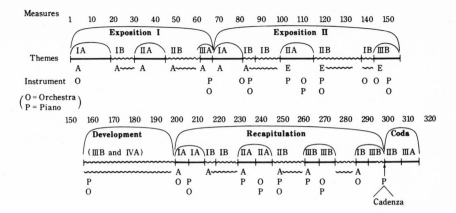

Rondo-sonata form. The rondo-sonata form is basically a rondo form, having a development section in place of one of the thematic sections as illustrated in Example 8–13. An unusual feature of this example is that the first and second themes both begin with the same triadic melodic pattern.

EXAMPLE 8–13. Mozart, *Quartet in D Major, K. 575,* last movement.

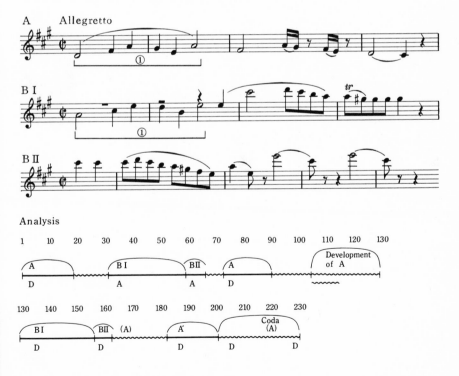

Free forms.   Most works of the Classical period can be analyzed in terms of the set forms previously described. Overtures to operas or ballets or independent concert overtures, for example, are often cast in sonata-allegro form. Some compositions, such as the *Fantasias* of Mozart or Beethoven are exceptions to this general rule. Because their formal structures do not follow any of the conventional patterns, they are said to be in free form.

EXAMPLE 8–14.   Mozart, *Fantasia in D Minor*, K. 397.

Multi-Movement Instrumental Forms

Sonata form.   The most important composite instrumental form of the Classical period is the *sonata form* that developed out of the *sonata da chiesa, sonata da camera* (suite), and the *Italian* and *French overtures* of the Baroque period. We must be careful to distinguish between sonata-allegro form (a single movement form) and sonata form (a composite form with several movements.) Most works in sonata form have four movements, but some compositions in sonata form have fewer or more movements. The chart in Example 8–15 summarizes the standard characteristics of Classical sonata form.

Works written in this composite form for one solo instrument, especially piano, or for an orchestral instrument with piano accompaniment are called *sonatas* (for example, Beethoven, *Sonata in F Minor for Piano*, Op. 2, No. 1). Works written in sonata form for chamber music combinations are named after the chamber group involved. A work in sonata form for a string quartet is called a *quartet,* (for example, Mozart's *Quartet in B-flat Major*, K.458); a work for three instruments is called a *trio;* and works for other combinations are similarly named. A work in sonata form for orchestra is called a *symphony.* Examples 8–16, 8–17, and 8–18 illustrate regular sonata form as well as some of the possible adaptations in the form.

Concerto.   The concerto grosso of the Baroque period was not an important form in the Classical period, but the solo concerto for piano, violin, or other instrument, with orchestral accompaniment, reached a high point of development in the Classical period. The Classical concerto is regularly in three movements, eliminating the minuet or scherzo movement. The first movement is in concerto-allegro form with double exposition and cadenza; the second movement is a slow movement in any form; and the last movement is a brilliant finale, often in rondo or sonata-allegro form. Cadenzas are sometimes indicated in the last two movements as well as in the first movement. (See Example 8–19.)

Other composite instrumental forms.   In addition to works in sonata or concerto form, other multi-movemented works with such titles as *divertimento, cassation,* and *serenade* are written for chamber music groups or orchestra. These are intended as light, entertaining works to be played at social events or for outdoor festivities, but some of them transcend this "occasional" character and are suitable for performance in the concert hall. Most works in this form have more than the four movements of the sonata or symphony.

EXAMPLE 8–15.   Standard characteristics of Classical sonata form.

	First Movement	Second Movement	Third Movement	Fourth Movement
Form	sonata-allegro	any (sonata-allegro, three-part song form, theme and variations, etc.)	minuet and trio or scherzo and trio	any (rondo, rondo-sonata, sonata-allegro, theme and variations, etc.)
Tonality	tonic	related key (dominant, parallel minor, etc.)	tonic	tonic
Tempo	fast	slow	moderate	fast	fast
Meter	any (simple quadruple, compound duple, etc.)	any	triple	triple	any
General	often most significant movement in terms of compositional technique and musical content	character ranges from quiet simplicity to deep pathos, depending on tempo, tonality, and other factors	dance-like and often graceful in character; usually homophonic in texture	often humorous in character, sometimes energetic, sometimes mysterious	generally more brilliant in character than the first movement

EXAMPLE 8-16. Haydn, Symphony No. 94 in G Major (Surprise)

	First Movement	Second Movement	Third Movement	Fourth Movement
Form	sonata-allegro	theme and variations	compound ternary	sonata-allegro (or rondo-sonata)
Tonality	G major	C major	G major	G major
Tempo	introduction: adagio cantabile main part: vivace assai	andante	allegro molto	allegro di molto
Meter	introduction $\frac{3}{4}$ main part $\frac{6}{8}$	$\frac{2}{4}$	$\frac{3}{4}$	$\frac{2}{4}$
General	clear, regular structure	theme itself in rounded binary form, followed by four variations and coda	robust, peasant-like minuet	lively and graceful in character

EXAMPLE 8-17. Haydn, Quartet in F Major, Op. 77 No. 2

	First Movement	Second Movement	Third Movement	Fourth Movement
Form	sonata-allegro	compound ternary	theme and variations	sonata-allegro
Tonality	F major	F major	D major	F major
Tempo	allegro moderato	presto, ma non troppo	andante	vivace assai
Meter	¢	$\frac{3}{4}$	$\frac{2}{4}$	$\frac{3}{4}$
General	first theme motive appears as counterpoint to second theme	called minuet, but has character of scherzo	note reversal of usual order of second and third movements	brilliant passage work, especially in first violin.

EXAMPLE 8–18. Beethoven, Quartet in C-sharp Minor, Op. 131.

	First Movement	Second Movement	Third Movement	Fourth Movement
Form	Fugue	rondo (ABACADCAB)	recitative	theme and variations (7 variations and coda)
Tonality	C♯ minor	D major	modulatory	A major
Tempo	adagio ma non troppo e molto espressivo	allegro molto vivace	allegro moderato-adagio	andante ma non troppo e molto cantabile
Meter	¢	$\frac{6}{8}$	c	$\frac{2}{4}$
General	quiet, almost religious or mystic character	simpler in texture and brighter in character than first movement	serves as transition between second and fourth movements	each variation in different tempo and character

EXAMPLE 8–18 (continued).

	Fifth Movement	*Sixth Movement*	*Seventh Movement*
Form	sectional	one-part song form	sonata-allegro
Tonality	E major	G♯ minor	C♯ minor
Tempo	presto	adagio quasi un poco an-dante	allegro
Meter	¢	3/4	¢
General	humorous scherzo with irregular form, inserted tempo changes, use of ponticello	leads without pause to last movement	first theme based on motive from fugue theme of first movement

EXAMPLE 8-19. Beethoven, Concerto in D Major for Violin and Orchestra, Op. 61.

	First Movement	*Second Movement*	*Third Movement*
Form	concerto-allegro	large binary song form	rondo
Tonality	D major	G major	D major
Tempo	allegro, ma non troppo	larghetto	fast
Meter	C	C	6 8
General	cadenza between recapitulation and coda	cadenza between this and last movement	cadenza before coda

Single-Movement Vocal Forms

Recitative. The recitative in Classical operas and oratorios, like that of the Baroque period, was written in either *secco* or accompanied style. Classical composers showed exceptional skill in providing appropriate accompaniments to underline the meaning of the text, especially in the accompanied recitatives.

Aria. The Classical aria tended to move away from the shallow display of virtuosity that marked many Baroque operatic arias; it also moved away from rigid adherence to the da capo form. Again, great skill in suggesting atmosphere and meaning is evident in the accompaniment.

Song. Mozart, Haydn, and Beethoven wrote several songs based on a simple, almost folk-song form, with each verse set to the same music. They also wrote more extended *Lieder*.

Chorus. Many choruses in Classical oratorios are similar in style and structure to Baroque models, featuring either imitative polyphonic texture throughout or an alternation of polyphonic and homophonic textures. Others show the influence of Classical instrumental music in their usage of developmental procedures and their increased emphasis upon the orchestra. Some short choruses or vocal canons on light or humorous texts were written for informal performance.

Multi-Movement Vocal Forms

Opera. Operas of the Classical period show significant advances in style and technique. Some Baroque characteristics, such as emphasis on virtuoso singing and spectacular stage effects, were eliminated; more attention was paid to the effective use of the orchestra, chorus, and vocal ensembles. A better balance was achieved between drama and music and the protagonists were more effectively characterized. One feature of Baroque opera which was continued was the division of the music into set pieces or "numbers."

Both *opera seria* and *opera buffa* were written, but the stereotyped distinctions between the two were less apparent, especially in a work such as Mozart's *Don Giovanni*. A third type of operatic genre, *Singspiel* (German: sung drama) was cultivated in this period. It was written in German instead of Italian and contained some sections of spoken dialogue. Mozart's *Die Entführung aus dem Serail (Abduction from the Seraglio)* and *Die Zauberflöte (The Magic Flute)* are examples of this type.

Many of the characteristics of Classical opera can be seen in the first act of Mozart's *Le Nozze di Figaro (The Marriage of Figaro)*. Mozart's librettist, Da Ponte, used Beaumarchais' play of the same name as the basis for his text. The principal characters are: Count Almaviva (baritone); Figaro, his valet (bass); Countess Almaviva (soprano); Susanna, her maid (soprano); Dr. Bartolo (bass); Marcellina, his former servant (mezzo-soprano); Cherubino, a page (a male role sung, however, by a soprano or mezzo-soprano); Don Basilio, a music master (tenor); Don Curzio, a judge (tenor); Antonio, a gardener (bass); and Barbarina, his daughter (soprano).

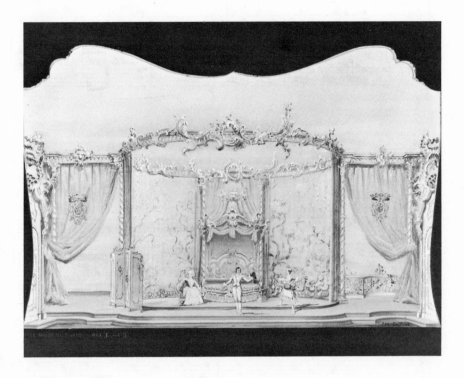

Marriage of Figaro, Act. I. Setting by C. M. Cristini. Used by permission.

Marriage of Figaro, Act One

No. 1, Duet. Figaro and Susanna are planning for their wedding which is to take place this day. Figaro is measuring the floor of the room that will be their bedroom; Susanna is admiring the new hat she has made for her wedding.

The leaps in the "Figaro theme" (a) aptly accompany his gestures of measuring the room. The lyric line of the "Susanna theme" (b) suggests her delight in her new hat. By having the duet end with Figaro joining in with the "Susanna theme," Mozart subtly suggests that Susanna is, at this point, the dominant one of the couple. The form of the duet is: Introduction-a-b-a-b-recitative-b-Coda.

EXAMPLE 8–20.*

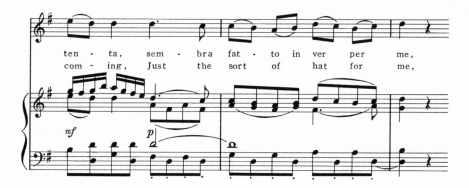

ten - ta, sem - bra fat - to in ver per me,
com - ing, Just the sort of hat for me,

Recitative. Susanna is displeased to learn that this room, located between the bedroom of the Count and that of the Countess, is to be their room. Figaro asks her to explain.

No. 2, Duet. Figaro points out that the room is conveniently located, for if the Count or the Countess should ring for them, they are close at hand. Susanna reminds him that the philandering Count might also find the room conveniently located, should he care to visit Susanna while Figaro is away. Figaro's jealousy is aroused.

Figaro's enthusiastic description of the room's location is sung in major (A). Susanna's warning about the dangers of the room's location is sung to a similar melody but in minor (B). The duet is in da capo form with an extended closing section.

EXAMPLE 8–21.

A Allegro
Figaro

Se a ca - so ma - da - ma la not - te ti chia - ma,
Sup - pos - ing one eve - ning my la - dy should want you,

EXAMPLE 8–21. continued.

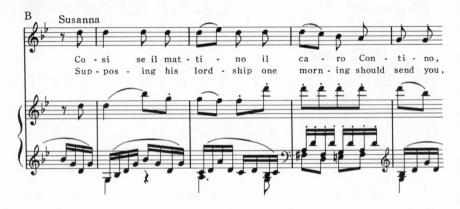

Recitative.   Susanna tells Figaro that the music master, Don Basilio, has told her of the Count's affection for her and adds that the Count is thinking of reviving an old custom according to which the first night of a bride in the service of a nobleman belongs to the nobleman. Susanna exits when the Countess rings for her. Figaro muses indignantly on the situation.

No. 3, Cavatina.   Figaro decides that if the count wants to "dance" (i.e., carry on a flirtation with Susanna), then he, Figaro, will play the tune. Determined to outwit the Count, he exits.

The first theme of the aria is a graceful minuet (A), underlining Figaro's words about the Count wanting to "dance." When Figaro speaks of his determination, the music changes to a fast, vigorous duple meter (B). The A section returns in an abbreviated form and a coda based on B ends the number.

EXAMPLE 8–22.

B Presto

L'ar - te scher - men - do,   l'ar - te a - do - pran - do,
Try   to de - ceive   me,   I'll   do   the   same   thing;

Recitative. Bartolo and Marcellina enter. Marcellina tells Bartolo that she has an old contract in which Figaro has promised to marry her. Bartolo agrees to help her, for he sees this as a chance to even the score with Figaro, who had been instrumental in helping the Count steal Rosina (the Countess) away from Bartolo in the past. (This incident is central to the plot of Rossini's *Barber of Seville*.)

No. 4, Aria. Bartolo sings of the joy of vengeance. He plans to confound Figaro, using all his skill as a lawyer. Bartolo exits.

The idea of stark vengeance is effectively portrayed by the stark unisons of the opening bars (A). The middle part of the aria is a typical "patter" section with rapidly repeated notes (C). The aria is in da capo form.

EXAMPLE 8–23.

A Allegro con spirito
Bartolo

La ven - det - ta,   oh,   la   ven - det - ta
Now for ven - geance! ah,   now for vengeance!

EXAMPLE 8–23. continued.

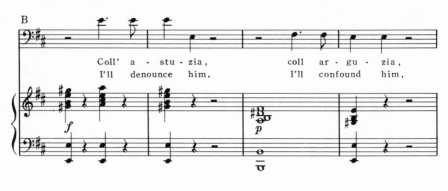

Recitative. Susanna enters and exchanges a few barbed remarks with Marcellina.

No. 5, Duet. Marcellina and Susanna parry sarcastic compliments. Marcellina exits after Susanna taunts her about her age.

The conflict between Marcellina and Susanna is mirrored in the conflict between the duplets of the violin melody and the triplets of the accompaniment. The voice parts are heard as obbligatos to the main violin melody.

EXAMPLE 8–24.

Recitative. Cherubino enters to tell Susanna that the Count has caught him in a compromising situation with Barbarina and has threatened to send him away unless the Countess intercedes for him. He sees that Susanna is carrying a ribbon belonging to his beloved godmother, the Countess. He takes it from Susanna and gives her a love poem he has just written, asking her to sing it for all the ladies of the castle.

No. 6, Aria. Cherubino sings of the wonder and ecstasy of love. He tells Susanna how he is languishing for love.

Mozart captures the breathless excitement of the young page in the rhythm of the accompaniment and the vocal line. Note the change of accompaniment that occurs when he sings of languishing for love. The aria is cast in open binary form.

EXAMPLE 8-25.

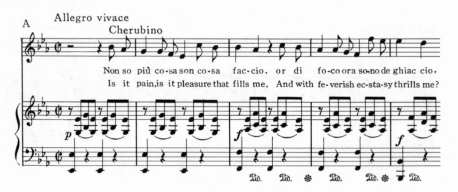

Recitative. The voice of the count is heard outside. Cherubino hides behind an armchair. The Count enters and declares his love for Susanna. Now the voice of Basilio is heard outside. The Count hides behind the same armchair as Cherubino sneaks around to sit in the chair. Susanna covers him with a dress as Basilio enters. Basilio tells Susanna that he is looking for Cherubino, who, he says, has been casting romantic glances at all the ladies in the castle, particularly at the Countess. When the Count hears this, he comes out of his hiding place to confront Basilio.

No. 7, Trio. The Count rages against the effrontery of Cherubino. Basilio slyly excuses himself for having found the Count and Susanna in a somewhat embarrassing situation. Susanna, overcome with shame and fear, almost faints. The Count recalls for Susanna how he had found Cherubino hiding under a tablecloth in Barbarina's room. He demonstrates by lifting the dress from the armchair and in so doing exposes the hapless Cherubino. Now Susanna is even more frightened and ashamed. The Count decries her frailty and faithlessness. Basilio takes delight in finding his suspicions of Susanna's affair with Cherubino seemingly confirmed.

In this complex ensemble number each character is given music which effectively brings out the meaning of his words and the nuances of his character. The dotted rhythms and pauses of the Count's theme (IA) suggest his anger. Basilio's theme (IB) has a conventional scalewise melody accompanied by unusual chromatic harmonies, suggesting the combination of servile deference and malicious sarcasm, which are his characteristics. The fluttering motives of Susanna's theme (IC) suggest her shame and fear. Note how these motives recur in the orchestra as Susanna recovers from her swoon in time to avoid sitting on Cherubino. For an especially effective use of musical material, listen to the passage in which the Count describes his discovery of Cherubino in Barbarina's room. At this point he was in the same role as Basilio is now, i.e., the role of one who discovers an embarrassing situation. Mozart captures the irony of this situation by having the Count tell of his discovery using the same scalewise melody and unusual harmony that Basilio used at the beginning of the number. The form of this number is an effective adaptation of sonata-allegro form.

EXAMPLE 8–26.

EXAMPLE 8–26. continued.

Recitative. The Count now realizes that Cherubino has overheard his declaration of love to Susanna.

No. 8, Chorus. A group of peasants enters to sing a song of praise to the Count. They are followed by Figaro, who is carrying a white veil.

As befits the simple nature of the peasants, the chorus is in a simple binary form with straightforward harmony and melody.

EXAMPLE 8-27.

Recitative.   Figaro asks the Count to put the veil on Susanna as a symbol of her virtue. Taking advantage of the presence of so many witnesses, Figaro tricks the Count into an assurance that the Count will not claim the privilege of spending the wedding night with Susanna.

No. 8a, Chorus.   The peasants exit with a repeat of their song of praise.

Recitative.   Cherubino offers to forget what he has overheard. The Count rewards him by making him an officer in the Count's regiment in Seville. The Count exits.

No. 9, Aria.   Figaro tells Cherubino he will now have to give up his frivolous life. He describes the excitement and glory of the military life.

The dotted rhythm of Figaro's theme in the opening duet returns in this aria. Now it assumes a military character to fit the text. The aria is in rondo form: a-b-a-c-d-a-d-Coda.

EXAMPLE 8-28.

From this point on the story becomes a tangled web of plot and counter-plot, adventure and misadventure, disguise and mistaken identity. The opera ends with the reconciliation of the Count and the Countess and the marriages of Figaro and Susanna, Cherubino and Barbarina. Among the musical highlights of the last three acts are the two arias of the Countess, *"Porgi amor"* ("Pour, O Love") and *"Dove Sono"* ("Are They Over"), and Susanna's aria *"Deh, vieni, non tardar"* ("Beloved, Don't Delay").

Religious music. Though religious music, in general, was not so much emphasized, Classical composers wrote some masses and oratorios that show a tendency toward the secular style of the opera or symphony. Some oratorios like Haydn's *The Seasons* are based on secular texts.

Representative Composers of the Classical Period

Karl Phillip Emmanuel Bach (German, 1714–1788). K. P. E. Bach is probably best known as the son of a famous father (J. S. Bach) and as the author of a text on keyboard playing *(The True Art of Playing the Clavier)* which gives valuable information on the performance of Baroque and Rococo music. His compositions, which include solo keyboard sonatas, concertos, chamber music, and choral music, are important landmarks in the development of pre-Classical and Classical forms and techniques.

Christoph Willibald Gluck (German, 1714–1787). Like Handel, Gluck was a cosmopolitan who lived and worked in Bavaria, Prague, Vienna, Milan, Venice, London, Paris, and elsewhere. He is known principally for his operas, *Orfeo ed Eurydice, Alceste, Armide,* and *Iphigenie en Tauride,* and others, which ushered in the operatic reforms of the Classical period.

Franz Joseph Haydn (Austrian, 1732–1809). Haydn spent the major portion of his creative life as court composer for the Esterhazy family. Living in relative isolation from outside musical influences and having at his disposal an excellent group of instrumentalists, Haydn developed new techniques and forms that were not only significant in themselves but also important influences on later composers.

He solved many of the problems inherent in the change from Baroque and Rococo styles to the Classical style. In his early symphonies he still used the Baroque texture of strong bass and soprano lines with the harmonic middle parts filled in by the continuo, but in his later works he achieved a more evenly balanced texture by distributing the harmonic parts among various instruments. In the preface to his *String Quartets*, Op. 33, he announced that they were written in a new manner; this new manner involved essentially a combination of the attractive melody of Rococo homophony with the richer texture of Baroque polyphony.

Boisterous peasant humor is often cited as a typical Haydn characteristic. This is an apt description of many of his minuets with their sturdy accents and folk-like themes and of many of his fast movement with their rollicking rhythms and unexpected pauses or turns of phrases. But it does not apply to all of Haydn's music. His slow movements vary from lyric simplicity to deep pathos; his other movements range from delicate, graceful minuets to complex, fugal finales.

Haydn is usually credited with the establishment of the sonata-allegro form, and it is true that we can trace the growth of this form in Haydn's works from a simple binary scheme to the fully developed sonata form with contrast of themes in the exposition and recapitulation, ingeniously worked out development sections, and interesting introductions and codas. However, other composers, such as those of the Viennese and Mannheim schools, also made significant contributions to the development of this form. Furthermore, in Haydn's own works the sonata-allegro form does not appear as often in a regular standardized form as we might expect. Haydn seems to delight in producing slight modifications in the form, such as introducing "false" recapitulations in the middle of the development section or omitting the return of the second theme in the recapitulation.

This refusal to be bound by strict rules extends also to Haydn's orchestration and harmony. He experimented freely with various orchestral combinations and instrumental techniques. He usually confined himself to simple major and minor triads, and seventh chords with harmonic progression by fifths, but on occasion he produced harmonies that are remarkably advanced. A striking, though probably coincidental, example is the passage in Example 8–29a, which contains an unusual harmony that Wagner later used (enharmonically changed) in his *Tristan und Isolde*.

EXAMPLE 8–29a.   Haydn, *Quartet in C Major*, Op. 54, No. 2., third movement.

EXAMPLE 8–29b.   Wagner, *Tristan und Isolde*, Prelude.

Haydn himself best expressed his attitude on rules in composition in the following passage in reply to the suggestion that all consecutive fifths should be banned from music.

> What do you mean? Art is free, and must not be confined by technical fetters. The ear—naturally, the cultured ear—must be the judge, and I feel myself as authorized as anybody else to make up rules. Such artificialities have no value; I should rather someone try to write a truly new minuet.[1]

Haydn wrote over 100 symphonies including:

Symphony No. 22 in E-flat Major (Philosopher):	Name refers to the serious academic character; unusual instrumentation includes two English horns.
Symphony No. 31 in D Major (Horn Signal):	Has four horns instead of the usual two.
Symphony No. 45 in F-sharp Minor (Farewell):	So-called because the last movement calls for the players to stop playing one by one and leave the stage, a not too subtle hint to Haydn's patron that the musicians wished to return to their homes after an extended tour with Count Ester-hazy.
Symphony No. 94 in G Major (Surprise):	Named after the unexpected loud chord in the slow movement, which was not written to wake up the sleepers in the audience as popular legend has it, but which, according to Haydn, was a novelty introduced so that the work could compete for the attention of the London audiences against the popular works of Haydn's former pupil, Pleyel.
Symphony No. 100 in G Major (Military):	So-called because of its use of military trumpet calls and percussion.
Symphony No. 101 in D Major (Clock):	Named because of the "ticking" accompaniment in the slow movement.
Symphony No. 103 in E-flat Major (Drumroll):	Begins with timpani roll.
Symphony No. 104 in D Major (London):	Last movement is based on a London street song.

Symphonies 82 to 87 are called the *Paris* symphonies because they were written for performance in that city. Symphonies 93 to 104 are called the *Salomon* symphonies or the *London* symphonies because they were written for the impressario, Salomon, to be performed in London. He also wrote 83 string quartets including:

---

[1] *Joseph Haydn, Leben, Briefe, Schaffen,* Willi Reich, ed. (Lucerne, Stocker 1946), in *Composers on Music,* trans. Sam Morgenstern, ed. (New York: Pantheon Books, A Division of Random House, Inc., 1956), p. 69. Used by permission.

Quartet in E-flat Major, Op. 33, No. 2 *(Joke)*:	Named because of the humorous pauses in the last movement.
Quartet in D Major, Op. 50, No. 6 *(Frog)*:	So-called because of the unusual bowing effects in the last movement.
Quartet in D Major, Op. 64, No. 5 *(Lark)*:	Name refers to soaring melody in the first movement.
Quartet in G Minor, Op. 74, No. 3 *(Rider)*:	So-called because of the "galloping" rhythm of the last movement.
Quartet in D Minor, Op. 76, No. 2 *(Quinten)*:	Called *Quinten* (Latin: fifths) because the opening theme of the first movement is based on the melodic interval of a fifth.
Quartet in C Major, Op. 76, No. 3 *(Emperor)*:	The second movement is a set of variations on a theme which became the Austrian national hymn. (See p. 232)

Haydn wrote many other chamber music compositions, including over 300 compositions for the baryton, an instrument played by his patron, Count Esterhazy. Haydn's choral works include masses, cantatas, and two famous oratorios, *The Creation* and *The Seasons*. He also wrote numerous compositions for piano, solo voice, and vocal ensembles, and 32 pieces for a musical clock. Of his several operatic works, none have remained in the current repertoire, except for *The Man in the Moon,* which recently enjoyed a modest revival spurred by the interest in space exploration.

Luigi Boccherini (Italian, 1742–1805).   Boccherini is known chiefly for his sonatas and concertos for cello, and for his chamber music.

Wolfgang Amadeus Mozart (Austrian, 1756–1791).   Mozart's middle name, Amadeus (Latin: beloved of God), possibly best describes him. But though the breadth and perfection of some of his masterworks may point to divine inspiration, the humor and the poignancy of his letters show his human traits.

> The golden mean—the truth in all things is neither known nor appreciated nowadays. To receive applause one must write things that are either so simple that a coachman can sing them, or else so incomprehensible that people like them just because no reasonable man can understand them. This is not what I wanted to speak to you about; I would like to write a book, a little critique on music with examples, but (note well) not under my own name. . . .[2]

> Your worthy letter has been safely received perceived, and from it I learn turn that my cousin buzzin' and you are tar very well. God be praised and thanked, we are also quite healthy wealthy. Today I got tot the letter getter from my Papa haha. I hope that you have dave received the letter better which I wrote you from Mannheim. All the better—better the all! But now for something sensible. . . .[3]

---

[2] Wolfgang Amadeus Mozart, letter to his father, Vienna, December 28, 1782.
[3] Wolfgang Amadeus Mozart, letter to his cousin, Mannheim, November 5, 1777.

Like Bach and Handel, Mozart and Haydn are often regarded as being very similar. However, a comparison of these two Classical composers reveals many interesting differences.

Haydn's long life began in obscurity and ended with his triumphant visits to England. Mozart's short life began with his highly successful tours as a child prodigy and ended with financial difficulties and a relative lack of recognition. Haydn was largely self-taught and developed his art in relative isolation from outside influences. During his early years, Mozart had the good fortune to have an excellent teacher, his father, Leopold; later he eagerly seized every opportunity to acquaint himself with many different styles and composers, assimilating them into his own uniquely personal musical expression. Haydn experimented and developed new forms and techniques; Mozart refined and perfected existing forms and techniques. Haydn's mode of expression tends to be more instrumental. Mozart's expression is more vocal; even in the fast movements of his instrumental works, he often writes a singing, lyric line.

Another difference between Haydn and Mozart sometimes cited is Mozart's more extensive use of chromaticism. We must be careful not to over-emphasize this use of chromaticism for at least two reasons. First, we should not expect to find extensive chromaticism such as we find in the twentieth century, but rather the controlled use of such chromatic tones as passing tones and other non-harmonic tones. The difference between Mozart's chromaticism and Schoenberg's chromaticism can be seen by comparing the theme of the minuet of Mozart's *Symphony No. 41 in C Major, K.551* (p. 228) with the first theme of Schoenberg's *Quartet No.3* (p. 349). Second, we should note that Haydn also used similar chromatic passages, especially in compositions he wrote after he became acquainted with Mozart and his music.

Mozart's works were chronologically catalogued by the nineteenth-century German musicologist, Koechel. They are designated according to their numerical position in this catalogue by the letter *K* followed by the appropriate number.

Mozart wrote 47 symphonies, of which the following are the most frequently performed: *Symphony No. 35 in D Major, K. 385 (Haffner); Symphony No. 36 in C Major, K. 425 (Linz); Symphony No. 38 in D Major, K. 504 (Prague); Symphony No. 39 in E-flat Major, K. 543; Symphony No. 40 in G Minor, K. 550; and Symphony No. 41 in C Major, K. 551 (Jupiter)*. The given nicknames refer either to the city of the first performance, to a patron of Mozart (Haffner), or in the case of *Jupiter*, probably to the grandeur of the work.

Mozart wrote over 50 concertos for piano, violin, or other orchestral instruments, some of them intended for performance with himself as soloist. He wrote 26 string quartets, including a set of 6 works dedicated to Haydn, and a set of 3 works dedicated to the King of Prussia.

Among his most famous string quartets are:

Quartet in B-flat Major, K. 458 *(Hunt)*	So-called because the opening theme resembles a hunting horn call.
Quartet in C Major, K. 465 *(Dissonant)*	The nickname refers to the unusual harmonic usage in the introduction to the first movement.

His other instrumental works include 17 sonatas for piano, 42 sonatas for piano and violin, and numerous other solo, chamber, and orchestral compositions. In addition to the *Requiem Mass,* he wrote other masses and religious choral music, songs for voice and piano, and other vocal works.

Of over twenty operas composed by Mozart, at least five hold a significant place in the standard repertoire:

Die Entführung aus dem Serail (The Abduction from the Seraglio) (1782). A *Singspiel* opera with a Turkish setting. Constanze and her maid Blondchen are held captive in a Turkish castle or *seraglio,* by Pasha Selim (a speaking part) and his harem guard, Osmin. Constanze's lover, Belmont and his servant, Pedrillo, seek to rescue the ladies but are captured themselves. At the close of the opera Pasha Selim relents and releases the four lovers, providing not only a happy ending to the story but a wonderful opportunity for a Mozartean finale.

Le nozze di Figaro (The Marriage of Figaro) (1786). See pp. 253–266.

Don Giovanni (1787). A *dramma giocosa* (comic play). The principal characters are the legendary lover, Don Giovanni; his servant, Leporello; and three of the Don's romantic conquests—Donna Anna, Donna Elvira, and the peasant girl Zerlina. Other characters include the Commandant, Donna Anna's father, who is slain by Don Giovanni; Don Ottavio, Donna Elvira's fiancee; and Masseto, Zerlina's fiancee. In the highly dramatic final scene the statue of the Commandant comes to drag Don Giovanni down to Hell. Musical highlights include the powerful overture, the humorous "Catalogue" aria of Leporello, Don Giovanni's serenade "Deh vieni alla fenestra" (Come to the window), and the ballroom music which, at one point, has three on-stage orchestras playing in three different meters.

Cosi fan tutte (Women Are Like That) (1790). An *opera buffa.* Don Alfonso lays a wager with Ferrando and Guglielmo that their fiancees, Fiordiligi and Dorabella will not be faithful. The men leave and return, disguised as Albanians, to make love to each other's fiancees. The maid, Despina, plays an important part in the ensuing complications. In the end the men reveal their identities and chastise their fiancees. Don Alfonso, having won his wager, brings about a reconcilitation.

Die Zauberflöte (The Magic Flute) (1791) A *Singspiel* opera. The main characters are the high priest, Sarastro; a young prince, Tamino; the Queen of the Night; her daughter, Pamina; a bird catcher, Papageno; his companion, Papagena; and a wicked moor, Monastatos. The complex and fantastic plot has many references to the ritual of the Masonic Order, of which Mozart was a member. Tamino, accompanied by Papageno, sets out to rescue Pamina from the temple of Sarastro. After many trials and ordeals Tamino and Pamina are united and Papageno finds a delightful companion in Papagena. Of special interest musically are the challenging coloratura arias of the Queen of the Night.

Ludwig van Beethoven (German, 1770–1827). Beethoven's motto, *"per aspera ad astra"* (Latin: through struggle to victory) suggests the keynote of his character and his music. He struggled against the physical affliction of increasing deafness, composing even when he could hear music only in his "mind's ear." He struggled against what he considered the servile role which society allotted to the musical artist, demanding that his music be supported by his patrons, not written for them. He struggled against the fetters of arbitrary and artificial rules and conventions in music, striking out in new directions in form and technique.

This sense of struggle reveals itself in such statements as the following from his notebook of 1812–1813:

> Do everything, do your utmost, to work out what is necessary for the long journey. You must seek everything—the fulfillment of your most divine desire— but you must seize it by observing the same steadfast way of thinking.

Beethoven's life and works may be divided into three chronological or stylistic periods. The works of his early, or "apprentice," period (c.1790– 1801) can be said to point toward the past. They show clearly the influence of Haydn, Mozart, and other composers in their adherence to traditional form and techniques, but they nevertheless contain many striking examples of Beethoven's uniquely personal style. The works of the middle, or "journeyman," period (1801–1817) seem to be written for Beethoven's own time and place. They can be characterized by an expansiveness, strength, and individuality that stem from Beethoven's confident command of his craft. The works of the late, or "master," period (c.1817–1827) point toward the future. In these works Beethoven experiments with unusual ways of handling the elements and forms of music, and parts of these works still sound advanced to the twentieth-century listener.

Ultimately, such general descriptions as these prove inadequate, and we must regard each of Beethoven's masterworks as a unique creation, revealing even within a single movement an incredible range of expressive possibilities.

Perhaps the most striking and all-pervasive characteristic of Beethoven's style is his consummate skill in the use of the temporal element. Some of his works are built almost entirely on a relentlessly reiterated rhythmic pattern; others are based on a variety of rhythms with striking syncopations and unexpected changes of meter and tempo.

The tonal element in Beethoven's music ranges from the relatively strict diatonicism of some of the early works to the extensive chromaticism of the later works, or from the short, pregnant motives of some of his allegro movements to the broad, lyric lines of some of his adagios. Powerful accents and sudden changes in dynamics are usually regarded as a hallmark of his style, but many of his works do not show these characteristics. Beethoven explored all the possibilities of the textural element from strict imitative polyphony to simple homophony; his harmonic usage varies from simple triadic harmony to striking dissonances.

Formally, Beethoven's works range from early works written in established patterns to later works in which the number of movements may vary from one to seven. Occasionally Beethoven expanded the sonata-allegro movement by increasing the number of themes in the first and second theme groups, lengthening the development section, and changing the coda into what is, in effect, a second development section. The scherzo may be counted among his formal innovations, even though the term had been used before.

Beethoven composed nine symphonies, all of which remain in the standard orchestral repertoire.

Symphony No. 1 in C Major, Op. 21	Shows influence of Haydn. Unusual features of the symphony are the tonic seventh chord which opens the first movement and the humorously hesitant introduction to the scale-wise theme of the last movement.
Symphony No. 2 in D Major, Op. 36	Again, Haydn's and Mozart's influences are apparent.
Symphony No. 3 in E-flat Major, Op. 55 *(Eroica)*	The original dedication of this work to Napoleon was withdrawn by Beethoven when he learned that Napoleon had proclaimed himself Emperor. (See pp. 232–234 and pp. 238–239.)
Symphony No. 4 in B-flat Major, Op. 60	Like all of the even-numbered symphonies of Beethoven, this work shows less sense of drama and passion than the odd-numbered symphonies.
Symphony No. 5 in C Minor, Op. 67	The first movement is based on a four note motive and is notable for its brevity, power, and unity. The second movement is a theme and variations. The third movement, a mysterious scherzo, leads without pause to the triumphant finale in which trombones, piccolo, contra-bassoon, and percussion are added to the usual Classical instrumentation.
Symphony No. 6 in F Major, Op. 68 *(Pastoral)*	Beethoven himself described the work as a "recording of sentiments rather than a painting in tone." He provided the following subtitles for each movement: I—Serene impressions awakened by arrival in the country, II—By the brook, III—Merry gathering of country folk, IV—The storm, V—Shepherd's song, glad and thankful feelings after the storm.
Symphony No. 7 in A Major, Op. 92	Wagner called this work the "apotheosis of the dance." Each movement is based on a particular rhythmic idea, heard throughout the movement.

I $\frac{6}{8}$ ♩. ♫ ♫ ♩. ♫ ♫ | II $\frac{2}{4}$ ♩ ♫ | ♩ ♩ |

III $\frac{3}{4}$ ♩ | ♩ ♪ ♪ ♩ | ♩ ♪ ♪ ♩ | ♩ ♩ ♩ | IV $\frac{2}{4}$ ♪ ♫ ♪ ♪ |

Symphony No. 8 in F Major, Op. 93	The slow movement, with its steady "ticking" rhythm in the woodwinds has reference to the metronome, invented in Beethoven's time by Maelzel. Beethoven was one of the first composers to use the metronome to indicate precise tempos.
Symphony No. 9 in D Minor, Op. 125 *(Choral)*	The finale includes parts for vocal soloists and chorus, based on Schiller's *Ode to Joy.* The symphony is in cyclic form; themes from the first three movements are brought back in the finale.

Beethoven wrote five concertos for piano and orchestra (including No. 5, the *Emperor* concerto), a concerto for violin and orchestra, and other orchestral music, including the following overtures:

Fidelio } *Leonore,* Nos. 1, 2, 3 }	{ All four works written at various times as over- { tures for Beethoven's opera, *Fidelio.*
Egmont	Part of incidental music Beethoven wrote for the Goethe play.
Prometheus	Part of music Beethoven wrote for a ballet.

Other overtures are: *Coriolanus; King Stephen; Ruins of Athens; Namensfeier (Celebration of the Name); Weihe des Hauses (Dedication of the House).*

His chamber music includes 17 works for string quartet, 11 trios, and various other works. Among his best known works in this medium are:

Three Quartets, Op. 59, No. 1, 2, 3 *(Rasoumovsky)*	Named after the Russian ambassador to Vienna. Each quartet contains a reference to Russian folk themes.
Quartet in F Minor, Op. 95 *(Serioso)*	One of Beethoven's most compact and powerful chamber music compositions.
Trio in D Major, Op. 70, No. 1 *(Ghost)*	The nickname refers to the mysterioso slow movement.

Beethoven also wrote ten sonatas for violin and piano, including *Op. 24 in F Major (Spring)* and *Op. 47 in A Major (Kreutzer);* and five sonatas for cello and piano. Of his 32 piano sonatas, the following are among the most famous: *Op. 13 in C Minor (Pathetique); Op. 53 in C Major (Waldstein); Op. 57 in F Minor (Appasionata); Op. 81a in E-flat Major (Les Adieux or Farewell);* and *Op. 106 in B-flat Major (Hammerklavier).*

In the field of vocal music, Beethoven wrote a *Mass in C* and a *Missa Solemnis (Solemn Mass) in D,* an oratorio, *Christus am Ölberg (Christ on the Mount of Olives),* and numerous other works.

His one opera, *Fidelio,* may be regarded as a hymn to conjugal love and to political liberty, two ideas which occupied much of Beethoven's thinking. *Fidelio* probably demanded more of Beethoven's time and creative energy than any other work. He once spoke of the opera to his friend, Georg August Griesinger, in the following words:

> My Fidelio was not understood by the public, but I know that it will yet be valued; nevertheless, although I know what *Fidelio* is worth, I know just as clearly that the symphony is my true element. When sounds stir within me, I always hear the full orchestra; I know what to expect of instrumentalists, who are capable of almost everything, but with vocal compositions I must always keep asking myself; can this be sung?[4]

We have included Beethoven in the Classical period because of his chronological and geographical proximity to the Viennese Classical composers, Haydn and Mozart; stylistically, however, most of his greatest compositions belong to the Romantic period. Like the twin-headed god, Janus, who looked both backward and forward, Beethoven brought the Classical period in music to its culmination and, at the same time, launched music on the path toward the Romantic period.

---

[4] Ludwig van Beethoven, statement to Georg August Griesinger, c. 1824, in *Beethoven: Letters, Journals and Conversations,* trans. Michael Hamburger, ed. (New York: Pantheon Books, A Division of Random House, Inc., 1952), p. 212. Used by permission.

chapter 9

The Romantic Period

The terms *Romantic* and *Romanticism* are borrowed from literature, where they refer to the fact that early nineteenth-century writers such as Novalis and Tieck had turned to the Romanesque period of the eleventh and twelfth centuries for literary inspiration and subject matter. In music, the term *Romantic* refers specifically to the period extending roughly from 1815 to 1900. The term may also be used in a general sense, in opposition to the term classical, to denote any composition, composer, or period marked by such characteristics as subjectivity, emotionalism, longing, exuberance, imbalance, asymmetry, picturesqueness, and fantasy.

The Romantic period shows several significant contrasts of styles. Some composers continued to write absolute music in the traditional forms of the Classical period; others wrote program music in such new forms as the symphonic poem or the character piece. Some composers of the period were intensely national, basing their music on the folk stories or the folk music of their native lands; others were international, seeking a more universal mode of musical expression. The musical expression of the Romantic period ranges from the intimacy of the solo piano to the large dimensions of grand opera, from the simplicity of a *Song Without Words* of Mendelssohn to the complexity of a symphony by Brahms.

The stylistic contrasts of the Romantic period can also be considered in terms of time and place. It is customary to divide the period chronologically into three subperiods—early Romanticism (c.1815–1850), middle Romanticism (c.1850–1890), and late Romanticism (c.1890–1920). Early Romantic composers continued the Classical emphasis on abstract music, especially in their instrumental works. The composers of the middle Romantic period tended more toward programmatic expression. Late Romantic composers also emphasized program music, incorporating new musical techniques (see p. 341). Geographically, significant national schools developed in Russia, Norway, Poland, Bohemia, and other countries. Nationalism in music, achieved by the incorporation of elements from folk music or subjects from folklore, became a significant movement, especially in the middle Romantic period.

The Formal Element in the Romantic Period

Classical composers tended to build their themes out of short motives which lend themselves to developmental treatment; Romantic composers showed a preference for broader, more lyric, non-motivic thematic construction. Exceptions to this general rule, however, can be seen in the works of many composers, especially in the music-dramas of Wagner, with their *leitmotiv* technique.

In terms of larger musical units, Romantic composers tended to avoid the clarity, balance, regularity, and precision of Classical composers. Phrases and periods of irregular lengths were often used. Cadences were often elided or avoided, providing for a more continuous flow of music. Larger musical units were delineated with less precision and clarity than in the Classical period, and there was a general avoidance of stereotyped formal patterns.

Classical balance between the principles of repetition, variation, and contrast was replaced by Romantic emphasis on variation and contrast. Though literal repetition was avoided, Romantic composers sometimes did exploit the principle of *cyclic form* in which thematic material from one movement of a large work reappears (usually in a varied manner) in other movements.

Single-Movement Instrumental Forms

Sectional forms. Binary, ternary, compound ternary, rondo and other sectional forms continued to be used in the Romantic period, but in general these forms were not so regular as in the Classical period.

Two important sectional forms of the Romantic period are the *character piece* and the *stylized dance movement. Character piece* is a generic term for works bearing such titles as *prelude, intermezzo, nocturne, impromptu, song without words, phantasy,* and *bagatelle.* These were usually written for piano, but they also appeared in chamber music and symphonic literature of the period. Occasionally, such works were written as descriptive program music. More often, the title indicates only a general mood as, for example, the quiet mood of a *nocturne.* Similar works, with such titles as *etude* or *study,* usually have a pedagogical as well as a purely musical purpose. The ternary structure of Example 9–1 is fairly typical for this genre. Compare this with a Classical ternary form, and note the freer construction here.

EXAMPLE 9–1. Chopin, *Nocturne in C-sharp Minor,* Op. 27, No. 1.

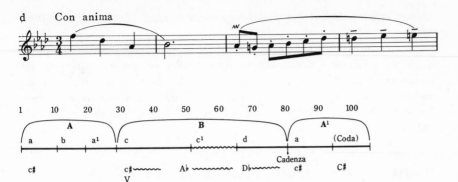

Stylized dance movements of the Romantic period, such as the *waltz, polonaise, mazurka,* and *polka,* were written in free sectional forms.

Variation forms. The theme and variations form was used for movements of a symphony, a sonata, or frequently for independent pieces. Some variations, such as Brahms' *Variations on a Theme of Haydn,* feature significant contrasts of mood, character, and technique. Others, such as *Caprice No. 24* of Paganini, described in Example 9–2, provide opportunity for virtuoso display of the various technical possibilities of an instrument. Compare the original version of this Paganini Caprice with the Liszt Etude and the Brahms Variations based on it to see how the same musical material can be used idiomatically for violin or piano.

EXAMPLE 9–2. Paganini, *Caprice No. 24.*

Theme		binary form
Variation	1	arpeggios with spiccato bowing
Variation	2	bariolage (string crossing)
Variation	3	slow theme in octaves (double stops)
Variation	4	high chromatic scales
Variation	5	broken octaves
Variation	6	thirds and tenths (double stops)
Variation	7	triplet neighbor-tone figures
Variation	8	triple stops
Variation	9	pizzicato executed with fingers of left as well as right hand
Variation	10	high legato melody
Variation	11	broken chords and rapid arpeggios
Finale (coda)		rapid arpeggios

Fugal form. As in the Classical period, strict fugal forms were seldom employed, but fugal techniques were used occasionally in other forms.

      Sonata-allegro form.   Some of the early Romantic composers wrote in a Classical sonata-allegro form; other composers expanded and varied the form. Example 9–3 is interesting for the way in which one key motive ① appears in various forms throughout the piece. New themes, based on this motive, appear both in the development section and in the coda.

EXAMPLE 9–3.   Brahms, *Symphony No. 2 in D Major,* first movement.

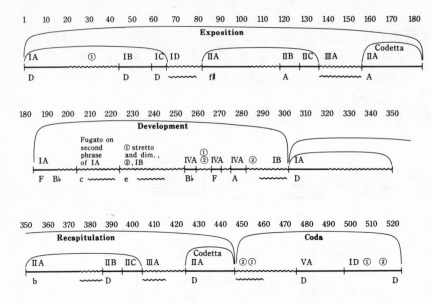

Free forms. The *symphonic poem,* or *tone poem,* is the most significant new instrumental form of the Romantic period. It may be defined as a single-movement instrumental work, based on some extra-musical or programmatic idea such as a poem, an historical event, a character, a drama, a scene from nature, or other subjects. Example 9–4 is written in a free sectional form; other tone poems are based on such forms as theme and variations, rondo, or sonata-allegro.

EXAMPLE 9–4. Smetana, *The Moldau* from the symphonic cycle *Má Vlast* (My Fatherland)

Musical
Sections   *Programmatic description* (in Smetana's words)

A   In the shade of the Bohemian forest two springs arise, one warm and
          bubbling, the other cool and calm. Their waves, rippling gaily over
          the rocks, unite and glisten in the sunlight. As the brook winds through
          Bohemia's valleys, it grows into a mighty river—

B   *The Moldau*

C   Through dense forests it flows, from which are heard the gay sounds of a hunt.

D   It flows through verdant meadows and lowlands where a peasant wedding is being celebrated with jubilant song and dance.

E   In the mysterious stillness of the night, wood and water nymphs revel on the river's moonlit surface (theme a). Fortresses and castles, projecting skyward on the surrounding slopes, remain as mute witnesses of the bygone glories and splendors of knighthood (theme b).

B¹   (*The Moldau* theme)

F   The river, now confined by rocky crags, foams as it plunges noisily through the valley.

B²   After the churning St. John Rapids, *the Moldau* flows in majestic peace toward Prague where it is welcomed by the noble ancient fortress of—

G   Vysehrad—

Coda and then, broadening out, vanishes into the distance.

Overtures to operas, ballets, and other stage works are often similar to tone poems of the Romantic period. Example 9–5 is interesting for its incorporation of programmatic elements within the framework of the sonata-allegro form; other overtures may be written in free form or other forms.

EXAMPLE 9–5.   Mendelssohn, Overture to *A Midsummer Night's Dream.*

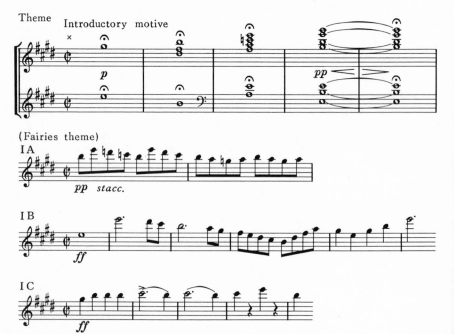

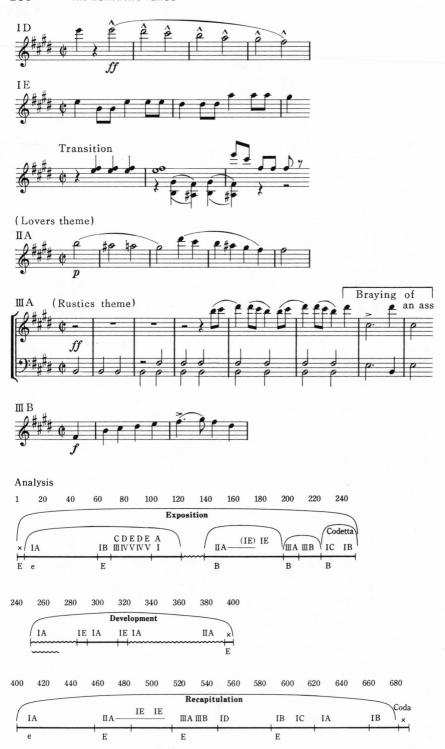

EXAMPLE 9–6. Brahms, Sonata in D Minor for Violin and Piano, Op. 108.

	First Movement	*Second Movement*	*Third Movement*	*Fourth Movement*
Form	sonata-allegro	sonatina	ternary with coda	sonata-rondo
Tonality	D minor	D major	F-sharp minor	D minor
Tempo	allegro	adagio	un poco presto e con sentimento	presto agitato
Meter	¢	$\frac{3}{8}$	$\frac{2}{4}$	$\frac{6}{8}$
General	structurally regular	no development section	middle section is development of first section	elements of both sonata form (including development) and rondo form (main theme returns several times)

EXAMPLE 9–7. Dvořák, Quintet in A Major for Piano and Strings, Op. 81.

	First Movement	*Second Movement*	*Third Movement*	*Fourth Movement*
Form	sonata-allegro	dumka (rondo) ABACABA	ternary	sonata-allegro
Tonality	A major	F-sharp minor	A major	A major
Tempo	allegro ma non tanto	alternates between slow and fast tempos	furiant (presto)	allegro
Meter	c	$\frac{2}{4}$	$\frac{3}{4}$	$\frac{2}{4}$
General	some unusual key relations between sections	dumka is a slavic elegy	scherzo with some Bohemian folk-like character	development has a fugato on the opening motive

The term overture, or concert overture, is also used for other instrumental compositions that have no connection with a stage work. Character pieces, such as those discussed under sectional forms, may also be written in free form.

Multi-movement Instrumental Forms

Sonata. The sonatas for piano or piano and one orchestral instrument of the early Romantic period are similar to Classical models. In the later Romantic periods, the sonata is somewhat neglected, except by such composers as Brahms. Note how Example 9–6 adheres to Classical form.

Chamber music. Chamber compositions in Classical sonata form were written by early Romantic composers, but the form was not as popular with later composers. Programmatic or nationalistic elements sometimes appear in chamber music compositions of the Romantic period. This can be seen in Example 9–7.

Symphony. The symphony was a significant form during the entire Romantic period. Among innovations in the form made by Romantic composers are the use of cyclic form, the introduction of programmatic or nationalistic elements, the addition or elimination of movements, and the substitution of new forms for those of the Classical model. Berlioz' *Symphonie Fantastique* is one of the earliest and most significant works to incorporate extensive programmatic elements in a symphony.

EXAMPLE 9–8.   Berlioz, *Symphonie Fantastique.*

Programmatic description (in Berlioz' words)	*Musical description*
(Preface) A young musician of extraordinary sensibility and overflowing imagination in a paroxysm of despair caused by unhappy love has poisoned himself with opium. The drug is too feeble to kill him, but plunges him into a heavy sleep accompanied by the weirdest visions. His sensations, emotions, and memories, as they pass through his diseased brain, are transformed into musical images and ideas. The beloved one herself becomes to him a melody, a recurrent theme (idée fixe) which haunts him everywhere.	
First Movement: Reveries, Passions: First he remembers that weariness of the soul, that indefinable longing, that somber melancholy and those objectless joys which he experienced before meeting his beloved. Then the volcanic love with which she at once inspired him, his delirious suffering, his return to tenderness, his religious consolation.	Irregular sonata-allegro form with introduction and coda. In quadruple meter with changes of tempo. The beloved is represented by IA theme. Second theme is based on motives of first theme.

I Ideê fixe
  Allegro agitato e appasionato assai

Second Movement: A Ball: At a ball, in the midst of a noisy, brilliant fête, he finds the loved one again.

A fast waltz in ternary form. A variation of the idée fixe appears in the middle section and the coda.

II Valse
  Allegro non troppo

Ideê fixe

Third Movement: In the Country: On a summer's evening in the country he hears two herders who call each other with their shepherd's melodies. The pastoral duet in such surroundings, the gentle rustle of the trees softly swayed by the wind, some reasons for hope that had lately come to his knowledge, all unite to fill his heart with long-missed tranquillity, and lend brighter colors to his fancies. But SHE appears anew, spasms contract his heart, dark premonitions appear to him. What if she proved faithless? One of the shepherds resumes his rustic tune, the other does not follow. The sun sets—far away there is rumbling thunder—solitude—silence.

Introductory duet of oboe and English horn, followed by a theme and four variations, ending with a coda like the introduction.

III Introduction
  Adagio

Theme

Ideê fixe

Fourth Movement: March to the Scaffold: He dreams he has killed his loved one, that he is condemned to death and led to the execution. A march, now gloomy and ferocious, now solemn and brilliant, accompanies the procession. Noisy outbursts are followed without pause by the heavy sound of measured footsteps. Finally the idée fixe, like a last thought of love, appears for a moment, to be cut off by the fall of the axe.

A march based on a scalewise theme alternating with trio section for winds. Near the end the idée fixe appears in the clarinet, followed by a loud short chord (beheading), and the movement concludes with full major chords.

IV March
Allegretto non troppo

Fifth Movement: Dream of a Witches' Sabbath: He sees himself at Witches' Sabbath surrounded by a fearful crowd of spectres, sorcerers, and monsters of every kind, united for his burial. Unearthly sounds, groans, shrieks of laughter, distant cries, to which others seem to respond! The melody of his beloved is heard, but it has lost its character of nobleness and timidity. Instead, it is now an ignoble dance tune, trivial and grotesque. It is *she* who comes to the Sabbath! A howl of joy greets her arrival. She joins the diabolical orgy. The funeral knell, burlesque of the *Dies Irae.* Dance of the Witches. The dance and the *Dies Irae* combined.

Free Form.
Introduction, burlesque of the *Idée Fixe, Dies Irae,* Witches' Dance (fugal), transition, Witches' Dance fugue combined with *Dies Irae.*

EXAMPLE 9-9. Schumann, Concerto in A Minor for Piano and Orchestra.

	First Movement	*Second Movement*	*Third Movement*
Form	irregular sonata-allegro	ternary	sonata-allegro
Tonality	A minor	F major	A major
Tempo	allegro affetuoso(several changes)	andantino grazioso	allegro vivace
Meter	C and 2/4	2/4	3/4
General	Movement opens with orchestra chord, brief piano cadenza, and then the first theme which then dominates most of the movement. Cadenza before coda.	First theme played antiphonally between solo piano and orchestra. Second theme in orchestra with piano accompaniment.	First theme returns between recapitulation and coda. Second theme is very syncopated. No cadenza.

Concerto. The Romantic concerto differs from the Classical concerto in its generally freer form, its more demanding virtuoso writing for the solo instrument, and its more symphonic character. The double exposition is often replaced by a single exposition and, occasionally, transition sections are written to connect one movement to the next without pause. Not only in the cadenza, but throughout the concerto, the soloist is called upon to execute difficult passages and special effects which exploit the technical possibilities of the instrument and the virtuoso skill of the performer. The orchestra plays an important role in the Romantic concerto, often performing thematic passages while the soloist either plays accompanying figures or is silent. A typical form may be seen in Example 9–9.

Ballet. Many independent ballets, not connected with an opera, were written during the Romantic period. Romantic ballet is a form of musical theater in which a story is told through dancing, pantomime, and scenic effects. It is accompanied by orchestral music that enhances and underlines the stage action. The music is often organized as separate pieces, each of which is in a sectional form or in a free form governed by the stage action.

Suite. In contrast to the Baroque suite with its established order of movements, the Romantic suite is a free succession of movements sometimes drawn from ballets or incidental music to plays, sometimes originally composed around a central story or idea. Suites were usually written for orchestra, but a few were written for piano or chamber combinations. Example 9–10 indicates the use of sectional forms in the separate movements or numbers of a ballet suite. The original ballet has many more numbers than the suite.

EXAMPLE 9–10. Tchaikowsky, *Nutcracker Suite.*

Overture Miniature	sonatina form (no development)
March	ternary form
Dance of the Sugar Plum Fairy	ternary form
Trepak	ternary form (second part begins with rhythmic motive of first part)
Arabian Dance	sectional $ABA^1B^1A^2$
Chinese Dance	one-part form (two contrasting phrases)
Dance of the Toy Flutes	ternary form
Waltz of the Flowers	sectional AABBAABB CCDDCC $AABBA^1A^1$ coda

Miscellaneous composite forms. Some Romantic composers wrote composite forms that did not fit any of the traditional schemes thus far given. Often, these consisted of a series of short character pieces related to a central idea or program. Schumann's *Carnaval,* for example, is a set of

21 short character pieces for piano, most of which are based on a four-note motive (A-E♭-C-B). In German musical notation these notes spell the name of a town in Bohemia (A-S-C-H) which was the home of Schumann's sweetheart, Ernestine von Fricken.

Preambule	Introductory piece
Pierrot ⎫ *Arlequin* ⎭	Characters from classic French pantomime; Pierrot is sad, Arlequin is mischevious
Valse noble	A slow, graceful waltz
Eusebius	The pensive, introverted side of Schumann's character.
Florestan	The vigorous, extroverted side of Schumann's character
Coquette	A flirt
Replique	A reply (echoes of the flirt's theme are also heard)
Papillons	Butterflies (A reminiscence of an early work by Schumann)
Lettres dansantes	Dancing letters, A.S.C.H. and S.C.H.A. (musical letters in Schumann's name)
Chiarina	A musical portrait of Clara Wieck, who later became Schumann's wife
Chopin	A beautiful tribute to the composer
Estrella	A musical portrait of Ernestine von Fricken
Reconnaissance	Recognition. Perhaps alluding to the masks worn by characters at a carnival.
Pantalon et Colombine *Valse Allemande*	The two lovers from classic French pantomime. German waltz
Paganini	A brilliant display piece in the style of the violin virtuoso
Aveu	A declaration of love
Promenade	A walk
Pause	A lively movement, the title is probably intended to be satiric
March des "Davidsbuendler" contre lês Philistins	March of the Society of David against the Philistines. The Society of David was a group of revolutionary young musicians; the Philistines represented the conservative public.

Single Movement Vocal Forms

Recitative and aria.   The secco recitative with only basso continuo accompaniment was not employed in the Romantic period. The differentiation between recitative and aria became gradually less clear until the two merge as one in the "unending melody" of the music-dramas of Wagner.

Songs. The Lieder (German: songs) of the German Romantic composers are among the most characteristic expressions of the Romantic period. The texts are often taken from major Romantic poets, the melodic line is expressive and closely adapted to the text, and the piano part transcends the role of mere accompaniment to become an equal partner in the projection of the mood and meaning of the text. Though German composers such as Schubert, Schumann, Brahms, and Wolf seem to dominate the form, composers such as Fauré and Duparc in France and Tchaikowsky and Mussorgsky in Russia also made significant contributions.

Three types of formal organization are used in Romantic *Lieder:* (1) *simple strophic form,* in which each verse of the text is set to the same music; (2) *modified strophic form,* which is similar to simple strophic organization except that slight alterations are made in the music to some of the verses to accommodate changes in the mood or meaning of the text; and (3) *through-composed* form in which completely different music is written for some or all of the verses. The following examples of Schubert's illustrate these three types.

EXAMPLE 9–11.   Schubert, "Heidenröslein" (text by Goethe).

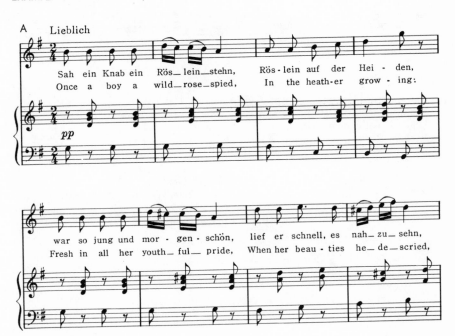

EXAMPLE 9–11. continued.

sah's_ mit_ vie - len_   Freu - den.   Rös - lein, Rös - lein, Rös - lein_ rot,
Joy_ in his heart was_   glow - ing.   Lit - tle wild rose, wild-rose_ red,

Rös lein auf der Hei - den.
In the heath- er grow - ing.

second stanza

Knabe sprach, ich breche dich, Röslein auf der Heiden!
Röslein sprach, ich steche dich, dass du ewig denkst an mich,
Und ich will's nicht leiden.
Röslein, Röslein, Röslein rot, Röslein auf der Heiden.

third stanza

Und der wilde Knabe brach's Röslein auf der Heiden;
Röslein wehrte sich und stach, half ihr doch kein Weh und Ach; musst' es eben
   leiden.
Röslein, Röslein, Röslein rot, Röslein auf der Heiden.

second stanza

Said the boy, "I'll gather thee, in the heather growing!"
Said the rose, "I'll pierce thee that thou may'st remember me, thus reproof
   bestowing."
Little wild rose, wild rose red, in the heather growing.

third stanza

Thoughtlessly he pulled the rose, in the heather growing;
But her thorns their spears oppose, vainly he laments his woes, with pain his hand
   is glowing.
Little wild rose, wild rose red, in the heather growing.

EXAMPLE 9–12.   Schubert, "Du bist die Ruh" (text by Rückert).

EXAMPLE 9–12. continued.

Treib an - dern Schmerz____ aus__ die__ ser__ Brust!
Chase ev - 'ry pain ____ from__ out__ this__ breast,

voll sei dies Herz____ von dei - ner Lust,____
Calm - ing this heart____ to joy - ful rest,____

von__ dei - ner____ Lust.____
to__ joy - ful____ rest.____

A¹ (Altered)

Dies Au - gen - zelt, von
Let thy pure light My

EXAMPLE 9–12. continued.

hellt, _____   o _ füll' _ es _ ganz, _____
bright, _____   Fill _ thou _ my _ soul, _____

o _ füll' _ es _ ganz! _____
Fill _ thou _ my _ soul! _____

EXAMPLE 9-13. Schubert, "Erlkönig" (text by Goethe).

① Schnell (♩=152)
②

EXAMPLE 9-13. continued.

(Father)

Mein Sohn, was birgst du so bang dein Ge-
My son, what makes thy sweet face grow so

(Son)

sicht? Siehst, Va - ter, du den
white?" "See, fa - ther, 'tis the

Erl - kö - nig nicht? den Er - len-
Erl king in sight! The Erl - king

(Father)

kö - nig mit Kron und Schweif? Mein
stands there with crown and shroud!" My

EXAMPLE 9–13. continued.

nicht, was Er - len - kö - nig mir lei - se ver - spricht?
hear The Erl - king whisper so low in mine ear?"

(Father)

Sei ru - hig, blei - be ru - hig, mein Kind: in dür - ren
"Be tranquil, then be tranquil, my child, 'Mong with - er'd

(Erlkönig)

Blattern säuselt der Wind. „Willst fei - ner— Kna - be, du
leaves the wind blow-eth wild." "Wilt come proud_boy, wilt thou

mit mir gehn? mei - ne Töch - ter sol - len dich war - ten schön; mei - ne
come with me? Where my beau - teous daugh-ter doth wait for thee; With my

etc.

EXAMPLE 9–13. continued.

Töch - ter füh - ren den nächt - li - chen Reihn und wie - gen und tan - zen und
daugh - ter thou'lt join in the dance ev - 'ry night, She'll lull thee with sweet songs to

sin - gen dich ein.   Sie wie - gen und tan - zen und sin - gen dich ein."
give thee de - light,   And lull thee with sweet songs to give — thee de - light."

(Son)

Mein Va - ter, mein Va - ter, und siehst du nicht
My fa - ther, my fa - ther, And can'st thou not

dort Erl - kö - nigs Töch - ter am dü - stern Ort?
trace The Erl - king's daughter in yon dark place?"

decresc.

(Father)

Mein Sohn, mein Sohn, ich seh es ge -
"My son, my son, the form you there

nau,   es schei-nen die al-ten Wei-den so grau.
see   Is on-ly the hol-low grey wil-low tree."

cresc.
ff

(Erlkönig)

Ich
"I

lie-be dich,mich reizt dei-ne schö-ne Ge-stalt,   und bist   du nicht
love thee well, with me thou shalt ride on my course,   And   if   thou'rt un-

pp

(Son)

wil-lig, so brauch ich Ge-walt."   „Mein Va-ter mein
will-ing, I seize thee by force!"   " My fa-ther! My

fff

EXAMPLE 9-13. continued.

er   reicht   den   Hof mit Müh und
He   reach'd   that house with toil and

Recit

Not;   in sei nen Ar-men das Kind   war tot.
dread,   But in his arms,lo! his child lay dead!

Andante

fp   *pp*   *p*   *f*

Other single movement vocal forms.   Choruses, vocal ensembles, and other Romantic single movement vocal forms are somewhat similar to those of the Classical period. Example 9–14 illutrates what might be called modified motet form, including sections in homophonic texture as well as sections in polyphonic texture. Notice that the opening thematic material does return later in the composition, thus creating a rounded or "closed" form.

EXAMPLE 9–14. Brahms, "How Lovely Is Thy Dwelling Place" from *The German Requiem.*

Introduction

a
How

How
p

Orchestra   *Chorus* How

EXAMPLE 9–14. continued.

EXAMPLE 9-14. continued.

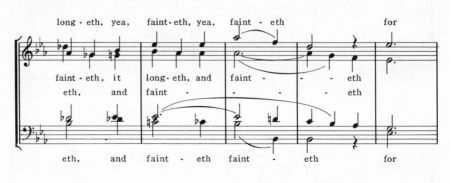

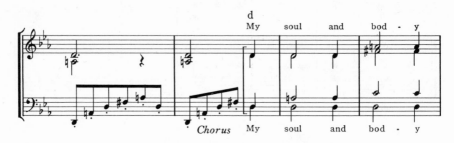

EXAMPLE 9–14. continued.

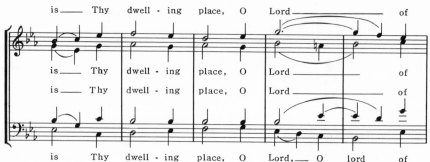

EXAMPLE 9-14. continued.

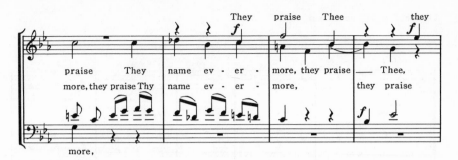

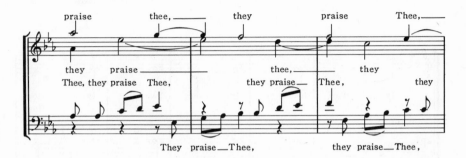

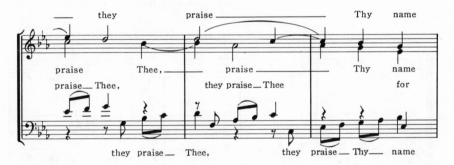

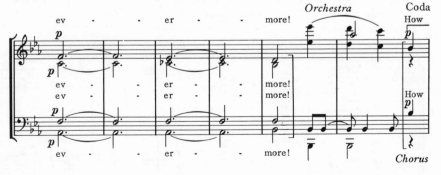

EXAMPLE 9–14. continued.

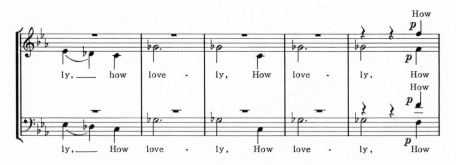

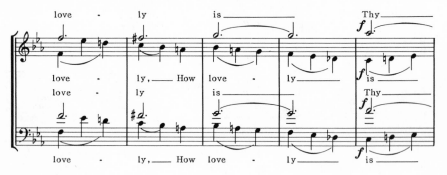

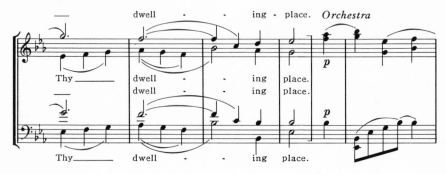

Multi-Movement Vocal Forms

Opera. Opera is not only an extremely important and popular form of the Romantic period, but it is also a highly varied form, representative of several different national styles.

Italian Romantic opera continued the development of the Classical Italian tradition. Plots ranging from the melodrama of *opera seria* to the humor of *opera buffa* are set in "number style," featuring arias, recitatives, ensemble numbers, and orchestral sections. The new musical techniques of the Romantic period allow for greater expressiveness and characterization. The orchestra effectively underscores the dramatic situation. Characters are sometimes identified musically by the use of a "signature theme," that is, a particular melody that is played when they enter a scene or when they are mentioned by another character.

Verdi's *Rigoletto* may be taken as a representative work in this genre. His librettist, Francesco Maria Piave, based the text for this opera upon Victor Hugo's controversial play, *Le Roi s'amuse.* To avoid censorship problems, which could have arisen because of the play's uncomplimentary portrayal of royalty, the plot of the opera was changed from nineteenth-century France to sixteenth-century Mantua. The principal characters are: The Duke of Mantua (tenor); Rigoletto, the court jester (baritone); Gilda, his daughter (soprano); Sparafucile, a hired assasin (bass); Maddalena, his sister (contralto); and Count Monterone, a courtier (bass).

The original title of the opera, *La Maledizione* (The Curse), gives the basic theme of the opera, the curse of a wronged father upon another father. The "curse theme" (a) is the basis of the prelude to the opera.

EXAMPLE 9–15a.

a   The curse theme

The action of the first two acts of the opera may be briefly summarized. The opera opens at a gay party in the Duke's palace. The festivities are interrupted by the entrance of Count Monterone, who accuses the Duke of having ruined his daughter's honor. Rigoletto, who has been assisting the Duke in his amorous adventures, taunts Monterone. Monterone hurls a curse at Rigoletto and leaves. Later, a group of courtiers abduct the young girl, Gilda, whom they believe to be Rigoletto's mistress. They take her to the palace and the Duke seduces her. Rigoletto vows revenge on the courtiers and the Duke.

Act III opens on an unusual stage setting. The left half of the stage is the ground floor of a rustic inn; the right half is a street leading down to the river Mincio. As the curtain opens Sparafucile and Maddalena are seated at a table in the inn, while Rigoletto and Gilda peek into the room from outside through a crack in the wall.

(In the following analysis of Act III, the division of the music into separate pieces is indicated by the original numbering of Verdi's score. In several places listed below as recitative, the orchestra is playing thematic material while the voices have recitative-like passages in strict tempo.)

No. 15. Rigoletto tells Gilda that she will now see how faithless the Duke is. (recitative) The Duke enters and asks for food and lodging. (recitative) He gives his view on the fickleness of women. (aria)

EXAMPLE 9–15b.

No. 16. Maddalena enters and the Duke begins a flirtation with her. (aria)

EXAMPLE 9–15c.

She lightheartedly rebuffs him. Then we hear the four characters expressing their individual thoughts—Gilda laments her lover's faithlessness (d); Maddalena coquettishly parries the Duke's advances (e); the Duke continues to press his flirtation (f); and Rigoletto vows vengeance upon the Duke (g). The characters sing individually, in duos, trios, or (as shown in Example 9–15 d, e, f, g) all together in quartet.

EXAMPLE 9–15 d, e, f, g.

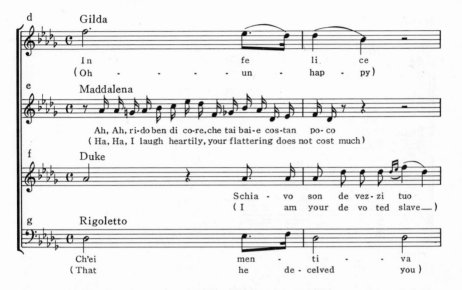

No. 17. Rigoletto instructs Gilda to disguise herself as a boy and flee to Verona. She exits. Sparafucile comes outside and concludes arrangements with Rigoletto for the assassination of the Duke. Rigoletto gives him half of his fee and instructs him to have the Duke's body in a sack when he returns at midnight. (recitative) Rigoletto exits. An approaching storm is heard (h).

EXAMPLE 9–15h.

Sparafucile returns to the inn. The Duke retires to a bedroom on the second floor still voicing his views on the fickleness of women (b). Maddalena implores Sparafucile to spare the Duke's life, but her brother is unwilling to give up the other half of the fee due him for the assassination. (recitative)

No. 18. Gilda returns in boy's clothing. She overhears Sparafucile finally

agree to spare the Duke's life and to kill instead the next person to enter
the inn and substitute this body for that of the Duke. Gilda decides to
sacrifice her life for the Duke. (recitative) Then Gilda implores heaven for
strength (i), as Maddalena and Sparafucile discuss their plan (j and k).
(trio)

EXAMPLE 9–15 i, j, k.

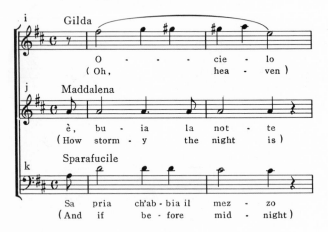

As the storm (h) reaches a climax, Gilda enters the inn and is stabbed by
Sparafucile. The storm gradually subsides. (orchestra interlude)

No. 19. Rigoletto returns and receives from Sparafucile a sack with a
body in it. He gives Sparafucile the rest of the money and goes toward the
river with the sack, gloating over his revenge. (recitative) Just then he
hears the voice of the Duke from the bedroom above. (b)

No. 20. Horrified, Rigoletto opens the sack to discover it contains his
daughter, fatally wounded. Gilda tells him of her sacrifice and promises
to pray for Rigoletto's soul in heaven. (aria and duet)

EXAMPLE 9–15 l.

Gilda dies in Rigoletto's arms. He cries out "the curse" (a) and collapses as the curtain falls.

French grand opera continues the tradition of the Baroque and Classical French opera, with its emphasis on virtuoso singing, spectacular staging and brilliant ballet. It is less passionate in character than its Italian and German counterparts.

French opera comique is similar to German *Singspiel* in that it is written in the national language and includes passages of spoken dialogue. The term *opera comique* does not necessarily imply a humorous plot; the most famous opera in this genre, Bizet's *Carmen,* is a tragedy. In the early part of the Romantic period *opera comique* was differentiated from grand opera by its generally lighter, simpler character; later the two styles merged into one unified style of French opera.

French opera lyrique combines aspects of opera comique and grand opera. It features sentimental plots set to melodious music. *French opera bouffe* has humorous plots set to light music.

German music drama represents an idealistic attempt to fuse music, poetry, drama, and the visual arts into one unified art form or *Gesamtkunstwerk*. In contrast to Italian Romantic opera with its separate numbers, music drama consists of a continuous flow of musical material with no applause points and no distinction between recitative style and aria style. This is often referred to as "unending melody." *Leitmotives,* short musical fragments representing characters, ideas, emotions, or objects, are used as a unifying factor. These are somewhat similar to the "signature themes" of Italian Romantic opera, but are generally shorter, used more extensively, and developed more effectively. The treatment of leitmotives in music drama is often compared to the treatment of themes in a sonata-allegro development section; in both cases it is possible to develop dramatic tension by the transformation, juxtaposition, and combination of the musical material. The expanded orchestra of the Romantic period plays an important role in music drama, sometimes dominating the singers and stage effects through its power and significance. Many of the aspects of the music drama style can be seen in the first act of *Die Meistersinger* (German: The Mastersingers).

Die Meistersinger is set in sixteenth-century Nuremberg. The principal characters are Walther von Stolzing, a young knight (tenor); Hans Sachs, a Mastersinger and shoemaker (bass-baritone); David, his apprentice (tenor); Veit Pogner, a Mastersinger and goldsmith (bass); Eva, his daughter (soprano); Magdalena, her nurse (mezzo-soprano) and Beckmesser, a Mastersinger and the town clerk (bass).

The prelude to the opera introduces the basic theme of the opera, the conflict between the new artistic ideals of the young knight, Walther, and the conservative tradition of the Mastersingers. We hear first the sturdy theme of the Mastersingers.

Die Meistersinger, Act I. Setting by C. M. Cristini. Used by permission.

EXAMPLE 9–16a.

This is followed by a lyric theme associated with Walther.

EXAMPLE 9–16b.

Next, Wagner writes a fanfare-like theme representing the banners of the various guilds.

EXAMPLE 9–16c.

The first part concludes with a broad theme representing traditional art.

EXAMPLE 9–16d.

The transition following is based on a syncopated motive which suggests yearning.

EXAMPLE 9–16e.

The second part of the prelude is devoted to two motives, the first signifying love.

EXAMPLE 9–16f.

The second indicates passion.

EXAMPLE 9–16g.

This leads to the third part of the prelude which features a motive representing the apprentices. This motive is the same as the Mastersinger's except that the note values are half as long (diminution).

EXAMPLE 9–16h.

This is interrupted by a rhythmic variation of the passion motive (g) and by a new motive representing joy.

EXAMPLE 9–16i.

All three motives appear in various combinations and lead to a climax in which the Mastersinger theme is heard (a).

In the concluding section of the prelude the Mastersingers' motive, the banner motive in diminution, and the motive of Walther's love are presented simultaneously.

EXAMPLE 9–16j.

The union of these themes in the music can be taken to represent the reconciliation of these elements in the drama. The coda of the prelude, based on the joy motive (i) leads without pause to the opening scene.

The curtain opens on a church interior. The congregation is singing the final stanza of a chorale.

EXAMPLE 9–16k.

Since   to   thee___ the   Sav _____ ior   came

Walther and Eva exchange loving glances, represented in the orchestra by the motives of Walther (b), love (f), and passion (g). The congregation leaves and Walther speaks to Eva. She sends her nurse, Magdalena, away on the pretext of finding her kerchief. Walther asks if Eva is married. Magdalena returns to urge her to leave the church. A motive representing David is heard.

EXAMPLE 9–161.

The young apprentice himself appears to tell them of the preparations that are being made for the Mastersinger song trial. Walther is seeking admission to the Mastersinger guild so that he can compete in the contest of song and win the hand of Eva. Eva and Magdalena leave as Walther passionately declares his love for Eva and his determination to win the contest.

Eventually, with the aid of the kindly Hans Sachs, and despite the machinations of the jealous Beckmesser, Walther does win the contest and the hand of Eva. Musical highlights of the rest of the opera include Walther's Prize Song, Sachs' monologue, "Wahn, Wahn," ("Mad, Mad") and the festive final scene.

Choral music. Though religious choral music did not occupy the important position in Romantic music that it did in Baroque music, there were nevertheless many outstanding oratorios, masses, and requiems written in the Romantic period. In addition, some composers such as Mahler, following the example set by Beethoven's *Ninth Symphony,* introduced chorus or solo voice into one or more movements of their symphonies.

Song cycles. A song cycle, or *Liederkreis,* is a set of songs written by one composer and based usually on texts by one poet. Often the texts are based on a central theme, and occasionally the music is unified by repetition of the same music at significant points in the cycle. Schubert's *Die Winterreise* (The Winter Journey) and Schumann's *Dichterliebe* (Poet's Love) are excellent examples of this form.

Representative Composers of the Romantic Period

Niccolò Paganini (Italian, 1782–1840). Paganini is best known as a violinist of almost legendary ability and as a composer of virtuoso works for the violin.

Carl Maria von Weber (German, 1786–1826). Weber inaugurated German Romantic opera with such works as *Der Freischütz* (The Free Shooter), *Euryanthe,* and *Oberon.*

Gioacchino Rossini (Italian, 1792–1868). Rossini's operas, including *Il Barbiere di Siviglia* (The Barber of Seville), *L'Italiana in Algeri* (The Italian in Algiers), and *Semiramide* are among the most significant examples of the early Italian Romantic opera. Other composers of this school include Gaetano Donizetti (1797–1848) and Vicenzo Bellini (1801–1835).

Franz Peter Schubert (Austrian, 1797–1828). Like Beethoven, Schubert is a transitional composer whose works have both Classical and Romantic characteristics. His Classical traits are manifest in his general adherence to traditional abstract forms in his instrumental works. His Romantic characteristics are evident in his songs, which masterfully capture the essential mood of the text in the melodic line and in the accompaniment. Even his instrumental works seem to be vocally oriented with broad lyric lines, rather than short, cogent motives. Schubert's music is predominantly homophonic in texture, with interesting innovations in harmonic progressions and modulations.

Of his nine symphonies, the best known and most frequently performed are:

Symphony No. 8 in B Minor (Unfinished)	Only two of the traditional four movements were completed.
Symphony No. 9 in C Major (Great)	Schumann called this the "symphony of heavenly length."

His chamber music comprises 22 piano sonatas and over 30 other works including:

Quartet in D Minor (Death and the Maiden)	The second movement is a set of variations on Schubert's song of the same name.
Quintet in A Major for Piano Violin, Viola, Cello and Bass (Trout)	The fourth movement is a set of variations on Schubert's song of this name.

Schubert wrote over 600 songs for voice and piano including "Der Erlkönig" (The Erl King), "Der Wanderer" ("The Wanderer"), "Ave Maria," "Standchen" ("Serenade"), and "Heidenröslein." His song cycles include "Die Schöne Müllerin" ("The Beautiful Miller") and "Die Winterreise" ("The Winter Journey"). He also wrote operas, operettas, melodramas, incidental music to dramas, and various religious choral works.

Hector Berlioz (French, 1803–1869). Berlioz himself describes his own music in the following passage from his memoirs: "The prevailing characteristics of my music are passionate expression, intense order, rhythmical animation, and unexpected turns."

In addition to this, we may point to Berlioz's contributions to orchestration both in his works, which often call for greatly expanded instrumentation and special effects, and in his treatise on orchestration, which remained a standard text for composers and students for over 100 years. He also is important for his formal innovations, especially the use of the idée fixe, a theme with programmatic connotations that recurs in various forms throughout the movements of a composition. Among his most famous works are:

Symphonic Fantastique	See pp. 287–289.
Harold in Italy	A program symphony based on Byron's *Childe Harold*, featuring a prominent solo viola part, originally written for Paganini.
Roman Carnival Overture	Based on themes from his opera *Benvenuto Cellini*.
Romeo and Juliet	A "dramatic symphony" for orchestra, chorus, and soloists, based on poetic commentary on the Shakespeare play.
Damnation of Faust	A dramatic cantata for orchestra, chorus, and soloists, with staging and ballet, based on scenes from Goethe's *Faust*. Best known from concert performances of such excerpts as the "Rakoczy March," the "Dance of the Sylphs," and the "Minuet of the Will-of-the Wisps."

Felix Mendelssohn (German, 1809–1847). Mendelssohn's contributions to the world of music include not only his many compositions, but also his work as a conductor, teacher, and performer. He is perhaps best known for his light, fanciful scherzo passages with soft, fast staccato string passages and emphasis on the lighter woodwind instruments, and his lyric, almost sentimental melodies. Although his music does show a wider gamut of expression than this, it tends in general toward Classical balance and restraint rather than toward Romantic exuberance and passion. His view on meaning in music is indicated in this passage:

> There is so much talk about music, and yet so little is said. For my part, I believe that words do not suffice for such a purpose, and if I found they did suffice I would finally have nothing more to do with music. People often complain that music is too ambiguous, that what they should be thinking as they hear it is unclear, whereas everyone understands words. With me it is exactly the reverse, and not only with regard to an entire speech, but also with individual words. These, too, seem to me so ambiguous, so vague, so easily misunderstood in comparison to genuine music which fills the soul with a thousand things better than words. The thoughts which are expressed to me by music that I love are not too indefinite to be put into words, but on the contrary, too definite.[1]

He wrote five symphonies and several concert overtures including:

Symphony No. 3 in A Minor, Op. 56 (Scotch)	Inspired by Mendelssohn's visit to Scotland. Second movement has "scotch snap" rhythms.

[1] Felix Mendelssohn: *Letters*, Gisella Selden-Goth, ed. (New York: Pantheon Books, A Division of Random House, Inc., 1945), p. 313. Reprinted by permission.

Symphony No. 4 in A Major, Op. 90 *(Italian)*	Inspired by Mendelssohn's visit to Italy. Last movement is an Italian dance, the Saltarello.
Symphony No. 5 in D Minor, Op. 107 *(Reformation)*	Composed for the celebration of the establishment of the German Reformed (Protestant) Church. The last movement contains references to the Dresden Amen, representing Catholicism, and the Lutheran chorale, "A Mighty Fortress Is Our God," representing Protestantism.
Hebrides (or *Fingal's Cave*), *Overture*	Inspired by his visit to Scotland.
Overture to Calm Sea and Prosperous Voyage	Inspired by two poems of Goethe.
Overture and Incidental Music to A Midsummernight's Dream	Written for the Shakespeare play. The music includes a delightful scherzo and the famous wedding march, used as the recessional at many marriage ceremonies.

Frédéric Chopin (Polish, 1810–1849). The following quotations, one by a nineteenth-century composer and one by a twentieth-century composer, can give us some understanding of Chopin as a musical innovator and a Romantic nationalist.

> To him we owe the extension of chords, broken as well as unbroken, and ornamented chord figures, chromatic and enharmonic progressions of which his works offer such astounding examples; little groups of passing tones which are scattered over the melodic figure like brightly shimmering dewdrops....He discovered those remarkable harmonic progressions by means of which he impressed a serious character on pieces of music whose unimpressive themes did not seem to *demand* profound significance....He belonged to those whose charm unfolds especially when they avoid the beaten path.[2]

> Chopin is generally considered the first of the nationalist composers and he certainly was strongly influenced by the patriotic aspirations of the oppressed country. We must, however, distinguish between the Parisian Chopin of the Waltzes and Nocturnes and the national Chopin of the Mazurkas, Polonaises and Polish songs. But in reality he was no more national than Schumann or Beethoven or Mozart; his inspiration simply came from a new source. His period was the heyday of the romantic movement when everything had to be exotic....when Chopin appeared on the scene with his Polish rhythms and cadences, he was hailed as the first nationalist, though he was only building on his own foundations just as Beethoven and Mozart had built on theirs.[3]

Except for two concertos for piano and orchestra, a cello sonata, and some songs, all of Chopin's works were written for piano solo and were intended for his own performances as one of the leading nineteenth-century piano virtuosos. They include 27 etudes, 56 mazurkas, 12 polonaises, 14 waltzes, 24 preludes, and 19 nocturnes, among which the following are some

---

[2] Franz Liszt, "Friederich Chopin" in Arthur Holde, *Unpublished Letters by Beethoven, Liszt, and Brahms, Musical Quarterly* **XXXII** (1946), 283. Reprinted by permission.

[3] Ralph Vaughan-Williams, *National Music* (London: Oxford University Press, 1934), p. 98. Reprinted by permission.

of the best known. The titles refer more to the general mood of the work than to any specific program.

Etude in C Minor, Op. 10, No. 12 (Revolutionary)
Prelude in D-flat, Op. 28, No. 15 (Raindrop)
Polonaise in A-flat Major, Op. 53 (Military)

Robert Schumann (German, 1810–1856). German Romanticism is probably nowhere better epitomized than in the life and music of Robert Schumann. His early years were filled with activity as a composer, performer, and critic; his last years were spent in a mental institution, suffering from what present-day psychiatry would diagnose as manic-depressive psychosis, an illness characterized by emotional fluctuations from extreme elation to suicidal depression. In his own writings on music, which so eloquently champion and chronicle the music of the Romantic period, Schumann gives vivid evidence of a predisposition toward this illness, for he often writes under two pseudonyms: Florestan, characterized by exuberance and confidence, and Eusebius, characterized by submission and doubt.

These opposing characteristics in his life are mirrored in his music, which often contrasts strong themes, diatonic harmony and vigorous persistent rhythms against more yielding themes, chromatic harmonies, and subtle irregular rhythms. Schumann's piano writing is highly idiomatic and his songs are well written for the voice. His orchestral writing, however, is often criticized as being awkward and unimaginative.

His views on programmatic titles are given in the following excerpt:

> Titles for pieces of music, since they again have come into favor in our day, have been censured here and there, and it has been said that "good music needs no sign-post." Certainly not, but neither does a title rob it of its value; and the composer, in adding one, at least prevents a complete misunderstanding of the character of his music. If the poet is licensed to explain the whole meaning of his poem by its title, why may not the composer do likewise? What is important is that such a verbal heading should be significant and apt. It may be considered the test of the general level of the composer's education.[4]

Schumann's orchestral works include:

Symphony No. 1 in B-flat Major, Op. 38 *(Spring)*	Nickname refers to its gentle, pastoral character.
Symphony No. 2 in C Major, Op. 61	The opening motive of the first movement reappears in the scherzo and the finale.
Symphony No, 3 in E-flat Major, Op. 97 *(Rhenish)*	Inspired by a journey on the Rhine.
Symphony No. 4 in D Minor, Op. 120	Has aspects of cyclic form in the use of several motives throughout various movements of the symphony.

[4] Robert Schumann, *On Music and Musicians,* ed. Konrad Wolff, trans. Paul Rosenfeld (New York: Pantheon Books, A Division of Random House, Inc., 1946), p. 72. Reprinted by permission.

Concerto for Piano and Orchestra in A Minor, Op. 54	See p. 290.

He wrote many compositions for piano including:

Abegg Variations, Op. 1	Based on a musical theme derived from the letters of the name of his friend, Meta Abegg.
Papillons, Op. 2 *(Butterflies)*	Twelve character pieces depicting "butterflys of different colors."
Carnaval, Op. 9	See pp. 291–292.
Kinderscenen, Op. 15 *(Scenes of Childhood)*	A set of simple character pieces, including the famous "Träumerei" ("Reverie").
Kreisleriana, Op. 16	A set of character pieces based on a character created by E.T.A. Hoffmann.
Faschingsschwank aus Wien, Op. 26 *(Carnival Prank from Vienna)*	A set of character pieces recalling Schumann's visit to the Vienna Carnival.

Of his many vocal works the best known are such song cycles as *Dichterliebe (Poet's Love)* and *Frauenliebe und Leben (Woman's Love and Life).* He wrote 17 chamber music compositions for various combinations, including the *Quintet for Piano and String Quartet in E-flat Major,* Op. 44, the first significant composition for this medium.

Franz Liszt (Hungarian, 1811–1886). Liszt was one of the most typical and influential composers of the Romantic period. His colorful and eventful life began with his triumphs as a child prodigy, continued through liasons with two of the most fascinating women of the century, and ended with his death in the midst of a Wagner Festival at Bayreuth. He brought piano performance to the virtuoso level that Paganini had achieved with violin playing, established the practice of playing from memory, and made the solo recital an important means of musical presentation. His influence as a teacher extended not only to his many pupils, but through them to countless other pupils and "grandpupils," including some of the leading present-day performers.

As a composer, Liszt inaugurated the *tone poem* or *symphonic poem* (see p. 282). One of the unique features of his works in this form is the technique of *transformation of themes* in which a given theme is transformed into other themes with different programmatic connotations. Effective use of the enlarged Romantic orchestra and unusual harmonic progression (often by thirds) are other characteristics of his music.

His piano music can usually be identified by fast bravura scale and arpeggio passages or lyric, almost sentimental melodic passages. In all his music Liszt tends more toward free rhapsodic forms than toward strict repetition patterns.

Among Liszt's best known orchestral works are:

Faust Symphony	A program symphony based on Goethe's play.
Dante Symphony	A program symphony based on Dante's *Divina Commedia.*

Les Préludes   Symphonic poem based on Lamartine's poem.

Mazeppa   Symphonic poem based on Victor Hugo's poem.

He wrote 2 piano concertos, 20 Hungarian Rhapsodies, *Todtentanz* (variations on the *Dies Irae*), and many other works for piano and orchestra. Among his best known compositions for solo piano are: the *Mephisto Waltz;* three *Valse Oubliées (Forgotten Waltzes);* the *Sonata in B Minor;* and the *Transcendental Etudes.*

In addition he wrote many songs, choral compositions, and piano transcriptions or arrangements of works by other composers.

Richard Wagner (German, 1813–1883). Wagner's own music drama *Die Meistersinger* (pp. 321–325) gives probably the most eloquent statement of his role as an artist and of his philosophy as a man. Just as Walther struggled against the rigid rules and reactionary outlook of the Meistersinger to win recognition and laurels, so too Wagner struggled against the Philistinism and timidity of the nineteenth-century public to gain understanding and appreciation of his music. But Walther is not a complete portrait of Wagner. Hans Sachs, one of the most magnificently drawn characters in all opera, comes closer to representing Wagner's deeper *Weltanschauung,* or world view. The character of Beckmesser is an obvious and quite malicious caricature of Wagner's chief critic, Hanslick, who, as an ardent champion of the absolutist point of view in music, had little sympathy for Wagner's highly referential music.

Although he wrote several orchestral works, choral works, songs, and piano compositions, Wagner's chief contributions to music are his operas and music-dramas. Some of the aspects of Wagner's musical style have already been discussed under music drama (see p. 321), including the leitmotive technique, the idea of "unending melody," and the important role assigned to the enlarged orchestra.

One of the most striking characteristics of Wagner's music is the textural element. Wagner enlarged the harmonic pallette, both in terms of chord structure and chord progression, using colorful sonorities and unusual progressions. His extensive use of chromaticism went to the very limits of traditional major-minor tonality and, in some cases, even beyond these limits to a type of writing that prefigured the atonal and dodecaphonic techniques of the twentieth century. The richness of the harmonic and melodic elements in Wagner's music, together with his striking orchestral effects, causes many listeners to overlook another salient aspect of Wagner's style—his skill in polyphonic writing. However, polyphony was never an end in itself for Wagner, but more a means of expressing the conflicts and congruences of a dramatic situation.

Wagner's orchestration features frequent passages for *divisi strings,* expressive use of the brass section (he even had special instruments, the *Wagner Tuben* designed for use in *Der Ring des Nibelungen*), interesting doublings or combinations of instruments, and sensitive selection of orchestral timbres to bring out dramatic or emotional effects. The powerful Wagnerian orchestra could easily drown out the singers on stage. This problem was ingeniously solved in Wagner's *Festspielhaus* (German: Festival Hall) at Bayreuth by having the orchestra pit extended under the stage, thereby softening the sound of the orchestra.

Wagner wrote extensively on his ideas about musical theatre; the following quotation is from his book *Opera and Drama* (1851):

> I have made it the goal of this book to prove that by the collaboration of precisely *our* music with dramatic poetry a heretofore undreamt significance not only can, but *must* be given to drama: to reach that goal, I must begin with a complete exposure of the incredible error in which those are involved who believe they may await the higher fashioning of drama from the essence of our *modern opera,* i.e., from the placing of poetry in a contra-minded position toward music.

With the exception of two early works, *Die Feen (The Fairies)* and *Das Liebesverbot (The Forbidding of Love),* all of Wagner's operas and music dramas hold a significant place in the standard repertoire, both in terms of stage performance and concert performances of excerpts. For all of these works, Wagner wrote his own libretti.

Rienzi (1838–1840). Based on Bulwer-Lytton's novel and showing influence of French grand opera and Italian *opera seria.*

Der Fliegende Holländer (The Flying Dutchman) (1843). An opera in the German Romantic opera tradition, based on the legend of the man condemned to roam the seas until the love of a woman redeems him.

Tannhäuser (1845). A German Romantic opera based on the medieval legend of the Minnesinger, Tannhäuser. The basic theme of the opera is the conflict between sensuous love represented by the goddess Venus, and virtuous love represented by the mortal Elisabeth. The central episode of the opera is the contest of song at Wartburg. The best known musical excerpts include the overture and the "Pilgrim's Chorus."

Lohengrin (1848). Heathen magic and Christian mysticism both figure in this Romantic opera set in the tenth century. It is Wagner's first work in which "unending melody" replaces separate "numbers." Musical highlights include the preludes to each of the three acts, and the famous bridal march, used in present-day wedding ceremonies as a processional.

Der Ring des Nibelungen (The Ring of the Nibelungs) (1853–1874). A cycle of four music dramas based on medieval German and Scandinavian legends, including the following individual music dramas: *Das Rheingold; Die Walküre; Siegfried; Götterdammerung (Twilight of the Gods).*

No brief statement could possibly capture the essence of this gigantic musico-dramatic conception. Listeners can probably approach it best by first hearing such famous excerpts as "The Ride of the Walküre" or "Brunnhilde's Immolation Scene," which are frequently performed in concert, and then by studying the plot itself, together with such commentaries as those of George Bernard Shaw and Ernest Newman. The complete cycle takes four full evenings to present and is rarely given in its entirely, except at Bayreuth.

Tristan und Isolde (1859). Based on a Celtic legend, this music drama is an eloquent expression of passionate love.

Die Meistersinger von Nürnberg (1867). See pp. 321–325.

Parsifal (1882). As Tristan is a hymn to passionate love, this last work of Wagner, based on medieval legends, is a hymn to the power of redeeming love, purity, and religious faith.

Giuseppe Verdi (Italian, 1813–1901). Verdi was born in the same year as Wagner and, like him, devoted most of his creative life to the composition of works for the musical theater. Unlike Wagner, Verdi did not strike out in revolutionary new paths, but instead brought the tradition of Italian opera to its highest peak of development. His operas, except for parts of *Otello* and *Falstaff*, maintain the "number" form of division into set pieces. In Wagnerian music dramas, the orchestra plays the dominant role; in Verdi's operas, the vocal line is the most important feature, with the orchestra used mostly as accompaniment. However, even in an accompanying role, the orchestra in Verdi's operas can masterfully suggest the dramatic situation and emotional mood. Verdi's musical language is more traditional and conservative than Wagner's; but when the dramatic situation demands it, he writes dissonant harmonies, chromatic melodic lines, and unusual orchestral effects with consummate skill.

Verdi once said "I would be willing to set even a newspaper or a letter, etc., to music, but in the theater the public will stand for anything except boredom." Actually he was very careful about the selection and setting of his libretti and was fortunate to have librettists like Piave and Boito who provided ideal vehicles for his music. Among his 27 operas the following are the most frequently performed:

Rigoletto (1851). See pp. 317–321.

Il Trovatore (1853). Based on a Spanish play and set in fifteenth-century Spain, this tragic opera centers on the love triangle of Manrico, a young troubadour, Countess Leonora, and Count di Luna. The best known excerpt from the opera is the "Anvil Chorus."

La Traviata (1853). Based on Dumas' play *La Dame Aux Camelias,* this opera is set in the Paris of 1850 and is one of the earliest examples of an opera plot based on contemporary life. The central figures are the courtesan Violetta, the young student Alfredo, who loves Violetta and tries to lead her away from her life of pleasure, and Alfredo's father, the elder Germont, who causes Violetta to forsake Alfredo. In one of opera's most famous death scenes, Alfredo and Violetta are reunited in love. Musical highlights include Violetta's aria "Sempre libera" ("Always Free") and the elder Germont's aria "Di provenza il mar" ("A Province by the Sea").

Aida (1871). This spectacular grand opera, written for the dedication of the Suez Canal and set in ancient Egypt, includes such musical highlights as the atmospheric prelude to the first act, the "Triumphal March," Radames' aria, "Celeste Aida" (Heavenly Aida"), and the closing tomb scene.

Luisa Miller (1849) and *Don Carlos* (1867). These are both based on plays by Schiller.

Macbeth (1847), *Otello* (1886), and *Falstaff* (1893). All three are based on plays by Shakespeare. The latter two works, written near the close of Verdi's life, are usually regarded as his greatest operas. They show some influence of Wagnerian techniques but, more than this, they show the fullest development of Verdi's own musical style.

Of Verdi's works outside the field of opera, the best known are the *Requiem, Four Sacred Pieces for Chorus and Orchestra,* and the *String Quartet in E minor.*

Charles Gounod (French, 1818–1893). Of Gounod's 12 operas, *Faust* and *Romeo and Juliet* are the most frequently performed. He also wrote choral music, orchestral, and piano works.

Jacques Offenbach (French, 1819–1880). Offenbach wrote over 90 operettas including such popular works as *Orpheus in the Underworld, The Beautiful Helen,* and *La Perichole.* His opera comique, *The Tales of Hoffman,* is frequently performed.

César Franck (French, 1822–1890). Franck is noted primarily for his *Symphony in D Minor, Symphonic Variations for Piano and Orchestra,* and other works for piano, organ, and various chamber music combinations. His vocal works include the oratorio *Les Beatitudes.* Cyclic form and unusual harmonic progression are two important features of his music.

Bedřich Smetana (Czech, 1824–1884). Czech nationalism is apparent in such works as his opera *The Bartered Bride,* his cycle of 6 symphonic poems entitled *My Fatherland* (including the well-known *The Moldau*), and his *Quartet in E Minor (From My Life).*

Anton Bruckner (Austrian, 1824–1896). Bruckner is best known for the massive dimensions of his 9 symphonies and his religious works for chorus and orchestra.

Johannes Brahms (German, 1833–1897). Though written in the middle of the Romantic period, the music of Brahms represents a combination of Classical and Romantic traits. It is Classical in its emphasis on traditional forms and its avoidance of programmatic content; it is Romantic in its emphasis on subjective expression and its usage of chromatic melodic and harmonic materials.

Brahms' works, in general, exhibit a high degree of stylistic unity and may usually be recognized by certain characteristic features. Two features, which probably relate to his study of earlier music, are his masterful skill in polyphonic writing and his occasional usage of melodic and harmonic materials based on the church modes. Brahms' rhythms are often complex and striking, featuring such devices as two against three, augmentation, diminution, and unusual syncopations. His melodies are often based on the intervals of thirds and sixths. His harmonic usage ranges from simple triads to extended tertian structures. His orchestration is sometimes criticized as being too full and massive; however, as with all good orchestration, it is uniquely suited to the expression of his musical ideas. Instead of the graceful minuet of Mozart, the boisterous scherzo of Beethoven, or the elfin scherzo of Mendelssohn, Brahms often writes a type of movement called the *intermezzo,* which is usually in duple meter and moderate tempo and has a uniquely personal character and charm. The use of a basic motive or motto in various forms is also a characteristic of many of his compositions. (See p. 280).

Most of his orchestral works remain in the standard repertoire.

Symphony No. 1 in C Minor, Op. 68	Sometimes called the "Tenth" Symphony, indicating that it is a worthy successor to Beethoven's nine symphonies.
Symphony No. 2 in D Major, Op. 73	See pp. 280–282.
Symphony No. 3 in F Major, Op. 90	First movement is unified through the use of basic motive *(F-A-flat-f).*
Symphony No. 4 in E Minor, Op 98	The last movement is cast in the form of a *chaconne.*
Serenade in D Major, Op. 11	
Serenade in A Major, Op. 16	Written for small orchestra.
Variations on a Theme of Haydn, Op. 56a	Based on the "St. Anthony Chorale" which appears in Haydn's *Feldmusik in B-flat Major*
Academic Festival Overture, Op. 80	Written for the University of Breslau in gratitude for the honorary doctorate conferred upon Brahms, the work is based on several German student songs.
Tragic Overture, Op. 81	Written at the same time as Op. 80, but in strong contrast to its mood.
Hungarian Dances	Arranged by Brahms from the original piano works.

He wrote four works for solo instruments and orchestra: *Concerto No. 1 in D Minor for Piano and Orchestra,* Op. 15; *Concerto No. 2 in B-flat Major for Piano and Orchestra,* Op. 83; *Concerto in D Major for Violin and Orchestra,* Op. 77; and *Double Concerto for Violin, Cello, and Orchestra,* Op. 102.

Among Brahms' works for voices and orchestra the best known are the *Deutsches Requiem (German Requiem),* the *Schicksalslied (Song of Destiny),* and the *Alto Rhapsody.* His piano works include sonatas, rhapsodies, intermezzos, variations, ballades, and fantasies. His chamber music includes 24 works for various combinations. His songs range from the naive simplicity and humor of *Vergebliches Ständchen* (Serenade in Vain) to the deep solemnity of the *Vier Ernste Gesänge* (Four Serious Songs).

Georges Bizet (French, 1838–1875). Bizet is known for his opera comique *Carmen* and his incidental music to *L'Arlesienne. Carmen,* one of the most popular of all operas, is based on a play by Mérimée and includes such well-known excerpts as the "Toreador Song," the "Habenera," and the "Seguidilla."

Modest Mussorgsky (Russian, 1839–1881). Mussorgsky was a member of the so-called "Russian Five," a group of composers including Cui, Balakirev, Borodin, and Rimsky-Korsakov, who sought to incorporate Russian nationalistic traits in their music. Mussorgsky is best known for his opera, *Boris Godunov,* the piano pieces, *Pictures at an Exhibition* (later orchestrated by Ravel and others), and the orchestral piece, *A Night on Bald Mountain.*

Peter Ilyitch Tchaikowsky (Russian, 1840–1893). Though marked by some Russian characteristics, Tchaikowsky's music is more cosmopolitan than that of the "Russian Five." Heightened emotional expression, ranging from despair to exaltation and bordering at times on sentimentality, is usually cited as a dominant characteristic of Tchaikowsky's music. In view of this, it is interesting to note what the composer himself had to say about the translation of emotions into music:

> During the actual time of creative activity, complete quiet is absolutely necessary to the artist. In this sense every work of art, even a musical composition, is objective. Those who imagine that a creative artist can—through the medium of his art—express his feelings at the moment when he is moved, make the greatest mistake. Emotions—sad and joyful—can only be expressed retrospectively, so to speak. Without any special reason for rejoicing, I may be moved by the most cheerful creative mood, and vice versa, a work composed in the happiest surroundings may be touched with dark and gloomy colors.[5]

One of the most obvious features of Tchaikowsky's music is the extended sequence, used effectively for heightened emotional effect. Other features of his music are the essentially homophonic texture, the skillful use of the contrasting colors of orchestral sections, and the idiomatic, virtuoso writing for solo instruments.

Of his orchestral works, the best known are:

Symphony No. 4 in F Minor, Op. 36 (Fate)	A cyclic, quasi-programmatic symphony, unified by recurrences of the "fate" motive, first stated in the introduction.
Symphony No. 5 in E Minor, Op. 64	Unusual for its cyclic form and its use of a waltz for the third movement. The slow movement horn solo is one of Tchaikowsky's best known themes.

---

[5] Peter Ilyitch Tchaikovsky, "Letter to Mme. von Meck (Kamenka, June 24 (July 6) 1878), in Modeste Tchaikovsky, *The Life and Letters of Peter Ilyich Tchaikovsky,* trans. Rosa Newmarch (New York: Dodd, Mead & Company, 1905), p. 306. Reprinted by permission.

Symphony No. 6 in B Minor, Op. 74 (Pathétique)	So named because of its heightened emotional character. It begins and ends with slow movements. The middle movements are a dance-like, quintuple-meter movement, and a scherzo, which ranges from the mysterious to the martial in character.
Festival Overture (1812)	A bombastic work, including even the sound of a military cannon, written in celebration of the Seventieth Anniversary of Napoleon's Retreat from Moscow.
Fantasy Overture: Romeo and Juliet	A symphonic poem in sonata-allegro form based on elements of the Shakespeare play.
Concerto No. 1 in B-flat Minor for Piano and Orchestra, Op. 23 *Concerto for Violin and Orchestra, Op. 35*	Both of these concertos are among the most frequenty performed works in the repertoire.

Of Tchaikowsky's operas, only *Eugen Onegin* and *Pique Dame* remain in the standard repertoire. His ballets *Swan Lake, The Sleeping Beauty,* and *The Nutcracker* are frequently performed as stage works or as suites based on excerpts from the ballets. He also wrote many works for piano, chorus, chamber music combinations, and voice and piano.

Antonin Dvořák (Czech, 1841–1904). Dvořák was a Bohemian or Czech nationalist composer whose music shows influences of Brahms and Wagner. He spent some time as artistic director of the National Conservatory in New York, and in 1895 in *Harper's Magazine* he wrote the following description of American music during that period.

> The great American republic alone, in its national government as well as in the several governments of the States, suffers art and music to go without encouragement. Trades and commerce are protected, funds are voted away for the unemployed, schools and colleges are endowed, but music must go unaided, and be content if she can get the support of a few private individuals.

Among his best known works are:

Symphony No. 5 in E Minor, Op. 95 (from the New World).	The name refers to the fact that it was written during Dvořák's sojourn in America. It has references to Negro spirituals and American Indian tunes, but the over-all character of the work is more Bohemian than American. In modern editions it is sometimes listed as Symphony No. 9.
Concerto in B Minor for Cello and Orchestra, Op. 104	One of the most brilliant and frequently performed works in the repertoire.
String Quartet in F Major, Op. 96 (American)	So-called because of its usage of American folk melodies.

Edvard Grieg (Norwegian, 1843–1907). Grieg's music shows a combination of German Romantic techniques applied to Norwegian musical and dramatic themes. His best known works are the *Concerto in*

A Minor for Piano and Orchestra and the incidental music to Ibsen's play, *Peer Gynt.*

Nicolai Rimsky-Korsakov (Russian, 1844–1908). A member of the "Russian Five," Rimsky-Korsakov is recognized for his brilliant orchestration, both in his own compositions and in his orchestration of other composer's works. The suite *Scheherezade,* the tone-poem *Sadko,* and the opera *Le Coq d'Or (The Golden Cockerel)* are among his best known works.

Giacomo Puccini (Italian, 1858–1924). Puccini was the leader of the so-called *verismo* school of Italian opera, which sought to bring more realism to opera by using plots and characters from everyday life instead of from mythology and history, and by using continuous naturalistic recitative style rather than the number style of earlier Italian opera. The following are among his best known operas:

La Bohème (1896). Based on Murger's novel, and set in Paris around 1840, the opera is based on the humorous adventures, romantic liaisons, and poignant misfortunes of a group of young artists. It is not divided into traditional arias; however, certain excerpts, such as Mimi's "Mi chiamano Mimi" (They Call Me Mimi), Musetta's "Waltz Song," and Rudolfo's "Che gelida manina" ("Your Tiny Hand Is Frozen"), have gained special popularity.

Tosca (1900). Based on Sardou's drama and set in Rome in 1800, the plot, with its political intrigue, romantic love, and religious panoply, provided Puccini with opportunity for a broad range of effective music from Tosca's "Vissi d'arte" ("Love and Music") to Cavarodossi's "E lucevan le stelle" ("When the Stars Were Brightly Shining").

Madame Butterfly (1904). Based on the love of a Japanese girl and an American naval lieutenant, the opera ends with the tragic suicide of the Japanese girl when she learns that the lieutenant has forsaken her for his American wife. The most performed excerpt from the opera is "Un bel di" ("One Fine Day").

Hugo Wolf (German, 1860–1903). Wolf is known for his 300 songs, which are marked by extraordinary fidelity to the mood and meaning of the poetic text. He also wrote an opera, *Corregidor,* and some instrumental works.

Gustav Mahler (Austrian, 1860–1911). Mahler, the last great representative of Viennese Romanticism, wrote nine symphonies and left sketches for a tenth symphony, from which several performing versions have been reconstructed. His *Symphony No. 8 in E-flat Major* is called the *Symphony of a Thousand* because of the large instrumental and choral forces it requires. Other works for voices and orchestra are *Das Lied von der Erde (Song of the Earth), Des Knaben Wunderhorn (The Youth's Magic Horn), Das klagende Lied (The Sorrowful Song),* and *Lieder eines fahrenden Gesellen (Songs of a Wayfarer).*

chapter 10

The Contemporary Period

The tendency toward stylistic disunity reaches a high point in the music of the Contemporary period. It is impossible to label any one particular style as *the* Contemporary style; instead we have an incredibly wide range of styles and schools, from extreme conservativism to radical experimentalism. Some of the most significant schools are listed here.

Schools of Contemporary Music

Late Romanticism or Post-Romanticism. Many composers of this school reflect the powerful influence of Wagner, especially in terms of extensive melodic and harmonic chromaticism, enlarged orchestral resources, effective developmental treatment, and intense subjectivity.

Impressionism. Impressionism represents a predominantly French reaction against German Romanticism. The term Impressionism, first used in painting and poetry and then applied to music, denotes a type of art which seeks to evoke the evanescent essense of sensuous impressions rather than to record the reality of ethical expression or intellectual experience. Impressionist music is characterized by delicacy, subtlety, and vagueness achieved through usage of such devices as whole-tone, pentatonic, and other unusual scales; extended tertian and non-tertian chords; and parallel harmonic progressions. A unique timbre is sometimes achieved through use of divisi, muted strings, muted brass, light woodwinds, and delicate percussion effects.

Neo-Classicism or Neo-Baroque. In reaction to both late Romanticism and Impressionism, some composers turn to the musical thought of earlier periods for inspiration and orientation. In part, this leads to the adaptation of diatonic melodies and harmonies, clear texture and orchestration, and regular rhythms and forms. More significantly, it leads to a renewed emphasis on objectivity and craftsmanship rather than subjectivity and experimentation. Although the term *neo-Classic* is usually used to describe this movement, the term *neo-Baroque* would be more accurate, for most composers writing in this style use the Baroque rather than the Classical period as a source and ideal.

Expressionism. A counter-reaction to French Impressionist tendencies, Expressionism can be thought of as a return to and continuation of Wagner's musical developments leading into the twelve-tone school of Schoenberg and his disciples. The vague delicacy of Impressionist music is replaced by a vivid boldness, achieved through use of chromatic melodic lines, dissonant chords, irregular rhythms, thick textures, and massive orchestral timbres.

Primitivism. This is not so much a school in itself as a description of the early period of such composers as Stravinsky and Prokofiev. The music has harsh sonorities and highly irregular rhythms performed by full orchestra with an enlarged percussion section.

Nationalism. Many contemporary composers have returned to the folk music characteristics of their native countries, producing music that can be either conservative or radical depending upon the style of the individual composer.

The Twelve-Tone School (Dodecaphonic or Serial School). The most significant development of this school is in the tone-row technique (see pages 69–70). In later works of this school, other elements are serialized creating what might be called dynamic-rows, instrument-rows, or texture-rows.

Futurism or Bruitisme. This is a relatively insignificant stylistic development characterized by the use of noise in place of, or in addition to, musical sounds.

Chance music. Another esoteric and relatively insignificant development in contemporary music is the "composition" of works by random or chance procedures such as the one described under the paragraph about John Cage (see p. 382). Actually the idea of "chance music" is not altogether new; Mozart's *Musikalisches Würfelspiel* (*Musical Dice Game*) is a "composition" in which various musical fragments are to be combined according to the numbers which come up on several throws of dice.

Computer music. Some experimentation has been made in "programming" electronic computers with the information necessary to produce a composition, and then notating and performing the result.

Tape and electronic music. The latest tendencies in music involve the use either of tape-recorded natural sounds or electronically produced artificial tones. These sounds are altered to precise specifications of temporal, tonal, and other elements and arranged in simultaneous or successive patterns of great complexity and uniqueness, according to the will of the composer. The scores for these works resemble an engineering graph more than a musical score. (see p. 370)

"Popular" music and jazz. An interesting aspect of contemporary music has been the relationship of "art" music and "popular" music. On the one hand, the aesthetic difference between the two has widened in this century perhaps more than ever before. If we compare dance music of the nineteenth century, such as a waltz by Johann Strauss, with art music of the same period, such as a symphony by Brahms, we find obvious but not overwhelming differences. When we turn to our own century, however, the gap between the latest hit tune and an electronic composition is so large that the two seem to have almost nothing whatsoever in common.

In other aspects of contemporary music, we find that this gap between art music and entertainment music is effectively being bridged by jazz. Many contemporary composers have utilized elements of jazz in their music. The blues technique, with its repeated harmonic pattern, "blue notes," and general character, has been employed by Ravel and Copland. Ragtime rhythms and melodies have been adapted by Stravinsky and Barber. Some extended compositions, such as Milhaud's *Creation of the World,* have been based on jazz idioms. Conversely, jazz composers and performers have borrowed techniques and themes from contemporary composers and from composers of previous periods. A conscious attempt at bridging the gap between art music and jazz is the so-called "third stream" music, in which idioms and media of the two styles are effectively combined.

The Formal Element in the Contemporary Period

The wide variety of styles in the Contemporary period is especially apparent in the formal element. Late Romantic, post-Romantic, and Expressionist composers tend toward non-motivic construction; neo-Classic, neo-Baroque, and twelve-tone composers tend toward motivic construction. Some contemporary composers write in forms adapted from earlier periods; others cast their works in free forms based either on the implications of the basic musical content (for example, the variation possibilities inherent in a tone-row) or on the implications of extra-musical factors (for example, the requirements of a song text or a ballet plot). Though many new formal ideas have been incorporated in various contemporary works, these are unique for each specific work. No significant, widely adopted, new formal structure has yet emerged from the Contemporary period that could be compared to the Baroque cantata, the Classic sonata, or the Romantic tone-poem.

Two aspects of the formal element common to almost all styles of contemporary music are the preference for irregular phrase, period, and section lengths, and the emphasis on variation as a compositional principle. In general, contemporary compositions are more secular than sacred, more abstract than programmatic, and more objective than subjective.

Since this is the final section on the formal element, it is appropriate to consider the relationship of form and content in music. Preceding sections on form may have given the impression that musical forms are like predetermined molds into which a composer pours his musical content. This is not true. Musical content results *in* a form, not *from* a form. Just as scales do not produce melodies, form does not produce music. Two melodies can be analyzed as being similar because they both begin with an ascending minor scale; two movements can be analyzed as being similar because they both have a compound ternary form. However, the minor scale did not produce the melodies; the compound ternary form did not produce the movements.

This relationship of musical form and content is obvious in contemporary music, with its wide variety of formal structures, but is just as true of earlier music. Two minuets by Mozart, for example, may seem almost identical formally when analyzed superficially in terms of sectional relationships. A more penetrating analysis of each work, however, will reveal significant differences in terms of motive manipulation, phrase length, cadential formulas, and other aspects.

Forms of the Contemporary Period

Since, as we have pointed out above, there is so much diversity in the forms of contemporary music, we shall not attempt to generalize on the characteristics of individual single-movement or multi-movement forms but shall instead present analyses of some representative works.

Debussy's *Prélude à l'après-midi d'un faune* is often cited as an example of free form, but on close examination it is seen to be cast basically in a large three-part form. Each part is made up like a musical mosaic of many small motives in different tempos and textures, which gives an improvisatory character to the work.

EXAMPLE 10–1. Debussy, *Prélude à l'après-midi d'un faune* (Afternoon of a Faun). Permission for reprint granted by Editions Jean Jobert, Paris, copyright owners, and Elkan-Vogel Co., Inc., Philadelphia, agents.

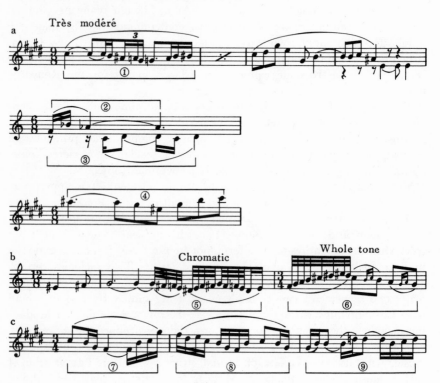

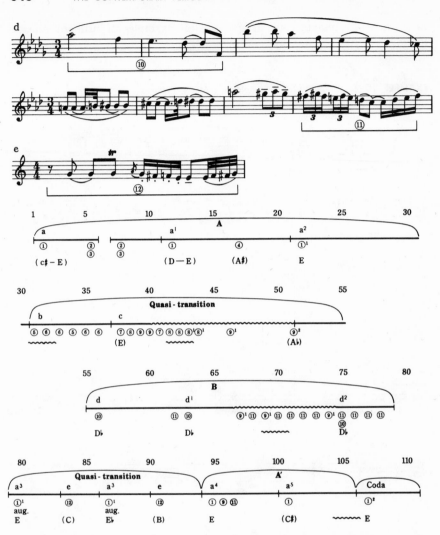

The full title of the next work to be analyzed is *Till Eulenspiegel's Merry Pranks, Set in the Old Time Roguish Manner—In Rondo Form—for Full Orchestra*. The composer, Richard Strauss, was always reluctant to give specific programs for his tone poems; he preferred to let the listener's imagination provide the story for his music. The programmatic analysis given here is a generally accepted one, based on hints he gave to his friends. The formal analysis shows the work to be in free sectional form, unified by the varied use of motives ① and ②. Why then did Strauss, in his title, indicate that the work was in "rondo form?" Was this his way of confounding the musical academicians, just as Till confounds the learned professors in the tone poem? In any case, this musical portrayal of a medieval *Taugenichts* (German:

ne'er do well) remains one of the greatest examples of brilliant musical humor and characterization.

EXAMPLE 10–2. Strauss, *Till Eulenspiegel's Merry Pranks.*

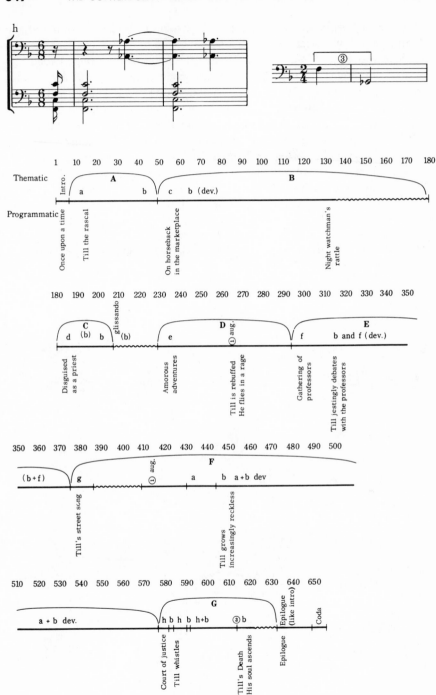

Arnold Schoenberg's *Quartet No. 3* is an especially clear example of the adaptation of Classical forms to modern techniques. We can analyze the work in two ways. First, we can see how the notes of the original tone row and its alterations are used in the themes, counter-themes, and accompaniments; the numbers on the themes refer to the numbered tones in the row. Second, we can analyze the work in terms of single movement forms. Although in our form graphs it appears that the form is quite regular and similar to Classical models, it does not sound this way mainly because Schoenberg does not bring back material in its original form. In the first movement, for example, the rhythms of the first and second themes are reversed in the recapitulation, while the pitches of the themes are the same as in the exposition, except for octave displacement.

EXAMPLE 10–3. Schoenberg, *Quartet No. 3*, Op. 30. Reprinted by permission of Gertrud Schoenberg.

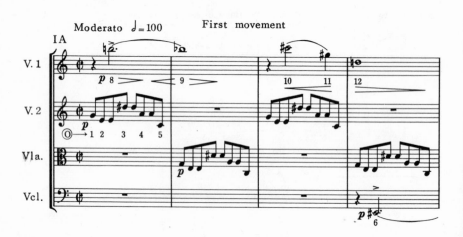

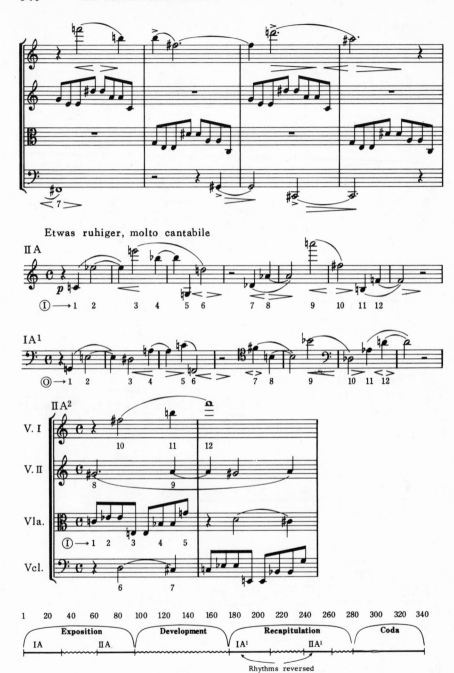

Etwas ruhiger, molto cantabile

EXAMPLE 10–3. continued.

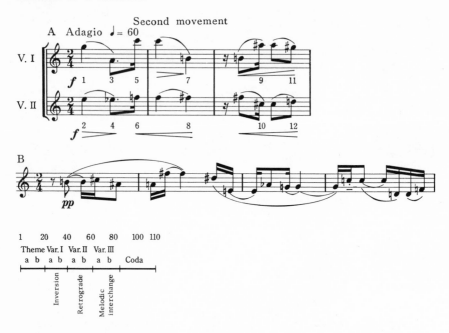

Second movement

A Adagio ♩ = 60

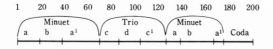

Third movement

Allegro moderato ♩ = 94

Fourth movement

Molto moderato ♩ = 76

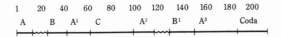

Bela Bartók's *Concerto for Orchestra,* with its brilliant orchestration, exciting rhythms, lyric melodies, clear-cut formal structure, and strong contrasts of mood, is one of the most accessible works in the modern repertoire. The title of the work refers to the fact that individual instruments and orchestral sections are treated in a soloistic or virtuoso manner, creating what might be called a contemporary adaptation of the concerto grosso principle, in which the concertino function is not assigned to a fixed group of instruments as in the Baroque period but is rather shared at different times by various instruments.

This work is an excellent example of Bartok's "arch form," both in terms of its single-movement forms and in terms of its over-all form. The form of the first movement, in particular, can be diagrammed in arch form as follows:

development

second theme   second theme

(exposition)   (recapitulation)

first theme   first theme

Note how the reversal of the first and second themes in the recapitulation contributes to the arch structure.

In terms of over-all form, the first and fifth movements balance each other as the two most vigorous movements; the second and fourth movements balance each other as the two lightest movements; and the third movement, with its "lugubrious" character, stands alone. Because of the relaxation of impetus from the first to the third movements, it would probably be more accurate to diagram this form as an inverted arch:

I   V

II IV

III

Bartók achieves a high degree of unity in this composition through the frequent use of the melodic interval of the perfect fourth in many themes. Other contrasting themes in the work are generally based on major and minor seconds.

EXAMPLE 10–4.   Bartók, *Concerto for Orchestra*. ©1946 by Hawkes & Son (London) Ltd. Reprinted by permission of Boosey & Hawkes Inc.

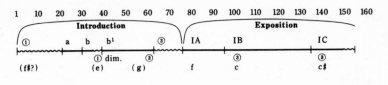

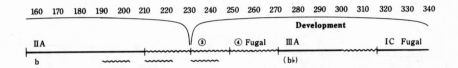

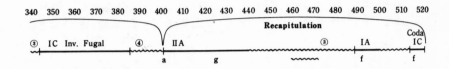

EXAMPLE 10–4. continued.

III Elegia (Elegy)

Intro I (based on ① of first movement)
Andante non troppo

(Based on ② of first movement)

c Poco agitato (based on a)

IV Intermezzo Interrotto (Interrupted Intermezzo)

a Allegretto

b Calmo

c Piu mosso

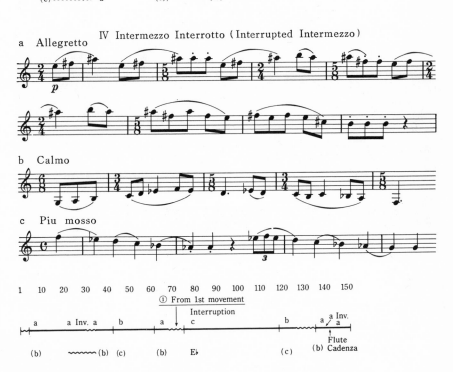

EXAMPLE 10–4. continued.

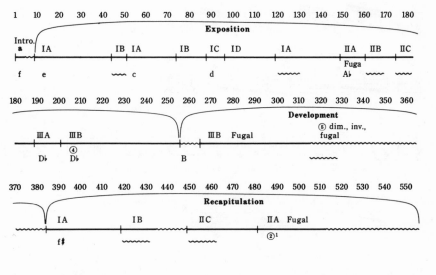

Igor Stravinsky's *Symphonie de Psaumes* (*Symphony of Psalms*) was composed "to the glory of God, and dedicated to the Boston Symphony Orchestra on the occasion of the 150th anniversary of its existence." The work is written for a large component of woodwinds and brass instruments, two pianos, harps, cellos, and basses. The violins and violas are, in a sense, replaced by the four-part mixed chorus. The text is in Latin and many of the themes show the influence of Gregorian chant in their modal tonality, limited range, conjunct motion, and repeated rhythms. Other interesting features of this score are the frequent use of rhythmic and melodic *ostinatos* (persistent repetitions), the clarity and effectiveness of the orchestration, and the unusual structure of the form.

EXAMPLE 10–5. *Symphonie de Psaumes.* Revised Version ©1948 by Boosey & Hawkes Inc. Reprinted by permission.

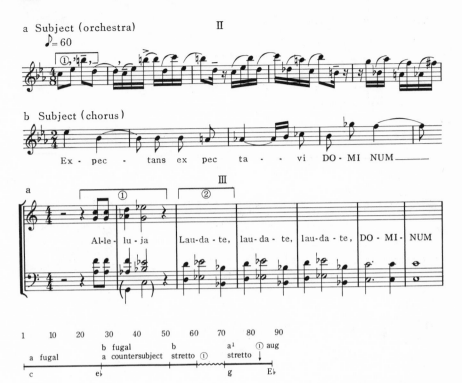

a Subject (orchestra)   II

b Subject (chorus)

Ex - pec - tans ex pec ta - - vi DO - MI NUM____

a   III
①   ②

Al-le - lu - ja   Lau-da - te, lau-da - te, lau-da - te, DO - MI - NUM

1   10   20   30   40   50   60   70   80   90
                    b fugal   b   a¹   ① aug
a fugal   a countersubject stretto ①   stretto ↓
c   e♭   g   E♭

EXAMPLE 10–5. continued.

1 10 20 30 40 50 60 70 80 90 100 110 120 130 140 150 160 170 180 190 200 210 220

a ③+④ b c d ① e c/④ f g/⑤/⑥ a

c C c e (c) c D E♭ c C

Alban Berg's opera, *Wozzeck,* is remarkable not only because of its usage of the twelve-tone technique but also because it is based upon a series of typical formal structures, most of them adapted from instrumental music. Each form is carefully chosen to meet the requirements of the text at that particular point in the opera. The libretto is based on a play by Büchner. The length and complexity of this work make it impossible to do more than list the various forms used and the corresponding dramatic situations.

EXAMPLE 10–6. Berg, Wozzeck.

MUSIC	DRAMA
ACT I	ACT I
Five Character Pieces	Exposition of the theme
Suite	Dialogue of Wozzeck and the Captain
Rhapsody	Dialogue of Wozzeck and Andres
March, Lullaby, and Scena	Scene in Marie's room
Passacaglia	Dialogue of Wozzeck and the Doctor (the repeated theme represents the Doctor's *idée fixe* about the relationship of nutrition and insanity)
Rondo	Marie's seduction by the Drum Major (the recurring theme represents sexual attraction)
ACT II	ACT II
Symphony in Five Movements	The development of the theme
Sonata-allegro	Wozzeck becomes suspicious of Marie

Invention and Fugue	The Captain and the Doctor taunt Wozzeck
Largo	Wozzeck accuses Marie of infidelity
Scherzo	Dance at the Inn
Rondo marziale	Scene at the barracks
ACT III	ACT III
Six Inventions	The catastrophe and epilogue
Invention on a theme	Marie reads the Bible
Invention on a note	Wozzeck murders Marie
Invention on a rhythm	Wozzeck at the tavern
Invention on a chord	Wozzeck's suicide
Invention on a key	(orchestral interlude)
Invention on triplets	Children at play

Roy Harris' *Symphony No. 3* represents an interesting twentieth-century adaptation of symphonic form—the symphony in one movement. The single movement is cast in five connected sections. Each section has its own distinct character, but the cyclic use of material from one section in other sections and the skillfully written transitions between sections give the work a strong sense of unity. Harris' melodic writing is remarkable for the way in which themes grow out of initial motives, not by deliberate formal techniques such as literal repetition, inversion, or other devices but rather through a process of organic development which is often more comprehensible to the ear than the use of traditional variation techniques. Note for example how the relationship between motive $(3)^1$ and motive $(3)^2$ is quite clear aurally even though the two motives are not strictly related by inversion or any other device.

EXAMPLE 10–7.   Harris, *Symphony No. 3 (1938)*. © 1939 by G. Schirmer Inc.
Reprinted by permission of the publisher.

EXAMPLE 10–7. continued.

In contrast to Harris' *Symphony No. 3*, with its emphasis on melodic development, the musical interest in Aaron Copland's *El Salon Mexico* is almost entirely in the rhythmic aspects. The work is a musical description of a "popular type dance hall in Mexico City," and its melodies, derived from folk and popular influences, are quite simple and similar, many of them being based on a first inversion major chord (motive ①). It is the exciting rhythm and the brilliant orchestration that give the work its character and distinction. The work is cast in a closed sectional form, and it is interesting to note that all the tonalities used in the piece are major.

EXAMPLE 10–8. Copland, *El Salon Mexico.* ⓒ 1939 by Aaron Copland; Boosey & Hawkes Inc., sole licensees. Reprinted by permission.

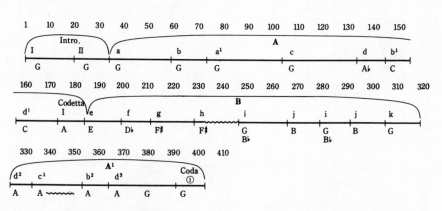

The graph given in Example 10–9 (p. 370) is from Karlheinz Stockhausen's Studie II, one of the first published scores of electronic music. This graph does not represent the entire work, but only a single page of the score. The top part of the score indicates frequency in cycles per second; the double line in the middle indicates duration in centimeters (76.2 cm = 1 second); and the lower part of the score indicates volume or intensity in decibels.

EXAMPLE 10—9. Stockhausen, No. 3 Elektronische Studien, Studie II. Copyright 1956, Universal Editions, Ltd., London, used by permission.

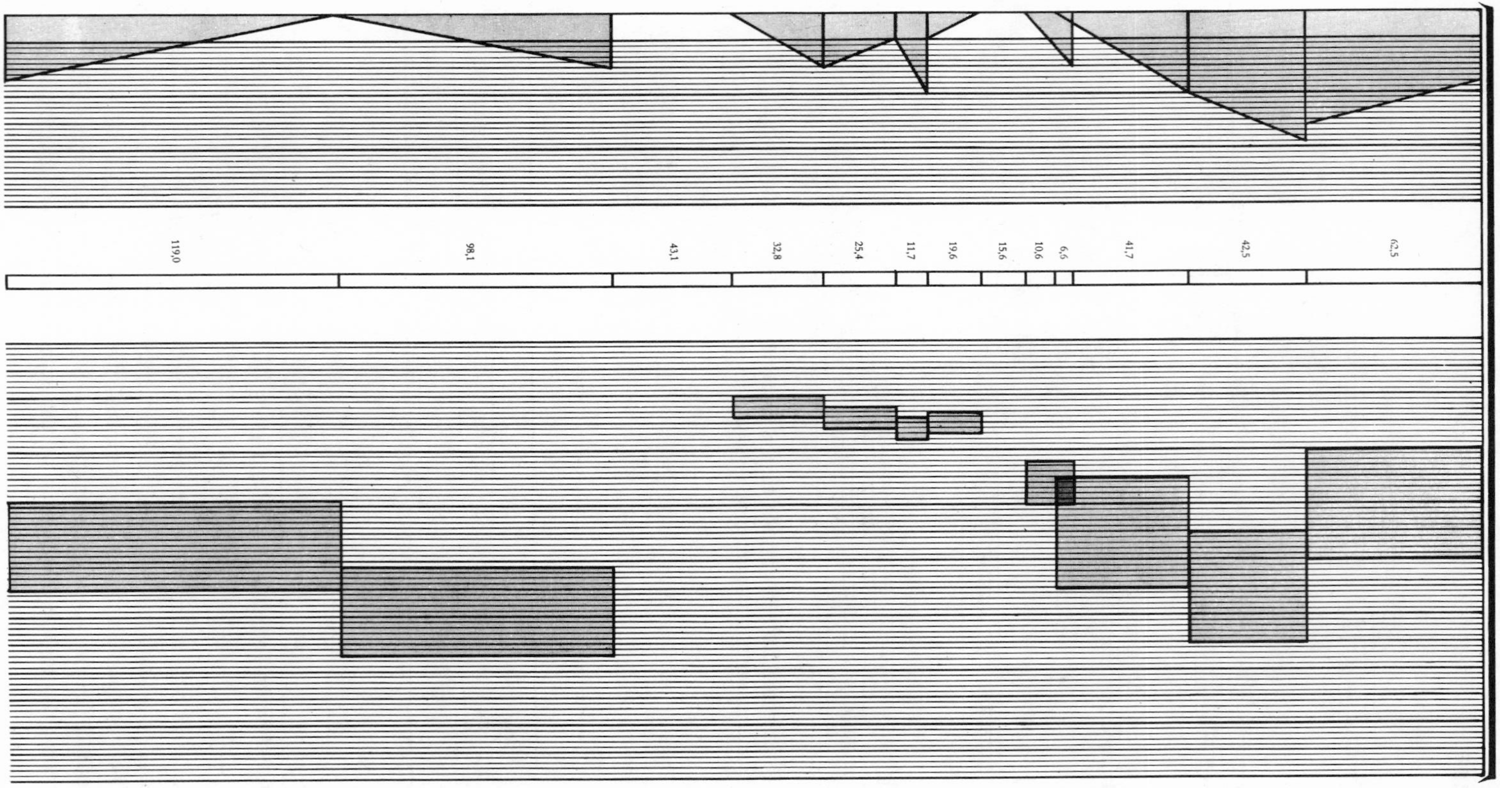

62,5
42,5
41,7
6,5
10,6
15,6
19,6
11,7
25,4
32,8
43,1
98,1
119,0

Representative Composers

Claude Debussy (French, 1862–1918). Founder and perhaps the only full-fledged representative of the Impressionist school, Debussy sought to create a musical style that could complement that of the Impressionist poets and painters. His musical technique owes something to such composers as Chopin, Mussorgsky, and Wagner (despite Debussy's antipathy toward him). His musical ideas were derived from literature, painting, and such exotic sources as Javanese gamelan music and American ragtime music. Most of the features discussed earlier under Impressionism apply to Debussy and are revealed in such orchestral works as these:

Prèlude à l'après-midi d'un Faune *(Prelude to the Afternoon of a Faun)*	See pp. 344–345.
Three Nocturnes	Three atmospheric symphonic poems (*Clouds, Festivals, Sirens*); the last adds a female chorus singing vowel sounds instead of words.
La Mer (The Sea)	Three symphonic poems based on the changing moods of the sea, entitled *From Dawn till Noon on the Sea, The Play of the Waves,* and *Dialogue of the Wind and the Sea.*
Images	Three symphonic sketches including *Gigues, Ibéria,* and *Ronde du Printemps. Ibéria,* the most frequently performed of the three is based on the composer's impressions of Spain.

His piano music includes: *Two Arabesques; L'Isle Joyeuse (Happy Island); Suite Bergamasque* (includes the famous *Claire de Lune*); *Jardins sous la pluie (Gardens in the Rain);* and *Hommage à Rameau* (a tribute to the eighteenth-century French composer).

He also wrote many songs including *Fêtes Galantes* and *Chansons de Bilitis,* chamber works including the *String Quartet in G Minor,* and one opera, *Pelléas and Mélisande,* based on Maeterlinck.

Richard Strauss (German, 1864–1949). Strauss began his career as a radical innovator whose expressionist tone poems and operas were shocking to the public at the turn of the century; he ended it as a conservative traditionalist whose last works seemed somewhat old-fashioned and out of date to the public after World War II. Throughout his career Strauss showed his ability to write colorfully and effectively for orchestra, to write memorable lyric melody, and to find new and unusual harmonic combinations and progressions.

He also wrote four string quartets, a concerto for violin, a concerto for piano, and other works for piano, voice and piano, chamber ensembles, and orchestra. His operas include the monodrama, *Erwartung (Expectation)*, *Die Glückliche Hand (The Lucky Hand)*, *Von Heute auf Morgen (From Today to Tommorrow)*, and the incomplete opera, *Moses and Aaron*.

Charles Ives (American, 1874–1954). Ives was trained as a musician but earned his living as an insurance broker. His works, mostly written before World War I, remarkably foreshadow such later contemporary techniques as polytonality, polymeter, polyrhythm, and the use of extensive dissonance; yet, many of them are based on diatonic New England folk and religious music. He has recently been "rediscovered," and such works as the following are receiving fairly frequent performances:

Sonata No. 2 for Piano (Concord, Mass.)	Movements are subtitled *Emerson, Hawthorne, the Alcotts, Thoreau.*
Symphony No. 3 (Holidays)	Movements are subtitled *Washington's Birthday, Decoration Day, Fourth of July, Thanksgiving.*
Three Places in New England	Movements are subtitled *The St. Gaudens in Boston Common; Colonel Shaw and his Colored Regiment; Putnam's Camp, Redding, Connecticut; The Housatonic at Stockbridge.*

Maurice Ravel (French, 1875–1937). Ravel's music is inspired by several diverse sources: the aesthetic concepts of French Impressionist poets and painters, the melodic and harmonic innovations of Debussy, the exotic coloring of Spanish and Oriental folklore, and the formal clarity of French Baroque composers such as Couperin. Though often compared to the works of Debussy, Ravel's compositions can be distinguished by their brilliant orchestration, clear texture, incisive rhythms, regular formal structure, extensive use of 11th and 13th chords, and skillful thematic development. His best known works include:

Daphnis et Chloé	Ballet, from which two orchestra suites were later drawn.
Boléro	Ballet, often played as a concert piece. One melody and one rhythmic accompaniment figure are repeated throughout in a variety of orchestrations that build a steady crescendo from the beginning to the end of the piece.
La Valse	A "choreographic poem" for orchestra that cleverly and somewhat sardonically parodies the style of Johann Strauss.
Ma Mère L'Oye	A piano suite, orchestral suite, and ballet based on Perrault fairy tales, including "Sleeping Beauty" and "Beauty and the Beast."
L'Enfant et les sortilèges (The Child and the Sorcerers)	A one-act fantasy opera based on Colette.

L'Heure espagnole *(The Spanish Hour)*	A comic opera about a clock maker and his unfaithful wife.
Tzigane	A rhapsody for violin and orchestra.

He also wrote several chamber compositions, songs, and other works for solo piano and orchestra.

Manuel de Falla (Spanish, 1876–1946). His best known works are two ballets, *El Amor Brujo (Love, the Magician),* and *El Sombrero de tres picos (The Three-Cornered Hat),* notable for their effective use of Spanish folk music.

Ernest Bloch (Swiss-American, 1880–1959). Works such as *Schelomo,* a rhapsody for cello and orchestra, show Bloch's usage of elements of Jewish folk music in a neo-Romantic style.

Heitor Villa-Lobos (Brazilian, 1881–1959). Villa-Lobos makes colorful and effective use of elements of Brazilian folk music in such compositions as his *Choros* for various instrumental and vocal combinations or in his *Bachianas Brasillieras,* in which he sets melodies based on Brazilian idioms in Bach-style counterpoint.

Béla Bartók (Hungarian, 1881–1945). Composers such as Liszt and Brahms had made some obvious use of Hungarian (more accurately "Gypsy") music, but it remained for Bartók and his compatriot, Zoltán Kodály, to undertake extensive research on true Hungarian folk music and then to incorporate it not only in narrowly nationalistic compositions but also in works of absolute music. Bartók's melodies, like those of much Hungarian folk music, are often built on unusual scale forms, but they are written with a clear feeling of tonic. His harmonies range from simple triads to highly chromatic, dissonant, polytonal sonorities. His style ranges from serene slow movements with regular rhythms to frenzied fast movements with complex, syncopated rhythms. One of his chief contributions to form is the arch form (see p. 351).

His *Concerto for Orchestra* (pp. 351–357), *Third Piano Concerto, Violin Concerto,* and *Viola Concerto* are frequently performed. His six string quartets are among the major contemporary contributions to chamber music literature. They make use of many special effects such as glissando, *col legno,* harmonics, and double, triple, and quadruple stops. He also wrote six volumes of piano music, entitled *Mikrokosmos,* which are intended primarily for piano instruction, but are also performed as concert pieces.

Igor Stravinsky (Russian-American, 1882–   ). Stravinsky once wrote, "The artist imposes a culture upon himself and ends by imposing it upon others."[2] This is an apt description of one who has at various

---

[2] Igor Stravinsky, *Poetics of Music in the Form of Six Lessons,* trans. Arthur Knodel and Ingolf Dahl (Cambridge, Mass.: Harvard University Press, 1947), p. 56. Copyright 1947 by the President and Fellows of Harvard College. Reprinted by permission.

periods in his creative life assimilated virtually all the major tendencies of this century and who has, in turn, been a dominant influence on the musical life of this period.

In his early Russian period (c.1910–1920), Stravinsky could be classified as a post-Romantic, nationalist, or primitivist composer. He drew upon Russian folklore and folk music for themes, upon his studies with Rimsky-Korsakov and his knowledge of other contemporary composers for techniques. His music of this period, with its shattering dissonances, frequent changes of meter, intricate rhythms, fragmentary chromatic melodies, and unusual orchestration at first shocked the musical world and then brought forth acclaim and emulation.

His second, or French, Period (c.1918–1923) was international in character, including several works based on American jazz style. Partly through economic necessity and partly through artistic conviction, Stravinsky, in this period, wrote more for small chamber ensembles, often with unusual instrumentation.

In his neo-Classic period (c.1920–1952), he turned back to such diverse sources as classic Greek drama, the Catholic liturgy, Pushkin, and Hogarth for subject matter, and to Bach, Pergolesi, Weber, Mendelssohn, and Tchaikowsky for musical ideas. The characteristic quality of many of these works results from contemporary adaptations of Baroque forms and techniques. They often feature diatonic melodies created, like many themes of Bach, from the expansion of an initial motive. These are set, however, in polyphonic or homophonic textures which yield a high degree of dissonance through free voice leading. The Baroque concerto grosso principle of opposing units of instruments is used, but with modern instrumentation and orchestral effects. The Baroque practice of writing movements with no dynamic change or with "terraced dynamics" is observed, but with contemporary dynamic extremes and unusual accents.

In his latest stylistic development, beginning about 1952, Stravinsky has gradually adopted the techniques of the twelve-tone school. Throughout these stylistic metamorphoses, Stravinsky's music has maintained its own uniquely personal characteristics. In particular, his vital rhythms, often cast in relentless *ostinatos,* are a clearly recognizable feature of his works in all periods. His rigorous sense of craftsmanship is evident in every composition from a short piano piece to a full-length opera or ballet.

Stravinsky's ballets, mostly written for the impressario Diaghilev, are not only among his most significant compositions, but are also representative of his various styles of composition. They are performed as complete ballets or as concert pieces and include:

L'Oiseau de feu *(The Firebird)*	Based on a Russian lenged, the music ranges from the quiet "Berceuse" to the frenetic "Final Dance," and shows the influence of Rimsky-Korsakov.

Petrouchka	Based on the story of puppets who come to life and act out scenes of love and tragedy, and then again become lifeless dolls, this brilliant score contains such novel techniques as bi-tonality, and polyrhythms.
Le Sacre du Printemps *(The Rite of Spring)*	"Scenes of pagan Russia" revolving around the ancient custom of sacrificing a virgin to the gods of fertility. The score features harsh dissonances, unusual orchestration, and irregular rhythms.
Les Noces (The Wedding)	A neo-Classic work with unusual scoring for chorus, soloist, four pianos, and percussion.
Histoire du Soldat *(The Soldier's Tale)*	A combination of dance, narration, drama, and music, based on a libretto by Ramuz.
Jeux des Cartes *(The Card Party)*	A "ballet in three deals" in which the dancers represent playing cards.
The Flood	A twelve-tone work originally written for television.

His other orchestral works range from such serious works as his *Symphony in Three Movements* to *Ragtime for Eleven Instruments, Ebony Concerto for Clarinet and Swing Band,* and a *Circus Polka* "composed for a young elephant."

His choral works include the *Symphony of Psalms,* (pp. 357–359) *Oedipus Rex* (an opera-oratorio), and *Canticum Sacrum ad honorem Sancti Marci nominis* (Sacred Song to Honor the Name of St. Mark). He also wrote some works for solo piano, voice and piano, and various chamber ensembles.

Stravinsky's writings on the aesthetics of music have the same vitality and clarity of expression that his music does:

> Composing for me, is putting into an order a certain number of these sounds according to certain interval-relationships.[3]

> I call your attention to this all-important point: consider on the one hand the conscious effort and patient organization that the composing of a work of art requires, and on the other hand the judgment—which is at least hasty and of necessity improvised—that follows the presentation of the work. The disproportion between the duties of the person who composes and the rights of those who judge him is glaring, since the work offered to the public, whatever its value may be, is always the fruit of study, reasoning, and calculation that imply exactly the converse of improvisation.[4]

> ...the musical sense cannot be acquired or developed without exercise. In music, as in everything else, inactivity leads gradually to the paralysis, to the atrophying of faculties.[5]

Anton Webern (Austrian, 1883–1945). Webern's twelve-tone compositions are extremely brief and compact; his entire creative output lasts less than four hours in performance time. He has been a strong influence upon many of the younger contemporary composers.

[3] *Ibid.* p. 37.
[4] *Ibid.* p. 132.
[5] *Ibid.* p. 135.

Alban Berg (Austrian, 1885–1935). Berg's earliest works are written in the style of post-Romanticism; even his later, fully twelve-tone works are written with Romantic subjectivity, occasionally using triadic harmony and melodies that sound almost tonal because they are based on tone rows emphasizing melodic seconds and thirds. His fame rests primarily on two operatic masterpieces, *Wozzeck* (pp. 362–363), and *Lulu,* an uncompleted opera based on a play by Wedekind. Other major works include the *Violin Concerto* and the *Lyric Suite for String Quartet.*

Sergei Prokofiev (Russian, 1891–1953). There are many contemporary composers, such as Schoenberg, whose music is more discussed than performed; there are others, for example, Prokofiev, whose music is more performed than discussed. From the primitivism of some of his early works to the neo-Classical style of his some of his later works, his music has achieved a balance between simplicity and complexity and between traditionalism and experimentation, which has made at least a significant part of it highly accessible to the listening public. He himself has described his style as follows:

> The first was the classical line, which could be traced back to my early childhood and the Beethoven sonatas I heard my mother play. This line takes sometimes a neo-classical form (sonatas, concertos), sometimes imitates the 18th-century classics)...The second line, the modern trend,...at first...took the form of a search for my own harmonic language, developing later into a search for a language in which to express powerful emotions....Although this line covers harmonic language mainly, it also includes new departures in melody, orchestration, and drama. The third line is the *toccata,* or the "motor," line traceable perhaps to Schumann's *Toccata....*The fourth line is lyrical: it appears first as a thoughtful and meditative mood, not always associated with the melody, or, at any rate, with the long melody....I should like to limit myself to these four "lines," and to regard the fifth, "grotesque" line which some wish to ascribe to me, as simply a deviation from the other lines. In any case I strenuously object to the very word "grotesque"....I would prefer my music to be described as "Scherzo-ish" in quality, or else by three words describing the various degrees of the Scherzo—whimsicality, laughter, mockery.[6]

He wrote seven symphonies, five piano concertos, two violin concertos, various chamber compositions, and numerous piano compositions including ten sonatas. He is perhaps best known for the following works:

Lieutenant Kije	Background music for a film, from which a suite was later taken.
Peter and the Wolf	A "symphonic fairy-tale for young and old." A narrator tells the story, and various instruments represent the characters.
Classical Symphony	Prokofiev's first symphony is a brilliant example of neo-Classicism in which forms and techniques of Mozart and Haydn are combined with modern techniques.

---

[6] Sergei Prokofiev, "Autobiography" from *S. Prokofiev,* ed. S. Shlifstein, trans. Rose Prokofieva (Moscow: Foreign Languages Publishing House, 1959), p. 36–37. Reprinted by permission of Progress Publishers.

Romeo and Juliet	Ballet based on Shakespeare.
Cinderella	Ballet based on the familiar fairy tale.
Love for Three Oranges	Fairy-tale opera, from which the march is often extracted and played as a separate concert piece.

Darius Milhaud (French, 1892–   ).   Milhaud is the best known and most prolific member of a group of French Contemporary composers known as *Les Six* (French: the Six), which also includes Louis Durey, Georges Auric, Francis Poulenc, Germaine Tailleferre, and Arthur Honegger. Unlike the Russian Five, this group of young French composers was not closely united behind a common cause, but rather shared a general tendency of reaction against older German and French composers. Milhaud is probably best known for two ballets: *La Création du Monde (The Creation of the World)* and *Le Boeuf sur le Toit (The Bull on the Roof),* the music to which reflect his interest in American jazz.

Walter Piston (American, 1894–   ).   Rhythmic energy, contrapuntal texture, and dissonant but basically diatonic harmony are among the stylistic features of Piston's music. Especially in his earlier works, he was identified with the neo-Classic and neo-Baroque schools; his later works are in a personal style that is more difficult to classify. He has written seven symphonies, many chamber music compositions, and the ballet, *The Incredible Flutist.* In addition to his activity as a composer, Piston has also taught for many years at Harvard and has written excellent texts on harmony and counterpoint.

Paul Hindemith (German, 1895–1963).   Hindemith was one of the most varied and prolific composers of the twentieth century. He has written works for virtually all solo instruments or instrumental combinations in styles ranging from neo-Classicism to neo-Romanticism. Both as a theorist and as a composer, Hindemith developed a melodic style that made free and extensive use of chromaticism, but was always based on a tonic center. His music is marked by clear formal structure and skillful polyphonic texture. His best known works include:

Mathis der Maler (Matthias the Painter)	Opera based on the life of the fifteenth-century painter, Matthias Gruenewald. A suite of three excerpts is frequently performed in concert.
Das Marienleben (The Life of Mary)	Song cycle to poems of Rilke.
Nobilissima Visione	Ballet on the life of St. Francis of Assisi. A suite of excerpts is often performed in concert.
Symphonic Metamorphosis on Themes by Weber	An orchestral composition with witty references to oriental music and American Jazz.
When Lilacs Last in the Dooryard Bloom'd	Setting of Walt Whitman's poem for chorus and orchestra.
Der Schwanendreher (The Swancatcher)	For solo viola and orchestra. One of several works which Hindemith wrote for his own performance as a viola soloist.

Carl Orff (German, 1895–   ). Simple diatonic melodies and harmonies set to forceful, reiterated rhythms are the characteristic elements of Orff's compositions, such as the cantata, *Carmina Burana,* and the opera, *Die Kluge* (German: The Clever Girl). Rhythm is also of paramount importance in his highly significant writings and methods of elementary music education.

Howard Hanson (American, 1896–   ). A neo-Romantic style is revealed in Hanson's works such as his *Second Symphony (The Romantic Symphony)*; his opera, *Merry Mount;* and his choral work, *Lament for Beowulf.*

Virgil Thomson (American, 1896–   ). In his opera, *Four Saints in Three Acts* and in his music for the motion picture, *The Plow that Broke the Plains,* Thomson writes in an extremely clear and uncomplicated style that contrasts strongly with the complex compositions of his contemporaries. He is also a prominent music critic.

Roger Sessions (American, 1896–   ). Sessions' style is difficult to classify because it reflects influences of several schools including expressionism, neo-Romanticism, and dodecaphonicism. Many of his works, such as his symphonies and sonatas, have very complex rhythmic, melodic, and textural ideas, making them difficult for both performer and listener. Others, such as his suite of incidental music for the play, *The Black Maskers,* are more accessible.

George Gershwin (American, 1898–1937). Gershwin is perhaps best known to the general public for his musical comedies, *Of Thee I Sing* and *Girl Crazy,* and for his many popular songs. In compositions such as the folk-opera, *Porgy and Bess,* the symphonic poem, *An American in Paris,* and the fantasy for piano and orchestra, *Rhapsody in Blue,* however, he showed his ability to combine elements of jazz with elements of art music.

Roy Harris (American, 1898–   ). A conscious nationalism in subject matter, themes, and style are revealed in Harris' best known compositions; the *Symphony No. 3,* (pp. 363-366) the *Folksong Symphony,* and the overture, *When Johnny Comes Marching Home.*

Aaron Copland (American, 1900–   ). Copland's music shows a variety of influences from neo-Classicism and American nationalism to the twelve-tone school. In his best known works, the ballets, *Billy the Kid, Rodeo,* and *Appalachian Spring,* he writes in a diatonic, consonant, homophonic style, with strong rhythmic impulse and highly effective orchestration. He has written several valuable books on music, such as *Music and Imagination,* in which he points out, "An important requirement for subtle listening is a mature understanding of the natural differences of musical expression to be anticipated in music of different epochs....To approach all music in the vain hope that it will soothe one in the lush harmonies of the late nineteenth century is a common error of many present day music lovers."[7]

William Walton (English, 1902–   ). Written in a neo-Romantic style, remarkable especially for its melodic lyricism, Walton's best known works include his oratorio, *Belshazzar's Feast,* and his music for such films as *Major Barbara* and *Hamlet.*

Luigi Dallapiccola (Italian, 1904–   ). Italy's most prominent twentieth-century composer, Dallapiccola uses the twelve-tone technique in a lyric and expressive style in such works as his opera, *Il Prigioniero.*

Dimitri Shostakovich (Russian, 1906–   ). The directives of the Soviet government have influenced Shostakovich somewhat in his choice of subject matter; the music of Beethoven, Bach, and Mahler, and contemporary composers have been more significant influences on his musical style. Often complex and dissonant, his music is also marked by warm lyricism and rhythmic incisiveness. His best known works include the *Symphony No. 5,* the *Symphony No. 7 (Leningrad)* and the "Polka" from the ballet, *The Age of Gold.*

Elliott Carter (1908–   ). Carter's music is characterized by highly complex and imaginative rhythmic usage, emphasis upon contrapuntal texture, a uniquely personal adaptation of the twelve-tone technique, and exploration of unusual instrumental timbres. Though not an extremely prolific composer, he has won recognition for such compositions as his two string quartets and his *Double Concerto for Harpsichord and Piano with Two Chamber Orchestras.*

Samuel Barber (American, 1910–   ). Barber's musical style combines elements of neo-Classicism and neo-Romanticism. Among his best known compositions are the *Adagio for Strings,* the two *Essays for Orchestra,* and his opera, *Vanessa.*

William Schuman (1910–   ). Schuman's early interests were in jazz and business administration. He turned from these to compose such works as the *American Festival Overture,* the cantata, *A Free Song,* and three symphonies, which are all written in what might be described as an American adaptation of the neo-Classic or neo-Romantic style. Schuman, however, has never completely deserted his early interests. His experience with jazz has left its imprint in the rhythmic vitality which marks much of his writing. His administrative experience has equipped him to assume such positions as music director of a publishing firm, director of the Juilliard School of Music, and, most recently, director of the New York Lincoln Center for the Performing Arts.

[7] Aaron Copland, *Music and Imagination* (Cambridge, Mass.: Harvard University Press, 1952), p. 14. Copyright 1952 by the President and Fellows of Harvard College. Reprinted by permission.

John Cage (American, 1912–   ). A radical and controversial innovator, Cage has experimented with "chance music" and such unusual instruments as the "prepared piano," a piano with various objects placed on the strings inside the instrument. His *Imaginary Landscape* is a "chance music" composition resulting from the random sounds produced by twelve radios playing simultaneously on different stations.

Benjamin Britten (English, 1913–   ). An eclectic composer, Britten shows unique ability to write highly effective dramatic music in his operas such as *Albert Herring* and *Peter Grimes* and in his choral works such as the *Spring Symphony* and the *War Requiem*.

Leon Kirchner (American, 1919–   ). In his *Concerto for Violin, Cello, Ten Winds and Percussion,* Kirschner has used intricate rhythms, twelve-tone melodies, and dissonant harmonies; in his writings on music, he has stressed the importance of a continuity between the music of the past and music of the present and future.

Gunther Schuller (American, 1925–   ). Schuller has written works for such unusual combinations as four cellos, three trombones and piano, and four horns and bassoon, as well as works for the standard orchestra, such as his *Seven Studies on Themes of Paul Klee.* He is also recognized as an authority on the relationship of jazz and contemporary music and as a composer of "third stream" music.

Karlheinz Stockhausen (German, 1928–   ). Though he has written works for conventional instruments in serial style, such as the *Zeitmasse (Tempos)* for woodwind quintet, Stockhausen is principally identified as one of the foremost composers of electronic music. He has described electronic composition as follows:

> To compose electronic music means: to describe in mechanical and electro-acoustical terms that which sounds, and to think wholly in terms of machine, apparatus, wiring scheme; to reckon with unique production and any number of repetitions of the composition.[8]

To some people the recent developments in the electronic production and reproduction of music seem to portend an end to music as a vital art. They foresee a development in which the music of electronic computers and sound generators will reach such a stage of complexity that it will be impossible for the human ear to comprehend or appreciate it. Their forebodings might be epitomized in the macabre conception of a concert in which one machine listens to another.

To take this attitude is to put oneself in the company of those in every

---

[8] Stockhausen, "Electronic and Instrumental Music," in *die Reihe,* Vol. 5. English edition copyright 1961, Theodore Presser Co., in association with Universal Editions; used by permission.

age who have condemned the technical advances of the progressive musicians of their time. From Giovanni Maria Artusi's *Dissertation about the Imperfections of Modern Music,* written in 1600 to Henry Pleasant's *The Agony of Modern Music,* written in 1955, there have been scores of impassioned condemnations of contemporary music. In some cases these criticisms have been just and the composers attacked have sunk into a deserved oblivion; in most cases, however, the composers have survived this initial criticism to win general recognition and acceptance.

The outlook for music in our own time is in fact, especially propitious, for along with the discovery of new musical materials on the part of our contemporary composers has come the discovery of a vast amount of music literature from the past on the part of present day musicologists, theorists, and performers. The musician and the listener of today have a larger body of music available to them than at any other time in history. With this opportunity, however, has come the challenge to develop a wider knowledge and appreciation, and above all, the challenge to develop an active participation in music; for, without the active participation of an ever increasing number of people, the rich musical heritage that is now ours can atrophy and be forgotten, and the artistic advances which are within our grasp can degenerate and become sterile. With such active participation, however, we can move toward that deeper awareness of the past and the present, of the personal and the universal—which has always been music's unique contribution to mankind.

Index

Pronunciation Guide

Foreign words and proper names have approximate pronunciations indicated in in parentheses after the main entry. A key to the sounds employed is given below. It is impossible to indicate all the various nuances of vowel sound and length without employing a system such as the International Phonetic Transcription. To use this, however, would probably be confusing and cumbersome for most readers. Ideally the best way, if not the only way, to learn proper pronunciation is to hear the words spoken by a good native speaker of the language. The conscientious reader can, however, achieve an adequate comprehension and command of the terms used in this book by studying carefully the pronunciations given in the index.

Vowels:

a—as in *sat*
ah—as in *father*
ai—as in *raid* (but as a single vowel, not as a diphthong)
e—as in *get* (like the *ai* sound, but shorter. In concluding syllables in German it should be pronounced almost like the *a* in *along*)
ee—as in *see*
i—as in *hit* (like the *ee* sound, but shorter)
o—as in *hot*
oh—as in *go* (for concluding syllables in Italian it should be pronounced very short)
oo—as in *too*

Diphthongs:

ie—as in *lie*
oi—as in *ointment*
ou—as in *house*

Foreign vowels:

The following vowels have no equivalent sounds in English, but they may be approximated as indicated.

ö—*ai* (as in *raid*) through closely rounded lips
ü—*ee* (as in *see*) through closely rounded lips

Diphthongs:

The following consonants are to be pronounced according to normal English usage:

b, d, f, h, j, k, m, n, p, t, v, w, y, z.
g—hard as in *go*
l—generally brighter and more "palatized" (with the tongue closer to the roof of the mouth)
r—generally to be "rolled" especially at the beginnings of syllables.
s—always sibilant as in *so*.

Foreign consonants:

The following consonants have no equivalent sounds in English, but may be approximated as indicated.

kh—like the guttural Scotch *ch* in *loch*
nh—the nasal French *n*
xh—place the tongue as for the vowel *ee* (as in *see*) and emit a strong current of breath.
zh—like the *s* in *measure*.

Accent is indicated by capital letters. As a general rule vowels are long for accented syllables, short for unaccented syllables. The glottal stop is indicated with a diagonal line (/).

Musical compositions are listed in the index only when they are represented in the text by a musical example. For descriptions of other works, see the main biographical entry of the composer.

A

Abbreviation, 169
Abstract music, 176
A cappella (ah kah-PEL-lah), 105
Accelerando (ah-tchel-air-AHN-doh), 21
Accelérér (ah-sel-air-ai), 21
Accent, 15-17
Accidentals, 43-44, 46, 52
Accompagnato (ahk-kom-pahn-YAH-toh), 198
Accompaniment, 128-131
Acoustics, 5-7
Adagio (ah-DAH-joh), 19
Additive approach, 126-128
A due (ah DOO-ai), 102
Aerophones, 84
Affectueux (ah-fet-ü-ö), 83
Affetuoso (ahf-fet-too-OH-zoh), 83
Agitato (ah-jee-TAH-toh), 83
Agité (ah-zhee-tai), 83
Agnus Dei, 184
Agogic accent, 15
Aimable (ai-mahbl), 83
Allant (ahl-lahnh), 19
Allargando (ahl-lahr-GAHN-doh), 21
Allegro (ahl-LAI-groh), 19
Alleluia (ahl-lai-LOO-yah), 183
Allemande (ahl-mahnhd), 31
Allmählich (ahl-MAI-lixh), 21
Altered chords, 115-116
Altflöte (AHLT-flö-te), 84
Altklarinette (AHLT-klah-ri-NET-te), 84
Alto (ahl-toh), 85
Alto clarinet, 84, 85, 93
Alto clef, 45
Alto flute, 84, 92
Altonium, 95
Alto voice, 104
Amabile (ah-MAH-bee-lai), 83
Ambrosian hymn, 140
Amplitude, 6, 7, 9
Analysis of music:
  form, 174
  harmony, 117
Anapestic, 27
Ancient music, 10, 141, 181
Andante (ahn-DAHN-tai), 19
Anima, con (kohn AH-nee-mah), 83
Animato (ah-nee-MAH-toh), 83
Animé (ah-nee-mai), 83
Antecedent phrase, 161

Anthem:
  pre-Baroque, 187
  Baroque, 199
Anticipation, 120
Antiphonal texture, 139-140, 184
Appassionato (ahp-pahss-syoh-NAH-toh), 83
Appoggiatura (ahp-po-jah-TOO-rah):
  non-harmonic tone, 120
  ornament, 67
Arch form, 351
Arco (AHR-koh), 87
Ardent (ahr-dahnh), 83
Aria (AH-ree-ah):
  Baroque, 199
  Classical, 252
  Romantic, 292
Arioso (ah-ree-OH-soh), 199
Arpa (AHR-pah), 85
Arpeggio (ahr-PED-joh), 99
Arpeggio accompaniment, 129
Ars antiqua, 181
Ars nova, 181, 192
Articulation, 82-83
Art music, 225
A tempo (ah TEM-poh), 21
Atonal music (see Twelve-tone music)
Augmentation, 169
Augmented intervals, 47, 75-76, 112
Augmented triad, 113
Augmenter (ohg-mahnh-tai), 81
"Auld Lang Syne," 125
Auric, Georges (zhorzh oh-reek), 374
Ausdrucksvoll (OUS-drooks-fol), 83
Authentic cadence, 163
Avec force (ah-vek forss), 83
Avec verve (ah-vek vairv), 83

B

Bach, Johann Cristoph (YOH-hahn KRIS-tof bahkh):
  Sonata in C Minor, 148
Bach, Johann Sebastian (YOH-hahn se-BAHSS-tee-ahn bahkh), 219-222
  Brandenburg Concertos, 106, 210
  Cantata No. 16, 145-146
  Cantata No. 80, 200-205
  Cantata No. 190, 147

French Suite No. 5 in G Major, 208-209, 216-217
Fugue in C Minor from The Well-Tempered Clavier, Book I, 212-214
Herr Gott, dich loben wir, 145
Bach, Karl Phillip Emmanuel (kahrl FIL-lip ai-MAHN-oo-el bahkh), 266
Bagatelle, 278
Bagpipe, 94
Balakirev, Mily (MEE-lee bah-lah-kee-REF), 336
Ballade (bahl-lahd), 187
Ballata (bah-LAH-tah), 188
Ballet, 291
Ballet suite, 291
Band, 101
Banjo, 90
Barber, Samuel, 381
Bar form, 187
Bariolage (bah-ree-oh-lahzh), 279
Baritone horn, 85, 86, 95
Baritone voice, 104
Bar line, 16, 24
Baroque music, 10, 197-223
    early period, 10, 148, 197
    formal element, 197-198
    late period, 10, 197
    middle period, 10, 197
    temporal element, 31-32
    textural element, 145-148
    timbre-dynamic element, 105-106
    tonal element, 68
Bartók, Béla (BAI-lah BAHR-tohk), 375
    Concerto for Orchestra, 352-357
    Fifth String Quartet, 58, 63
    Mikrokosmos, 34
Baryton (BAH-ree-tohn), 90
Bass afterbeat accompaniment, 130
Bass-baritone voice, 104
Bass clarinet, 84, 85, 93
Bass clef, 45
Bass drum, 85, 97, 98
Bassklarinette (BAHSS-klah-ri-NET-te), 84
Basson (bah-sohnh), 84
Bassoon, 84, 85, 93, 94
Basso (BAHSS-soh), 104
Basso profundo (proh-FOOND-oh), 104
Bass staff, 45
Bass viol, 85, 86, 90
Bass voice, 104
Bayreuth (bie-ROIT), 332
Beams, 23-24
Beat, 15
Bebop, 35
Becken (BEK-en), 85
Beethoven, Ludwig van (LOOD-vig fahn BAIT-hoh-fen), 272-275

Concerto in D Major for Violin and Orchestra, Op. 61, 251
Quartet in G Major, Op. 18, No. 2, 226-227
Quartet in A Major, Op. 18, No. 5, 118
Quartet in F Major, Op. 59, No. 1, 62
Quartet in E Minor, Op. 59, No. 2, 30
Quartet in C-sharp Minor, Op. 131, 249-250
Sonata in C Major for Cello and Piano, Op. 102, No. 1, 78
Sonata in C Minor for Piano, Op. 13, 230-231
Sonata in A-flat Major for Piano, Op. 26, 177
Symphony No. 1 in C Major, Op. 21, 236-237
Symphony No. 3 in E-flat Major, Op. 55, 82, 119, 228-229, 232-234, 237-239
Symphony No. 5 in C Minor, Op. 67, 65, 66
Symphony No. 7 in A Major, Op. 92, 230
Symphony No. 9 in D Minor, Op. 125, 61
Bel canto (bel KAHN-toh), 197
Belebt (be-LAIPT), 83
Bells, 97
Berg, Alban (AHL-bahn bairk), 378
    Wozzeck, 362-363
Berlioz, Hector (hek-tohr bair-lee-ohz), 326-327
    Symphonie Fantastique, 287-289
Bewegt (be-VAIGT), 83
Bewegter (be-VAIG-ter), 21
Binary form, 175
    Baroque, 208-209
    Classical, 226
    closed, 209
    open, 209
    rounded, 209
Birnbaum, Johann Abraham, 222
Bi-tonal chords, 151
Bizet, Georges (zhohrzh bee-zai), 335-336
Bloch, Ernest, 375
Block chord accompaniment, 128
Blue notes, 70-71
Blues, 35
Boccherini, Luigi (loo-EE-jee bok-kai-REE-nee), 269
Borodin, Alexander ahl-leks-AHN-der BOR-oh-deen), 336
Bossa nova, 36
Bourrée (boo-rai), 216
Bowing, 87-90
Boy soprano, 104
Brahms, Johannes (yoh-HAHN-ness brahmz), 334-335

Clarinet Quintet in B Minor, Op. 115, 82
The German Requiem, Op. 45, 307-317
Piano Quartet in A Major, Op. 26, 118
Sonata in D Minor for Violin and Piano, Op. 108, 62, 286
Symphony No. 2 in D Major, Op. 73, 30, 280-282
Symphony No. 4 in E Minor, Op. 98, 160, 161
Brace, 102
Brass choir, 101
Brass instruments, 84-85, 86, 94-97
Bratsche (BRAH-tshe), 85
Breit (briet), 19
Breve, 29
Brio, con (kohn BREE-oh), 83
Britten, Benjamin, 382
Broken chord accompaniment, 129
Bruckner, Anton (AHN-tohn BROOK-ner), 334
Bruitisme (brüee-tizm), 342
Bugle, 97
Bugle tenor (bügl te-nohr), 85
Burgundian School, 181, 192
Buxtehude, Dietrich (DEET-rixh books-te-HOO-de), 218
Byrd, William, 193
   Motet: Ego sum panis vivus, 186-187

C

Caccia (KAH-tchah), 188
Caccini, Giulio (JOO-lee-oh kah-TCHEE-nee), 217
Cadences, 162-167
   Baroque, 198
   combined, 164-167
   harmonic, 162-163
   melodic, 164
   pre-Baroque, 182-183
Cadenza (kah-DEN-zah *or* kah-DEN-tsah), 242
Cage, John, 382
Caisse (kess), 85
Calando (kah-LAHN-doh), 21, 81
Camerata (kah-mai-RAH-tah), 217
Canon, 134, 138
Cantabile (kahn-TAH-bee-lai), 83
Cantata (kahn-TAH-tah), 145-147, 200-205
Cantus firmus (KAHN-tooss FEER-mooss), 140
Canzo (KAHN-tsoh), 187
Canzona (kahn-TSOH-nah), 192

Caressant (kah-ress-ahnh), 83
Carissimi, Giacomo (JAH-koh-moh kah-REESS-see-mee), 218
Carter, Elliott, 381
Cassa (KAH-sah), 85
Cassation, 245
Castanets, 97
Castrato (kah-STRAH-toh), 104
Cavalli, Piero Francesco (pee-YAIR-oh frahn-CHESS-koh kah-VAHL-lee), 218
Celesta, 86
Cello, 85, 86, 90, 91
Cembalo (CHEM-bah-loh), 85
Cesti, Marc' Antonio (mahrk ahn-TOH-nee-oh CHESS-tee), 218
Chaconne (shah-kohn), 175, 211
Chalumeau (shah-lü-moh), 93
Chamber music:
   Classical, 226-227, 232, 243, 245, 249-250
   Contemporary, 348-351
   instrumental, 99-101
   Romantic, 287
   vocal, 104
Chamber orchestra, 101
Chamber singers, 104
Chambonnières, Jacques Champion (zhahk shahnh-pyohnh shahnh-bohn-yair), 218
Chance music, 342
Change of tonality, 61
Chanson (shahnh-sohnh):
   Baroque, 199
   pre-Baroque, 191
Chant (*see* Gregorian chant)
Chantant (shahnh-tahnh), 83
Character, 83
Character piece, 278, 291-292
Chimes, 97
Chinese music, 181
Choir, 104-105
Chopin, Frédéric (fred-e-rik shoh-panh), 328-329
   Nocturne in C-sharp Minor, Op. 27, No. 1, 149, 278-279
Chorale (koh-RAHL):
   Baroque, 145, 199
   pre-Baroque, 187
Chorale prelude, 211
Chord, 113-119
   classification, 122-123
   distribution, 121-122
Chordophones, 84
Chorus, 104-105
Chorus (form):
   Baroque, 199
   Classical, 252
   Romantic, 307, 325

Chromatic chords, 115-116
Chromatic half step, 47
Chromaticism, 60
Chromatic scales, 50
Chromatic tones, 50
Church modes, 51-52, 59-60
Circle of fifths, 61
Cithara (KITH-ah-rah), 90
Clarinet, 84, 85, 92-93
Clarinette (klah-ree-net), 84
Clarinette alto (ahl-toh), 84
Clarinette basse (bahss), 84
Clarinette contrebasse (kohntr-bahss), 84
Clarinetto alto (klah-ree-NET-toh AHL-toh), 84
Clarino contrabasso (klah-REE-noh kohn-trah-BAHSS-soh), 84
Clarion, 93
Clarone (klah-RO-nai), 84
Classical music, 10, 225-275
  formal element, 225-226
  general characteristics, 225
  temporal element, 32
  textural element, 148-149
  timbre-dynamic element, 106-107
  tonal element, 68-69
Classical orchestra, 106
Clausula (KLOU-zoo-lah), 142, 185
Clevecin (klah-ve-sanh), 85
Claves (KLAH-vess), 97
Clavicembalo (klah-vee-CHEM-bah-loh), 85
Clavichord, 85, 97
Clavicordo (klah-vee-KOR-doh), 85
Clef signs, 45
Climax, 63-65
Closed binary form, 209
Close position, 121
Coda (KOH-dah), 235-236
Codetta (koh-DET-tah), 236
Col legno (kohl lai-nyoh), 90
Color (KOH-lohr), 142-143
Coloratura (koh-loh-rah-TOO-rah), 104
Combined cadences, 164-167
Complexity, 29
Complex meters, 25-26
Compline, 183
Composite organum, 141
Compound interval, 113
Compound meter, 17-18, 25
Compound ternary form, 227-230
Computer music, 342
Con anima (kohn AH-nee-mah), 83
Con brio (BREE-oh), 83
Concert band, 101
Concerti ecclesiatici (kohn-CHAIR-tee ai-klai-zee-AH-stee-chee), 205

Concertino (kohn-chair-TEE-noh), 105, 210
Concerto (kohn-CHAIR-toh):
  Baroque, 217
  Classical, 245, 251
  Romantic, 291
Concerto-allegro form, 242-243
Concerto grosso (GROSS-soh), 105, 217
  contemporary adaptations, 351
Concert overture, 287
Conducting, 16-17
Conductus (kohn-DOOK-tooss), 185
Con fuoco (kohn foo-O-koh), 83
Conjunct progression, 61
Con moto (kohn MOH-toh), 83
Consequent phrase, 161
Consistency, 29
Consonance:
  chords, 117
  intervals, 111-113
Consort, 215
Contemporary music, 10, 341-383
  attitudes toward, 382-383
  formal element, 343-344
  schools of, 341-343
  temporal element, 33-36
  textural element, 150-152
  timbre-dynamic element, 108
  tonal element, 69-71
Continuo (kohn-TEE-noo-oh), 105
Contour, 63-65
Contrabass clarinet, 84, 85
Contrabasso (kohn-trah-BAHSS-soh), 85
Contra-bassoon, 84, 85, 94
Contrafagotto (kohn-trah-fah-GOT-toh), 84
Contralto voice, 104
Contrary motion, 133
Contrast, 167-168
Contrebasse (kohnhtr-bahss), 85
Contrebasson (kohnhtr-bah-sohnh), 84
Copland, Aaron, 380-381
  El Salon Mexico, 368-369
Cor anglais (kohr ahnh-glai), 84
Cor-à-pistons (kohr-ah-peess-tohnh), 84
Corelli, Archangelo (ahr-KAHN-je-loh koh-REL-lee), 218-219
  Sonata da chiesa in E Minor, Op. 3, No, 7, 215-216
Cornet, 95
Cornet-à-pistons (kohr-net-ah-peess-tohnh), 84
Cornetto (kor-NET-toh), 84
Corno (KOR-noh), 84
Corno inghlese (KOR-noh een-GLAI-zai), 84
Corno ventile (KOR-noh ven-TEE-lai), 84

Corrente (kor-REN-tai), 32
Counterpoint, 136-138 (*see also* Textural element)
Countersubject, 211
Countertenor, 104
Couperin, François (frahnh-swah koo-peranh), 219
Courante (koo-rahnht), 32
Credo, 183
Crescendo (kre-SHEN-doh), 81
Cui, César (SAI-zahr küee), 336
Cycles per second, 6
Cyclic form, 278
Cymbales (sanh-bahl), 85
Cymbals, 85, 97

D

Da capo aria (dah KAH-poh AH-ree-ah), 199
Dactylic, 27
Dallapiccola, Luigi (loo-EE-jee dahl-lah-PEEK-koh-lah), 376
Dance music:
  Baroque, 31-32, 208-209
  Classical, 32
  Contemporary, 34, 35-36
  jazz, 35-36
  pre-Baroque, 31, 191-192
  Romantic, 33, 279, 291
Debussy, Claude (klohd de-bü-see), 222, 371
  Prélude à l'après-midi d'un faune, 344-345
Deceptive cadence, 163
Decibel, 6
Decrescendo (dai-kre-SHEN-doh), 81
Derivative approach, 119-125
de Falla (*see* Falla)
des Prez (*see* Josquin)
Détaché (dai-tah-shai), 89
Development, 235
Diatonic chords, 115-116
Diatonic half step, 47
Diatonic scales, 50
Diatonic writing, 60
Dies Irae (DEE-aiss EE-rai), 184-185, 289
Diminished intervals, 47, 75-76, 113
Diminished-minor seventh chord, 115
Diminished seventh chord, 115
Diminished triad, 113
Diminuant (dee-mee-nü-ahnh), 81
Diminuendo (dee-mee-noo-EN-doh), 81

Diminution, 169
Direction, pitch, 62-63
Disjunct progression, 61-62
Dissonance:
  chords, 117
  intervals, 112-113
Distant tonalities, 61
Divertimento (dee-vair-tee-MEN-toh), 245
Dodecaphonic (doh-dek-ah-FON-ik), 342
Dolce (DOHL-chai), 83
Dolente (doh-LEN-tai), 83
Dominant, 55
Dominant seventh chord, 115
Dorian mode, 51, 59
Dotted notes:
  articulation, 82
  duration, 24, 27
Double exposition, 242
Double flat, 43-44
Double leading tone cadence, 182
Double period, 159, 161-162, 174
Double-reed instruments, 94
Double sharp, 43-44
Double stop, 89
Doubling, 116, 121
Doubly dotted notes, 24
Doucement (dooss-mahnh), 83
Doux (doo), 81, 83
Down beat, 16-17
Down bow, 89
Dramatic soprano, 104
Dramatic tenor, 104
Drängend (DRENG/ent), 21, 81
Drum, 85, 86, 97-99
Duet, 100
Dufay, Guillaume (gee-yohm dü-fah-ee), 192
Dumka (DOOM-kah), 33, 386
Dunstable, John, 192
Duo, 100
Duparc, Henri (ahnh-ree dü-pahrk), 293
Duple meter, 16-18, 25
Duplet, 27, 28
Duration, 6-7
Durey, Louis (loo-ee dü-rai), 379
Dvořák, Antonin (AHN-toh-neen DVOR-zhahk), 337
  Humoresque, 125
  Quintet in A Major for Piano and Strings, Op. 81, 286
  Symphony No. 5 in E Minor, Op. 95, 56, 57, 128, 150
Dynamic accent, 15
Dynamics, 9, 81, 105 (*see also* Timbre-dynamic element)
Dynamic-row, 342

E

Early Baroque period, 10, 148, 197
Early Romantic period, 10, 277
Echappée (ai-shah-pai), 120
Edge-tone instruments, 92
Egyptian music, 181
Eighth note, eighth rest, 22
Eilig (IE-lixh), 19
Einfach (IEN-fahkh), 83
Ein wenig (ien VAI-nixh), 19
Elargissant (ai-lahr-zhee-sahnh), 21
Electronic music, 342, 365, 366, 382
Electronic organ, 99
Electrophones, 84
Eleventh chord, 115
Embouchure (ahnh-boo-shür), 92
En badinant (ahnh bah-dee-nahnh), 83
Encore plus (ahnh-kohr plü), 19
En diminuant (ahnh dee-mee-nü-ahnh), 21, 81
English Baroque opera, 200
Englisch Horn (ENG/lish horn), 84
English horn, 84, 85, 94
Enharmonic tones, 43
En mourant (ahnh moo-rahnh), 21, 81
En pressant (ahnh press-ahnh), 21, 81
En s'effaçant (ahnh sef-ah-sahnh), 21, 81
Ensembles:
  instrumental, 99-101
  vocal, 104-105
Entschlossen (ent-SHLOSS-en), 83
Episode, fugal, 211
Ersterben (air-SHTAIR-ben), 21, 81
Erstes Zeitmass (AIR-stess TSIET-mahss), 21
Escaped tone, 120
Espressivo (ess-press-SEE-voh), 83
Estampie (ess-tahnh-pee), 191
Ethos, 176
Etude (ai-tüd), 278
Etwas (ET-vahss), 19
Euphonium, 95
Exercises:
  formal element, 176-178
  temporal element, 36-38
  textural element, 153-157
  timbre-dynamic element, 108-109
  tonal element, 71-79
  use and importance, 10-12
Exposition, 235
Expressif (ex-press-eef), 83
Expression, 83
Expressionism, 341
Extension, 169

F

Fagott (fah-GOT), 84
Fagotto (fah-GOT-toh), 84
Falla, Manuel de (MAHN-oo-el de FAHL-lyah), 375
Falsetto (fahl-SET-toh), 103
Familiar style, 193
Fancy, 215
Fantasia:
  Baroque, 215
  Classical, 244
  pre-Baroque, 192
Fauré, Gabriel-Urbain (gah-bree-el-ür-banh foh-rai), 293
Feierlich (FIE-er-lixh), 83
Feminine cadence, 164
Fermata (fair-MAH-tah), 25, 199
Feurig (FOI-rixh), 83
Fifth, 47, 75-76, 111
Figure, 159, 160-161
Figured bass, 117
Fingering, 89
First inversion, 116
Flat, 43-44, 46
Flauto (FLOU-toh), 84
Flautone (flou-TOH-nai), 84
Flauto piccolo (FLOU-toh PEEK-koh-loh), 84
Flemish School, 193
Flexibility, 29-30, 31
Flicorno tenore (flee-KOR-noh te-NOH-rai), 85
Florentine opera, 200
Flöte (FLÖ-te), 84
Flugelhorn, 95
Flute, 84, 85, 92
Flûte (flüt), 84
Flûte alto (ahl-toh), 84
Folk music, 60, 78, 123, 225, 277, 342
Form, 9, 159, 343-344 (*see also* Formal element)
Formal element, 9, 159-176
  Baroque, 197-198
  Classical, 225-226
  Contemporary, 343-344
  pre-Baroque, 182
  Romantic, 277-278
Form graphs, use of, 178
Forms of music, 175
Fort (for), 81
Forte (FOR-tai), 81
Forte piano (pee-AH-noh), 83
Fortissimo (for-TEESS-see-moh), 81
Foster, Stephen, "Old Folks at Home," 124
Fourth, 47, 75-76, 111
Franck, César (sai-zahr frahnhk), 334

Free forms, 175
  Baroque, 215
  Classical, 244
  Contemporary, 346-347
  pre-Baroque, 192
  Romantic, 282
Free organum, 141
Free tone, 120
Frei (frie), 21
French Baroque opera, 200
French grand opera, 321
French horn, 84, 86, 95, 96
French overture, 209
French sixth, 122
Frequency, 6, 7
Frescobaldi, Girolamo (jee-ROL-ah-moh
  fress-koh-BAHL-dee), 218
Freudian psychology, 4
Freudig (FROI-dixh), 83
Froberger, Johann Jakob (YOH-hahn
  YAH-kob FROH-bair-ger), 218
Fugal forms, 175
  Baroque, 211-215
  Classical, 234
  Romantic, 279-280
Fugue (fyoog), 138, 175, 211-214
Full anthem, 187
Full cadence, 162
Fundamental, 6
Fuoco, con (kohn foo-O-koh), 83
Furiant, 386
Futurism, 342

G

Gabrieli, Giovanni (joh-VAHN-nee gah-
  bree-AIL-ee), 193-194
Gallant style, 225
Galliard (gahl-yahrd), 191
Gamba, 90
Gamelan, 365
Gavotte (gah-voht), 208-209, 216
Gefällig (ge-FEL-ixh), 83
Gehalten (ge-HAHL-ten), 83
Geheimnisvoll (ge-HIEM-niss-fol), 83
Gehend (GAI-hent), 19
Geige (GIE-ge), 85
Geistliche Konzerte (GIEST-lixh-e kon-
  TSAIR-te), 205
German Baroque opera, 200
German sixth chord, 122
Gershwin, George, 375
Gervaise, Claude (klohd zhair-vaiz),
  Pavanne and Gaillarde, 192

Gesamtkunstwerk (ge-SAHMT-KOONST-
  vairk), 321
Gesangvoll (ge-ZAHNG-fol), 83
Gestalt psychology, 4
Getragen (ge-TRAH-gen), 19, 83
Gigue (zheeg), 32
Giocoso (joh-KOH-soh), 83
Gioioso (joi-YOH-soh), 83
Glee, 105
Glee club, 105
Glissando (gleess-SAHN-doh), 89
Glockenspiel (GLOK-en-shpeel), 97
Gloria, 183
Gluck, Christoph Willibald (KRISS-toph
  VEEL-li-bahld glook), 266
Goliard (GOH-lee-ahrd), 181
Gong, 97
Gounod, Charles (shahrl goo-noh), 334
Grace notes (*see* Ornamentation)
Gracieux (grah-see-ö), 83
Graduale, 183
Gran cassa (grahn CAHSS-sah), 85
Grave (GRAH-vai), 19
Grazioso (graht-SYOH-zoh), 83
Great staff, 45
Greek music, 181
Gregorian chant, 31, 181, 183-184
Gregory, Pope, 181
Grieg, Edvard (ED-vahrd greeg), 337-338
Ground bass, 192, 211
Grosse caisse (grohss kess), 85
Grosse Trommel (GROHSS-e TROM-
  mel), 85
Guitar, 90

H

Habanera (ah-bah-NAI-rah), 35
Half cadence, 162-163
Half diminished seventh chord, 115
Half note, half rest, 22
Handel, George Frederick [in German the
  name is spelled and pronounced
  Georg Friedrich Händel] (GAI-ohrk
  FREED-rixh HEN-del), 222-223
  Messiah, 198-199, 205-207
Hanslick, Eduard, 3
Hanson, Howard, 380
Harfe (HAHR-fe), 85
Harmonic analysis, 117
Harmonic cadences, 162-163
Harmonic counterpoint, 136-137
Harmonic intervals, 111-113
Harmonic minor scale, 49-50
Harmonic progression, 117-118, 122-123

Harmonic rhythm, 118-119
Harmonics, 89
Harmonic tension, 117
Harmonization, 119-128
  additive approach, 126-128
  derivative approach, 119-125
Harmony, 111-128 (*see also* Textural
  element)
Harp, 85, 86, 99
Harpe (ahrp), 85
Harpsichord, 85, 97
Harris, Roy, 380
  Symphony No. 3, 364-366
Hautbois (oh-bwah), 84
Haydn, Franz Joseph (frahnts YOH-zef
  HIE-dn), 266-269
  Quartet in E-flat Major, Op. 33, No. 2,
    57
  Quartet in C Major, Op. 54, No. 2, 267
  Quartet in D Minor, Op. 76, No. 2, 62,
    78
  Quartet in C Major, Op. 76, No. 3, 232
  Quartet in F Major, Op. 77, No. 2, 248
  Symphony No. 94 in G Major, 127, 247
Heldentenor (HEL-den-ten-OHR), 104
Helicon, 95, 97
Hemiola (hem-ee-OH-lah), 32
Hindemith, Paul (poul HIN-de-mit), 379
Historicus, 205
Hoffmann, E.T.A., 3
Hold, 25
Homophonic texture, 128-131
Honegger, Arthur (ahr-tür on-egg-air), 379
Horn, 84, 86, 95, 96
Hungarian rhythm, 27
Hybrid texture, 138-139
Hymn, 187

I

Iambic, 27
Idée fixe (ee-dai feeks), 287-289
Idiophones, 84
Imperfect cadence, 164
Imperfect consonances, 112
Imitation, 134-135
Imitative polyphony, 134-135
Impressionism, 10, 69, 341, 365
Impromptu, 278
Improvisation, 152
Innig (IN-nixh), 83
Instrumental ensembles, 99-101
Instrumental ranges, 85-86
Instrumentation, 101
Instrument-row, 342

Instruments, 84-99
Intermezzo, 200, 278, 335
Intervals:
  harmonic, 111-113
  melodic, 46-47, 75-76
  patterns, 62
Intonazione (een-toh-nah-tsee-OH-nai),
  192
Introduction, 235
Introitus, 183
Invention, 215
Inversion:
  harmonic, 116
  melodic, 69-70, 170
Isorhythm, 142-143, 185
Italian overture, 209
Italian Romantic opera, 317
Italian sixth chord, 122
Ite missa est, 183, 184
Ives, Charles, 374
  Three Places in New England, 34

J

Jazz, 342-343
  temporal element, 35-36
  textural element, 152
  timbre-dynamic element, 101
  tonal element, 71-72
Jazz ensembles, 101
Jongleur (zhohnh-glör), 181
Josquin des Prez (zhohss-kanh dai prai),
  193
  Ave Maria, 138
Joyeux (zhwoi-ö), 83

K

Kettledrum, 85, 86, 97
Key, 55-61
Keyboard, 42-44
Keyboard instruments, 85, 86, 97-99
Key signatures, 52-54
Kirchner, Leon, 382
Klagend (KLAH-gent), 83
Klarinette (klah-ri-NET-te), 84
Klavichord (KLAH-vi-kord), 85
Klavier (klah-VEER), 85
Kleine Flöte (KLIE-ne FLÖ-te), 84
Kleine Trommel (KLIE-ne TROM-mel),
  85
Kontrabass (KON-trah-bahs), 85

Kontrabassklarinette (KON-trah-bahss-klah-ri-NET-te), 84
Kontrafagott (KON-trah-fah-GOT), 84
Kornett (kor-NET), 84
Kriegerisch (KREE-ger-ish), 83
Kuhnau, Johann (YOH-hahn KOO-nou), 219
Kyrie, 183

L

Landini, Francesco (frahn-CHESS-koh lahn-DEE-nee), 192
Landini cadence, 182
Ländler (LEND-ler), 33
Langsam (LAHNG-zahm), 19
Langsamer werden (LAHNG-zahm-er VAIR-den), 21
Large (lahrzh), 19
Largo (LAHR-goh), 19
Lasso, Orlando di (or-LAHN-doh dee LAHSS-soh) [also called Lassus (LAHS-sooss)], 193
Late Baroque period, 10, 197
Late Romantic period, 10, 277, 341
Lauds, 183
Laut (lout), 81
Lauter werden (LOUT-er VAIR-den), 81
Leading tone, 55
Leaning tone, 120
Lebhaft (LAIP-hahft), 19
Lebhaft bewegt (LAIP-hahft be-VAIKT), 83
Ledger lines, 45
Legato (lai-GAH-toh), 82, 89
Léger (lai-zhai), 83
Leggiero (lai-JAI-roh), 83
Leicht (liexht), 83
Leidenschaftlich (LIE-den-shahft-lixh), 83
Leise (LIE-ze), 81
Leiser werden (LIE-zer VAIR-den), 81
Leitmotiv (LIET-moh-TEEF), 321
Lent (lahnh), 19
Lento (LEN-toh), 19
Leonin (lai-oh-nanh), 192
Libéré (lee-bai-rai), 21
Libretto, 200
Lieblich (LEEB-lixh), 83
Lied (leet):
    Baroque, 199
    Classical, 252
    pre-Baroque, 191
    Romantic, 293-307
Liederkreis (LEED-er-kriess), 325
Linear counterpoint, 138

Liszt, Franz (frahnts list), 328, 330-331
Loudness, 6-7, 9
Lourd(loor), 19
Loure (loor), 216
Lully, Jean-Baptiste (zhahnh bah-teest lü-lee), 218
Lusingando (loo-zeen-GAHN-doh), 83
Lute (loot), 90
Luther, Martin, *A Mighty Fortress Is Our God*, 55
Lydian mode, 52, 59
Lyre, 90
Lyric soprano, 104
Lyric tenor, 104

M

Machaut, Guillaume de (gee-ohm de mah-shoh), 192
Madrigal, 188-191
Madrigal singers, 104
Maelzel, Johann (YOH-hahn MEL-tsel), 19
Maestoso (mah-ess-TOH-soh), 83
Magnificat, 183
Mahler, Gustav (GOOSS-tahf MAH-ler), 338
Majestueux (mah-zhess-tü-ö), 83
Major intervals, 47, 75-76, 112
Major-major seventh chord, 115
Major-minor seventh chord, 113-115
Major scale, 47-49, 50, 52-54, 58-59
Major triad, 113
Mandolin, 90
Mannheim School, 267
March, 32
Marimba, 97
Martelé (mahr-te-lai), 89
Martiale (mahr-see-ahl), 83
Marziale (mahr-tsee-AH-lai), 83
Masculine cadence, 164
Mass:
    Baroque, 208
    Classical, 266
    pre-Baroque, 183-184, 187
    Romantic, 325
Mässig (MAI-sixh), 19
Mässig laut (lout), 81
Mässig leise (LIE-ze), 81
Masque, 200
Mastersingers, 321
Matins, 183
Mazurka, 33, 279
Measure, 16
Mediant, 55

Medieval music, 10, 181
  temporal element, 31
  textural element, 140-143, 145
  tonal element, 68
Meistersinger (MIE-ster-ZING/er), 321
Melisma (me-LIZ-mah), 184
Melismatic setting of chant, 184
Melismatic organum, 142
Mellophone, 95
Melodic cadences, 164
Melodic intervals, 46-47, 75-76
Melodic minor scale, 49-50
Melodic ornamentation, 67-68
Melody, 9, 41 (see also Tonal element)
Melody, location of, 130
Membranophones, 84
Mendelssohn, Felix (FAI-liks MEN-dels-
    zohn), 327-328
  Concerto in E Minor for Violin and
    Orchestra, Op. 64, 67, 82
  Octet in E-flat Major, Op. 20, 66
  Overture to A Midsummer Night's
    Dream, Op. 21, 284-285
  Symphony No. 4 in A Major, Op. 90, 67
Meno (MAI-noh), 21
Meno mosso (MOSS-soh), 21
Men's chorus, 104
Mesto (MESS-toh), 83
Meter, 15-18 (see also Temporal element)
  multimeter, 34
  polymeter, 33
  time signatures, 25-26
  unusual meters, 34
Metronome, 19, 21
Mezzo forte (MED-zoh FOR-tai), 81
Mezzo piano (pee-AH-noh), 81
Mezzo soprano voice, 104
Middle Baroque period, 10, 197
Middle Romantic period, 10, 277
Milhaud, Darius (dah-ree-üss mee-yoh),
    379
Minor intervals, 46-47, 75-76, 112
Minor-major seventh chord, 115
Minor-minor seventh chord, 115
Minor scales, 49-50, 52-54, 58-59
Minor triad, 113
Minnesinger (MIN-ne-ZING/er), 181,
    187
Minuet, 32
Minuet and Trio form, 175, 227-230
Missa Solemnis (MISS-ah soh-LEM-niss),
    183-184
Misterioso (meess-tair-ee-OH-zoh), 83
Mixed chorus, 104-105
Mixolydian mode, 52, 60
Modal cadences, 164
Modality, 58

Mode, 51-52, 55-61
Moderato (moh-dair-AH-toh), 19
Modéré (moh-dai-rai), 19, 81
Modern music (see Contemporary music)
Modulation, 61
Moins (mwanh), 21
Moins vite (veet), 21
Molto (MOHL-toh), 19
Monody, 197
Monophonic texture, 111
Monteverdi, Claudio (KLOU-dee-oh
    mohn-te-VAIR-dee), 217-218
  Orfeo, 148
Mordent, 67
Morendo (mo-REN-doh), 21, 81
Morley, Thomas, Hard by a Crystal
    Fountain, 188-191
Mosso (MOSS-soh), 21
Motet (moh-TET), 175
  Baroque, 199
  isorhythmic, 142-143, 185
  modified (Romantic), 307
  Paris, 185
  thirteenth-century, 142, 185
  sixteenth-century, 185-187
Motion, pitch, 132-134
Motive, 159-160, 174
Moto, con (kohn MOH-toh), 83
Motto, 280
Mouvementé (moov-mahnh-tai), 83
Movement, 159, 162
Mozart, Wolfgang Amadeus (VOLF-
    gahng ah-mah-DAI-ooss MOH-
    tsahrt), 269-272, 342
  Concerto in A Major for Piano and
    Orchestra, K. 488, 242
  Fantasia in D Minor, K. 397, 244
  Marriage of Figaro, 241, 252-266
  Quartet in B-flat Major, K. 458, 161-162
  Quartet in D Major, K. 499, 167
  Quartet in D Major, K. 575, 243
  Symphony No. 39 in E-flat Major, K.
    543, 57, 60, 63
  Symphony No. 41 in C Major, K. 551,
    165, 228, 239-240
Multimeter, 34
Multiple octave divisions, 70
Munter (MOON-ter), 83
Musicia Enchiriadis, 141
Musica ficta (MOO-zi-kah FEEK-tah), 68
Musical units, 159-162
Music drama, 321
Music literature, periods of, 9-10
Music theory, elements of, 7-9
Mussorgsky, Modest (MOH-dest moo-
    SORG-skee), 336
Mute, 89, 92, 95

Mysterieux (mee-stair-ee-ö), 83
Mystic chord, 151

N

Nachlassen (NAHKH-lahss-en), 21, 81
Nachtanz (NAHKH-tahnts), 191
Nationalism:
   Contemporary, 342
   Romantic, 277, 287
Natural, 43-44, 46
Natural horn, trumpet, 94-95
Neapolitan opera, 200
Neapolitan sixth chord, 122
Neighbor tone, 120
Neo-Baroque, 341
Neo-Classicism, 341
Neumatic singing of chant, 184
Neumes, 31, 184
Nicht zu (nixht tsoo), 21
Ninth, 47, 75-76
Ninth chord, 115
Nocturne, 278
Noise, 5
Non-chord tones, 119-120
None, 183
Nonet, 101
Non-harmonic tones, 119-120
Non-imitative polyphony, 135
Non-legato, 82
Non-motivic construction, 160
Non-tertian chords, 115
Non troppo (nohn TROP-poh), 21
Notation, 8-9
   neumatic, 184-185
   pitch, 42, 44-46
   rhythm, 21-25
Note, 41, 159
Notre Dame, School of, 181, 192
Novachord, 99
Number of parts, 135
Number opera, 200, 252, 317, 321

O

Objectivity, 176
Oblique motion, 133
Oboe, 84, 85, 93, 94
Obrecht, Jakob (YAH-kop OH-brexht), 193
Occursus (oh-KOOR-sooss), 182
Ockeghem, Johannes (yoh-HAHN-nes
   OK-e-gem), 193
Octave, 47, 75-76, 111

Octave signs, 45-46
Octet, 101
Odo of Cluny, 3
Offenbach, Jacques (zhahk OF-en-bahkh),
   334
Offertorium, 183
Office, 183
Open binary form, 209
Open position, 121
Opera:
   Baroque, 200
   camerata, 217
   Classical, 252-266
   Contemporary, 362-363
   English Baroque, 200
   Florentine, 200
   French Baroque, 200
   French grand, 321
   German Baroque, 200
   Italian Romantic, 317-321
   Masque, 200
   music drama, 321
   Neapolitan, 200
   number, 200, 252, 317, 321
   Roman, 200
   Romantic, 317-325
   Venetian, 200
   verismo, 338
Opéra bouffe (oh-pai-rah boof), 321
Opera buffa (OH-pai-rah BOOF-fah), 200,
   252
Opéra comique (oh-pai-rah koh-meek),
   321
Opéra lyrique (oh-pai-rah lü-reek), 321
Opera seria (OH-pai-rah ZAIR-ee-ah),
   200, 252
Oratorio:
   Baroque, 205-207
   Classical, 266
Orchestra, 84-85
   Baroque, 107
   Classical, 106
   Contemporary, 108
   Romantic, 107
Orchestral score, 84-85, 102
Orchestration, 101
Ordinary, 183
Ordre, 216
Orff, Carl, 380
Organ, 85, 99
Organum (OHR-gah-noom), 140-142, 185
Orgel (OR-gel), 85
Orgue (ohrg), 85
Ornamentation, melodic, 67-68, 170
Ostinato (ohss-tee-NAH-toh), 357
Ottavino (ot-tah-VEE-noh), 84
Overblowing, 92, 94

Overtone, 6-7, 9
Overture:
  Baroque, 209
  French, 209
  Italian, 209
  Romantic, 284-285, 287

P

Pachelbel, Johann (YOH-hahn pahkh-EL-bel), 218
Paganini, Niccolò (NEEK-koh-loh pah-gah-NEE-nee), 325
  Caprice No. 24, 279, 285, 287
Palestrina, Giovanni Pierluigi da (joh-VAHN-nee pee-air-loo-EE-jee dah pah-less-TREE-nah), 193
  Missa, Te Deum, 144
Parallel fifths and octaves, 123-124
Parallel minor, 52-54
Parallel motion, 132-133
Parallel organum, 141
Parallel voice leading, 151
Paris motet, 185
Parlando (pahr-LAHN-doh), 103
Parody mass, 187
Partita (pahr-TEE-tah), 216
Passacaglia (pahss-sah-KAHL-yah), 175, 211
Passamezzo (pahss-sah-MED-zoh), 191
Passing tone, 120
Passion, 205
Passionné (pahss-yoh-nai), 83
Pas trop (pah troh), 21
Pathos, 176
Patterns:
  pitch, 62
  rhythm, 26-29
Patter song, 257
Pauke (POU-ke), 85
Pavanne (pah-vahn), 191-192
Pedal point, 211
Pentatonic scale, 51
Percussion ensemble, 101
Percussion instruments, 85, 86, 97-99
Perfect cadence, 164
Perfect consonances, 111-112
Perfect intervals, 47, 75-76, 111
Peri, Jacopo (yah-KOH-poh PAIR-ee), 217
Period, 159, 161, 174
Perotin (pair-oh-tanh), 192
Petite caisse (pe-teet kess), 85
Petite flût (flüt), 84
Peu à peu (pö ah pö), 21
Phantasy, 278

Phon, 6
Phrase, 159, 161, 174
Phrase group, 159, 161, 174
Phrygian cadence, 164
Phrygian mode, 51, 59
Physical characteristics of sound, 5-7
Piacévole (pee-ah-CHAI-voh-lai), 83
Pianissimo (pee-ah-NEESS-see-moh), 81
Piano (pee-AH-noh) (dynamics), 81
Piano, pianoforte (instrument), 41-44, 85, 86, 97
Piano trio, 100
Piatti (pee-AH-tee), 85
Piccolo, 84, 85, 92
Pitch, 6, 7
  contour, 63-65
  designation, 41-44
  direction, 62-63
  motion, 132-134
  notation, 42, 44-46
  patterns, 62
  progression, 61-62
Piston, Walter, 379
Più (pyoo), 19
Più mosso (MOSS-soh), 21
Pizzicato (peet-see-KAH-toh), 87
Plagal cadence, 163
Plainsong, 183
Plaisant (plai-sahnh), 83
Plötzlich (PLÖTS-lixh), 21
Plus (plü), 19
Plus animé (plüz-ah-ni-mai), 21
Poco (PO-koh), 19
Poco a poco, 21
Point of imitation, 185
Polarity of outer voices, 106
Polka, 33, 279
Polonaise (pohl-oh-naiz), 33, 279
Polychoral, 194
Polymeter, 33
Polyphonic texture, 131-138
Polyrhythm, 34
Ponticello (pohn-tee-CHEL-loh), 90
Popular music, 342-343
Portamento (pohr-tah-MEN-toh), 89
Portato (por-TAH-toh), 82
Posaune (poh-ZOU-ne), 84
Poulenc, Francis (frahnh-seess poo-lahnhk), 379
Pre-Baroque Music, 10, 181-194
  formal element, 182
  temporal element, 31
  textural element, 140-145
  timbre-dynamic element, 105
  tonal element, 68
Prelude:
  Baroque, 215

pre-Baroque, 192
Romantic, 278
Premier tempo (prem-yai tem-poh), 21
Prepared piano, 377
Presto (PRESS-toh), 19
Prime, 47, 183
Primitivism, 341-342
Program music, 176, 282, 284, 287-289
Program symphony, 287-289
Progression:
  harmonic, 117-118, 122-123
  pitch, 61-62
Progressive jazz, 35
Prokofiev, Sergei (SAIR-gai proh-KOH-fyef), 378-379
Prominence:
  melodic, 68
  rhythmic, 29
Proper, 183
Psychological characteristics of sound, 5-7
Puccini, Giacomo (JAH-koh-moh poo-CHEE-nee), 338
Puncta (POONK-tah), 191
Purcell, Henry, 219
Pure minor scale, 49

Q

Quadruple meter, 16, 18, 25
Quarter note, quarter rest, 22
Quadruple stop, 89
Quarter tone, 70
Quartet, 100, 245, 248-250
Quintet, 100-101
Quintuple meter, 16, 25-26

R

Rachmaninoff, Sergei (SAIR-gai rahkh-MAH-nee-nof), 372
Ragtime, 35
Ralentir (rahl-ahnh-teer), 21
Ralentissant (rahl-ahnh-tiss-ahnh), 21
Rallentando (rahl-len-TAHN-doh), 21
Rameau, Jean-Phillipe (zhahnh fee-leep rah-moh), 219
Range, 65-66
  instruments, 85-86
  voices, 104
Rapide (rah-peed), 19
Ravel, Maurice (moh-reess rah-vel), 374-375
Rebec, 19
Recapitulation, 235

Recitative (re-see-tah-TEEV), 32
  Baroque, 198
  Classical, 245, 252
  Romantic, 292
Recitativo accompagnato (rai-chee-tah-TEE-voh ahk-kom-pahn-YAH-toh), 198
Recitativo secco (SEK-koh), 198
Recitativo stromentato (stroh-men-TAH-toh), 198
Recorder, 94
Related tonalities, 61
Relative minor, 52-54
Renaissance music, 10, 181
  temporal element, 31
  textural element, 143-145
  timbre-dynamic element, 105
  tonal element, 68
Repeated chord accompaniment, 129
Repetition, 167-168, 175
Résolu (res-oh-lü), 83
Responsorial, 184
Rest, 22, 28
Retardation, 120
Retenu (rö-te-nü), 21
Retrograde, 69-70, 170
Retrograde inversion, 69-70, 170
Rhythm, 15, 29 (see also Temporal element)
Rhythmic activity, 131-132
Rhythmic characteristics, 29-31
Rhythmic notation, 21-25
Rhythmic patterns, 26-29
Rhumba, 35
Ricercare (ree-chair-KAH-rai), 192, 215
Ricochet (ree-koh-shai), 90
Rimsky-Korsakov, Nicolai (NIK-oh-lie rim-skee-KOR-sah-kof), 338
Rinforzando (reen-for-TSAHN-doh), 83
Ripieno (ree-pee-AI-noh), 105
Risoluto (ree-zoh-LOO-toh), 83
Ritardando (ree-tahr-DAHN-doh), 21
Ritenuto (ree-te-NOO-toh), 21
Ritornello(ree-tor-NEL-loh), 210
Rococo music, 10, 148, 225
Romanesque period, 181
Roman opera, 200
Romantic music, 10, 277-338
  early period, 277
  formal element, 277-278
  general characteristics, 277
  late period, 277, 341
  middle period, 277
  temporal element, 32-33
  textural element, 149-150
  timbre-dynamic element, 107
  tonal element, 69

Rondeau (rohnh-doh), 188
Rondo (RON-doh), 175, 230-231
Rondo-sonata, 243
Root, 116
Root position, 116
Rossini, Gioacchino (joh-AH-kee-noh ross-SEE-nee), 326
Round, 134
Rounded binary form, 209
Row, 69-70, 342, 348
Rubato (roo-BAH-toh), 21, 29-30

S

St. Martial, School of, 181
Saltarello (sahl-tah-REL-loh), 191
Sanctus, 183
Sarabande (sah-rah-bahnhd), 32
Saxophone, 86, 93-94
Scale degrees, 55
Scale properties, 55
Scales, 47-55
Scarlatti, Alessandro (ah-less-SAHN-droh skahr-LAH-tee), 219
Scarlatti, Domenico (doh-MEN-ee-koh), 4, 222
Scheibe, Johann Adolf, 222
Scheidt, Samuel (SAHM-oo-el shiet), 218
Scherzando (skair-TSAHN-doh), 83
Scherzend (SHAIR-tsent), 83
Scherzhaft (SHAIRTS-hahft), 83
Scherzo (SKAIR-tsoh), 32
Scherzo and trio form, 227-230
Schmeichelnd (SHMIEXH-elnt), 83
Schnell (shnel), 19
Schneller werden (SHNEL-er VAIR-den), 21
Schoenberg, Arnold (AHR-nolt SHÖN-bairk), 69, 372-373
    Pierrot Lunaire, 108
    String Quartet No. 3, Op. 30, 60, 62, 69, 348-351
Schubert, Franz Peter (frahnts PAI-ter SHOO-bairt), 326
    Du bist die Ruh, 295-299
    Erlkönig, 299-307
    Heidenröslein, 293-294
    Quintet in A Major for Piano and Strings, 137
    Symphony No. 8 in B Minor, 63
    Tod und das Mädchen, 65
Schuller, Gunther, 382
Schuman, William, 381
Schumann, Robert (ROH-bairt SHOO-mahn), 329-330
    Carnaval, Op. 9, 291-292
    Concerto in A Minor for Piano and Orchestra, Op. 54, 290
    Quintet in E-flat Major, Op. 44, 63
    Symphony No. 3 in E-flat Major, Op. 97, 30
Schütz, Heinrich (HIEN-rixh shüts), 218
Schwer (shvair), 19
Schwungvoll (SHVOONG-fol), 83
Score, 84-85, 102
Scotch snap, 27
Scriabin Alexander (ah-leks-AHN-der skree-AH-bin), 157, 372
Secco (SEK-koh), 198
Second (interval), 47, 75-76, 112
Second inversion, 116
Section, 159, 162, 174
Sectional forms, 175
    Baroque, 208-209
    Classical, 226-231
    Contemporary, 344-345
    Romantic, 278-279
Sehr (zair), 19
Sehr laut (lout), 81
Sehr leise (LIE-ze), 81
Semplice (sem-PLEE-chai), 83
Septet, 101
Sequence, melodic, 170
Sequence (form), 183, 185
Serenade, 245
Serial music, 342
Sessions, Roger, 380
Seventh chords, 113, 115
Seventh (interval), 47, 75-76, 112
Sext, 183
Sextet, 101
Sforzando (sfor-TSAHN-doh), 83
Sharp, 43-44, 46
Shaw, George Bernard, 3
Shawm, 94
Shostakovich, Dimitri (dee-MEE-tree shoss-tah-KOH-vich), 381
Sibelius, Jean (zhahnh see-BAIL-yooss), 372
Siciliano rhythm, 27
Sightsinging, 77-78
Signature theme, 317
Similar motion, 133
Simple (sanhpl), 83
Simple meter, 17-18, 25
Sinfonia (seen foh-NEE-ah), 209
Singing allegro, 69
Single-reed instruments, 92-94
Singspiel (ZING-shpeel), 252
Six, les (lai seess), 379
Sixteenth note, sixteenth rest, 22
Sixth, 47, 75-76, 112

Sixty-fourth note, sixty-fourth rest, 23
Slur, 82
Smetana, Bedřich (BAID-rixh SMET-ah-
 nah), 334
 The Moldau, 282-284
Smorzando (smor-TSAHN-doh), 21, 81
Snare drum, 85, 97, 98
Solo, 100, 102
Solovox, 99
Sonata-allegro form:
 Classical, 234-240
 Contemporary, 348-351
 with fugal techniques, 239, 240
 with programmatic elements, 284-285
 Romantic, 280-282, 284-285
 standard characteristics, 175, 234-236
Sonata da camera (soh-NAH-tah dah
 KAH-mai-rah), 216
Sonata da chiesa (kee-AI-zah), 215-216
Sonata form:
 Baroque, 215-216
 Classical, 245-250
 Romantic, 287
 standard characteristics, 245-246
Sonatina form, 241
Song:
 Baroque, 199
 Classical, 252
 Romantic, 293-307
Song cycle, 325
Song form, 226
Song without words, 278
Soprano voice, 104
Sordino (sohr-DEE-noh), 89
Sostenuto (soss-te-NOO-toh), 83
Sound, 5-7
Sousaphone, 95-97
Soutenu (soo-te-nü), 83
Spacing of parts, 136
Special instruments, 85, 86, 97-99
Spiccato (spee-KAH-toh), 89
Spinto (SPEEN-toh), 104
Spondaic, 27
Sprechstimme (SHPREXH-shtim-me),
 103
Staccato (stah-KAH-toh), 82, 90
Staff, 45
Statement, fugal, 211
Stile antico, 197
Stile moderno, 197
Stockhausen, Karlheinz (kahrl-hients
 shtok-HOU-zen), 382
 No. 3 Elektronische Studien, Studie II,
 369, 370
Stopping, 89
Strauss, Richard (RIXH-ahrt shtrouss),
 371-372

Till Eulenspiegel's Merry Pranks, 346-
 347
Stravinsky, Igor (EE-gohr strah-VIN-skee),
 375-377
 L'Histoire du Soldat, 108
 Petrouchka, 33
 Le Sacre du Printemps, 30, 34
 Symphony of Psalms, 358-361
Stretto (STRET-toh), 211
String bass, 85, 86, 90
Stringed instruments, 85, 86, 87-91
Stringendo (streen-JEN-doh), 21, 81
String orchestra, 101
String quartet, 100
String quintet, 100
String sextet, 101
String trio, 100
Stromentato (stroh-men-TAH-toh), 198
Strophic form, 293
Study, 278
Style, 9-10
Subdominant, 55
Subito (SOO-bee-toh), 21
Subject, 211
Subjectivity, 176
Submediant, 55
Suite:
 Baroque, 216-217
 Romantic, 291
Sul ponticello (sool pohn-tee-CHEL-loh),
 90
Sul tasto (sool TAHSS-toh), 90
Summaries:
 formal element, 176
 temporal element, 36
 textural element, 153
 timbre-dynamic element, 108
 tonal element, 71
Supertonic, 55
Sur la touche (sür lah toosh), 90
Suspension, 120
Sustained chord accompaniment, 129
Sweelinck, Jan Pieterszoon (yahn PEE-
 ters-zohn SVAI-link), 217
Swing, 35
Syllabic singing of chant, 184
Symphony:
 with chorus, 325
 Classical, 245, 247
 Contemporary, 363-366
 in one movement, 363-366
 with programmatic elements, 287-289
 Romantic, 287-289
Symphonic poem, 282
Symphonic wind ensemble, 101
Syncopation, 30-31

T

Tailleferre, Germaine (zhair-main tah-ye-fair), 379
Talea (TAH-lai-ah), 143
Tambourine, 97
Tamburo militaire (tahm-BOO-roh mee-lee-TAIR), 85
Tango, 35
Tanz (tahnts), 191
Tape music, 342
Tchaikowsky, Peter Ilyitch (PAI-ter IL-yitch chie-KOF-skee), 336-337
  Concerto in D Major for Violin and Orchestra, Op. 35, 64
  Nutcracker Suite, 291
  Symphony No. 4 in F Minor, Op. 36, 64
  Symphony No. 5 in E Minor, Op. 64, 64, 128
Te Deum (tai DAI-oom), 140-148
Telemann, Georg Philipp (GAI-org PHIL-ip TAIL-e-mahn), 219
Temple block, 97
Tempo, 15, 19, 21 (*see also* Temporal element)
Tempo primo (TEM-poh PREE-moh), 21
Temporal element, 7-9, 15-38
  Baroque, 31-32
  Classical, 32
  Contemporary, 33-36
  pre-Baroque, 31
  Romantic, 32-33
Temporal variations, 168-169
Tendre (tahnhdr), 83
Teneramente (ten-air-ah-MEN-tai), 83
Tenor, 140
Tenor clef, 45
Tenor drum, 97
Tenorhorn (te-NOHR-horn), 85
Tenor voice, 104
Tenth, 113
Tenu (te-nü), 83
Tenuto (tai-NOO-toh), 83
Ternary form, 175
  Baroque, 209
  Classical, 226-227
  Contemporary, 344-345
  Romantic, 278-279
Terraced dynamics, 105
Tertian chords, 115
Tessitura (tess-see-TOO-rah), 66-67
Textual music, 176
Textural element, 7, 9, 111-157
  Baroque, 145-148
  Classical, 148-149
  Contemporary, 150-152

pre-Baroque, 140-145
Romantic, 149-150
Texture (see also Textural element)
  homophonic, 128-131
  hybrid, 138-140
  monophonic, 111
  polyphonic, 131-138
Texture-row, 342
Texture variations, 171-173
Theme, 173-174
Theme and variations form, 175
  Baroque, 211
  Classical, 231-234
  Contemporary, 349
  pre-Baroque, 192
  Romantic, 279
Theme group, 235
Third, 47, 75-76, 112
Third stream music, 343
Thirteenth chord, 115
Thirty-second note, thirty-second rest, 23
Thomson, Virgil, 380
Thorough bass (*see* Figured bass)
Three-part form (*see* Ternary form)
Through-composed form, 293
Tie, 24
Timbale (tanh-bahl), 85
Timbre, 6, 7, 9
Timbre-dynamic element, 7, 9, 81-109
  Baroque, 105-106
  Classical, 106-107
  Contemporary, 108
  pre-Baroque, 105
  Romantic, 107
Timbre-dynamic variations, 171
Time signatures, 25-26
Timpani, 85, 86, 97, 98
Toccata (toh-KAH-tah):
  Baroque, 215
  pre-Baroque, 192
Tonal characteristics, 55-68
Tonal element, 7-9, 41-79
  Baroque, 68
  Classical, 68-69
  Contemporary, 69-71
  pre-Baroque, 68
  Romantic, 69
Tonality, 55-61
  change of, 61
Tonal variations, 170-171
Tone, 5, 41
Tone cluster, 115, 151
Tone color (*see* Timbre)
Tone poem, 282
Tone quality, 6, 7
Tone row, 69-70, 342, 348

Tonic, 55
Tonic accent, 15
Tout à coup (toot-ah-koo), 21
Tractus, 183
Transformation of themes, 330
Transition, 174
Transposition, 86-87, 171
Traurig (TROU-rixh), 83
Treble clef, 45
Treble staff, 45
Tremolo (TRAIM-oh-loh), 90
Très (trai), 19
Très doux (doo), 81
Très fort (for), 81
Triad, 113
Triangle, 97
Tribrachic, 27
Trill, 67
Trio (ensemble), 100
Trio (form), 245
Trio sonata, 100
Triple meter, 16-18, 25
Triple stop, 89
Triplet, 27-28
Triste (treest), 83
Trochaic, 27
Tromba (TROM-bah), 84
Trombone, 84, 86, 95, 96
Trommel (TROM-mel), 85
Trompete (trom-PAI-te), 84
Trompette (trohnh-pet), 84
Trope, 184
Troubadour (troo-bah-door), 181, 187
Trouvère (troo-vair), 181, 187-188
Trumpet, 84, 86, 95, 96
Tuba, 85, 86, 95, 96
Turn, 67
Tutti, (TOO-tee), 102, 105, 210
Twelve-tone music, 69-70, 151, 342, 348, 372-374
Twentieth-century music (*see* Contemporary music)
Two-part form (*see* Binary form)
Types of music, 176

U

Ukulele, 90
Unending melody, 293, 321
Unison, 47, 112
Unity and variety, 173
Un poco (oon PO-koh), 19
Unusual meters, 34

Upbeat, 16-17
Up bow, 89

V

Valve, 95
Variation forms, 175
    Baroque, 211
    Classical, 231-234
    Contemporary, 349
    pre-Baroque, 192
    Romantic, 279
Variation techniques:
    combined, 172-173
    temporal, 168-169
    textural, 171-172
    timbre-dynamic, 171
    tonal, 170-171
Vaughan Williams, Ralph, 328, 372
Venetian opera, 200
Ventilhorn (fen-TEEL-horn), 84
Verbreitern (fair-BRIE-tern), 21
Verdi, Giuseppe (joo-ZAIP-pai VAIR-dee), 333-334
    Rigoletto, 317-321
Verismo, (vai-REEZ-moh), 338
Verlöschen (fair-LÖSH-en), 21, 81
Verse anthem, 187
Vespers, 183
Vibra-harp, 97
Vibraphone, 97
Vibration, 5-7
Vibrato (vee-BRAH-toh), 89
Vielle (vee-el), 90
Viennese Classicism, 225
Vif (veef), 19
Villa-Lobos, Heitor (HIE-tohr VEEL-lah-LOH-boss), 375
Viol, 90
Viola, 85, 86, 90, 91
Viola da gamba (vee-OH-lah dah GAHM-bah), 90
Viola d'amore (dah-MOH-rai), 90
Violin, 85, 86, 90, 91
Violine (vee-oh-LEE-ne), 85
Violino (vee-oh-LEE-noh), 85
Violon (vee-oh-lohnh), 85
Violoncelle (vee-oh-lohnh-sel), 85
Violoncello, 85, 86, 90, 91
Virelai (veer-e-lai), 188
Vite (veet), 19
Vivace (vee-VAH-chai), 19
Vivaldi, Antonio (ahn-TOHN-yoh vee-VAHL-dee), 219
    The Seasons, 125

Vocal ensembles, 104-105
Voice leading, 123-124
Voices, 103-104
  ranges, 104
Vox organalis, 141
Vox principalis, 141

W

Wagner, Richard (RIXH-ahrt VAHG-
  ner), 222, 331-333
  Die Götterdämmerung, 107
  The Flying Dutchman, 150
  Lohengrin, 149
  Die Meistersinger, 150, 321-325
  Tristan und Isolde, 67, 267
Walton, William, 381
Waltz, 33, 279
Weber, Carl Maria von (kahrl mah-REE-
  ah fon VAI-ber), 326
Webern, Anton (AHN-tohn VAI-bern),
  377

Weniger (VAI-ni-ger), 21
Weniger bewegt (be-VAIKT), 21
Whole note, whole rest, 22
Whole-tone chords, 151
Whole-tone scale, 51
Wolf, Hugo (HOO-goh volf), 338
Women's chorus, 104
Wood block, 97
Woodwind choir, 101
Woodwind instruments, 84, 85-86, 90-94
Woodwind quintet, 100
Word painting, 186

X-Y-Z

Xylophone, 86, 97, 99
Zart (tsahrt), 83
Zärtlich (TSAIRT-lixh), 83
Zierlich (TSEER-lixh), 83
Zurückgehalten (tsoo-RÜK-ge-HAHL-ten),
  21
Zurückhalten (tsoo-RÜK-hahl-ten), 21